HANGING THE SHERIFF

HANGING

A BIOGRAPHY OF

the

University of Utah Press
Salt Lake City, 1987

HENRY PLUMMER

SHERIFF

R. E. Mather and
F. E. Boswell

Volume Twenty-One of the University of Utah
Publications in the American West
under the Editorial Direction
of the American West Center
Floyd A. O'Neil, Director

Library of Congress Cataloging-in-Publication Data

Mather, R. E. (Ruth E.), 1934–
  Hanging the sheriff.

  (University of Utah publications in the American
West ; v. 21)
  Bibliography: p.
  Includes index.
  1. Plummer, Henry Amos, d. 1864.   2. Outlaws—
Montana—Biography.   3. Outlaws—Idaho—Biography.
4. Sheriffs—Montana—Biography.   5. Vigilance
committees—Montana—History—19th century.
6. Frontier and pioneer life—Montana.   7. Montana—
History.   I. Boswell, F. E., 1941–   .   II. Title.
III. Series.
F731.P57M38   1987   978.6'01'0924   [B]   87–2125
ISBN 0-87480-300-4

CONTENTS

ILLUSTRATIONS

MAPS

ACKNOWLEDGMENTS

Special acknowledgments are due the following libraries and historical societies for the use of their materials and the help provided by members of their staffs:

Idaho Historical Society
Luna House Museum, Nez Perce County Historical Society
Nevada County Library, Nevada City, California
National Archives, San Francisco Branch
Sutro Library, San Francisco, California
California State Library
Stanford University Libraries
Bancroft Library, Berkeley
Searls Historical Library, Nevada City, California
Nevada State Library
The Church of Jesus Christ of Latter-day Saints Genealogical
    Library, Salt Lake City
South Dakota Historical Society
Montana Historical Society
California Historical Society

A special thanks should also go to Peggy Lee, editor-in-chief of the University of Utah Press, for her encouragement and support, and to Dr. Merle Wells for suggesting the project.

HANGING THE SHERIFF

INTRODUCTION

The story of the controversial events that took place at Bannack City, Montana, during its brief existence as a center of gold mining east of the Rockies is also the story of Henry Plummer. Yet an accurate and unbiased account of these events and his life has not before been written. Over a year after Sheriff Plummer was hanged, editor Thomas Dimsdale of the *Montana Post*, who did not live in Bannack and had not witnessed what took place there, wrote a series of articles about the unusual occurrence of a community hanging its own sheriff and later collected them into a book. During the intervening one hundred twenty years since the publication of Dimsdale's book, Henry Plummer's story has been retold many times with little change or added insight. Because Dimsdale's primary concern in telling the story was with morality rather than reality, accuracy and fairness were both of rather low priority to him, and, as a few scholars of Montana history have already pointed out, his account therefore cannot be considered a reliable source.

In brief summary of the familiar story, on a Sunday afternoon in May 1863, the miners of Bannack set in motion a series of history-making incidents by electing themselves a judge, sheriff, and coroner. The new sheriff, a likeable young man, but with the reputation of having been a desperado, received the largest majority of votes by far. A few days after the election, he made a long trip north to marry a young woman waiting there for him and then brought her back to Bannack. But after only two and one-half months of marriage, the bride, Electa, left to visit relatives, explaining that her husband would join her later. Electa's departure so soon after the wedding caused some talk, but otherwise was not particularly damaging to the sheriff's continuing popularity.

The town over which Sheriff Plummer presided was a part of the recently created Territory of Idaho and had sprung up nearly overnight after a group of Colorado miners, on their way to the badly overcrowded gold fields around Lewiston, discovered large quantities of loose gold along a creek bank. Unaware that Lewis and Clark had given this tributary of the Beaverhead River the name Willard's Creek, the miners called the stream the Grasshopper, in honor of the flurry of insects that whirred into flight at their every step. By late fall of 1862, the richness of the Bannack gold had been recognized, and as word spread, a rush to the Grasshopper diggings began. Though the miners had taken steps to bring order by electing their own law officers, President Abraham Lincoln also sent to the territory Chief Justice Sydney Edgerton, a former congressman from the state of Ohio, who brought along his nephew, a young lawyer named Wilbur Sanders, to serve as his secretary.

It was only natural that there would be a certain amount of friction between the newcomers, whose authority rested only on paper, and those already actively engaged in administering justice in the eastern Idaho gold camps, men selected for their experience and the respect they had earned from the miners. Despite the inroads of civilization Plummer was making in the booming mining districts, Edgerton and Sanders did not trust the miners' sheriff. They had heard rumors that Plummer had previously been a desperado and held him responsible for a rash of robberies and murders committed along the trails. In December of the same year Plummer was elected, Wilbur Sanders organized a group of citizens who were bent on conducting a speedier and less expensive form of justice. Without holding a public trial, they hanged two suspected criminals and then announced that one of the men just hanged had accused the sheriff of leading a double life—acting as a lawman while actually directing a gang of robbers. Surprising Plummer at home, they walked him, along with two of his deputies, to the town gallows. Though Plummer asked to speak to his sister-in-law, Martha Vail, with whom he was boarding, his request was denied. The three law officers were hanged.

Some Bannack residents were not convinced their sheriff had actually been an outlaw, but Thomas Dimsdale's newspaper articles assured them that Henry Plummer was indeed guilty as charged and praised the men who had hanged him. Accepting Dimsdale's account, and that of Nathaniel Langford, which followed many years later, historians of the West unanimously stereotyped Plummer as a notorious bandit masquerading as a lawman, a brilliant organizer of a band of roughs responsible for countless robberies and over one hundred murders. Unbelievable as it may seem, the verdict announced by a group of self-appointed men operating outside traditional forms of justice has never been seriously questioned. To date the decision reached by this unauthorized body after secret proceedings that did not even include an examination of the accused has been accepted as unequivocal fact, none of the historians taking into account a heritage of justice by which a person is considered innocent until proven guilty by fair trial.

Though Bannack was not part of a state at the time, it was in a territory of the United States to which the president had appointed a chief justice. As a matter of fact, Justice Edgerton lived only a few houses away from Plummer. In addition to this national government appointee, there was also a miners' court organized to insure justice for members of the district. But Plummer was brought before neither Edgerton nor the miners' court, nor before any tribunal for that matter, so we have no means of determining whether there was sufficient evidence against him to have convinced a jury other than by studying the accounts left and forming our own judgment. But when we attempt to do this, we discover that exactly half of the needed information is missing—the defense.

In examining the evidence Dimsdale and Langford presented,

we encounter both inaccuracies and fabrications, but neither of these creates the major obstacle to sorting out the truth about what happened at Bannack in the winter of 1863–64. The greatest difficulty arises from the bias dominating the reporting, a bias that would have been exposed at a trial through cross-examination. These two main accounts, Dimsdale and Langford, are doubly biased, being written specifically as evidence for the defense of those who carried out the hanging of an elected law officer and additionally as evidence for the prosecution of Plummer. Since both accounts were written in retrospect of proving Plummer a man of bad character, every detail was accordingly reshaped to fit the prescribed mold. Plummer was not allowed to present a defense in response to the charges brought against him, and others accused of being involved were also hanged without public trial, thus leaving posterity no testimony in the actual words of the accused.

Despite the obvious handicap created by using the accounts dictated by his executioners, the following chapters are an attempt to, for the first time, tell the story of Henry Plummer with some degree of objectivity for the purpose of revealing what sort of man he was. To overcome the handicap, Dimsdale and Langford will be balanced with less prejudiced writers, eyewitnesses whenever possible.

Most historians admit to knowing very little about Plummer. His widow faded into obscurity, leaving behind nothing more than several conflicting stories as to how she spent the remaining years of her life after her husband's death. In his biography, Dimsdale stated that his informants offered at least twenty different versions of Plummer's birthplace, none of which could be verified. In fact the only point of agreement on Plummer seems to be that of his guilt. But Plummer was far too complex a person for the simplistic approach taken by Dimsdale, who presents his subject as a mere symbol of evil. Plummer came West to fulfill a dream, bringing with him the qualities he needed to make it come true — intelligence, decency, and dedication. Yet the twelve formative years he spent in the gold camp culture also influenced his character, leaving him a curious blend of his straitlaced New England heritage and the freewheeling frontier environment. His personality is usually described as magnetic, although his acquaintances have the irritating habit of failing to mention exactly what traits attracted them. During the years spent researching Plummer's life and times, we have concluded that none of those who wrote about him really knew him well, not only because of his natural reticence, but because they were not his intimate friends. Therefore our most satisfactory method of becoming acquainted with him has been to listen carefully each time he speaks. His combined words gradually build up the portrait of a fascinating man, and the direct quotations that have been preserved, despite inexactness and prejudice of the reporter, form a consistent personality pattern that is the basis of our biography.

Employing tools of both scholar and genealogist, we have engaged in a long struggle with the past, coaxing it to give up its secrets; but while continuing to rely on what others said about Plummer, we met with little success. It was only as we came to know him well enough to trust his word that we finally resolved the disputed issue of his birthplace and family lineage. Still, Henry Plummer is an elusive man, protective of his privacy, and we must admit that some of the surprises we have unearthed only add to uncertainty and confirm the mystery of the man himself.

Sufficient material is available, however, to indicate that both Henry and Electa Plummer possessed noteworthy character traits, and their naive hopefulness on meeting each other created a love tragedy as haunting as any in our literary heritage. The story of Plummer's experiences in Montana revolves around the lives of two families with rather opposite goals and values: the Edgertons, who came West to further a political career, and the Vails, the missionary family Plummer married into and with whom he lived while serving as sheriff of Bannack.

Because Dimsdale completed such an effective character assassination, the reader, even after discovering that accusations are based mainly on intuition, still cannot shake the damaging impression built by an overwhelming mass of accumulated derogatory details encountered throughout his book. The image of Plummer as the one man responsible for all crime committed in the mining districts east of the Rockies is so firmly ingrained it is nearly impossible for even the most impartial of readers to drop old suspicions and view him with an open mind. We will therefore start our story with Electa and attempt to take a fresh look at Henry Plummer through her eyes.

PART I

MONTANA

ELECTA BRYAN

In the ten years Electa Plummer spent as a widow, the thought may have crossed her mind more than once that if her husband had not met her, he would not have been killed by vigilantes. She had come west with her older sister, Martha Jane, Martha's husband, James Vail, and their two small children: Mary, four years old, and Harvey, only two. Vail, a twenty-four-year-old schoolteacher from Ohio, had accepted a position as manager of Sun River government farm, set up to "civilize and Christianize" the Blackfeet, Piegan, and Blood Indians, by providing them agricultural equipment and instruction in farming. Just six days before the family's departure for the wilderness, Electa Bryan celebrated her twentieth birthday. [1]

The Vails were to take the new ship route being used by the gold stampeders, following the Missouri River all the way to its headwaters at Fort Benton, when its depth was sufficient to permit navigation. Their ship was the *Emilie*, a luxuriously equipped steamer, and the first sidewheeler to attempt the course. With the American flag fluttering in the breeze at the bow and smokestacks puffing black clouds astern, the *Emilie* began her three-thousand-mile voyage not on the Missouri, but on the Mississippi, leaving St. Louis on 14 May 1862 under the able command of Captain Joseph La Barge, known as the greatest steamboatman on the river. The ship's cargo was three hundred tons of general merchandise, mining tools, mules, horses, wagons, and what were labelled "Indian goods," which included supplies and equipment James Vail would need on the farm as well as supplies promised as an annual annuity to the tribes for having signed a peace treaty. Aboard were eighty-five cabin passengers, charged one hundred dollars per person, and on deck, fifty-three more passengers, charged a lesser price. James Vail and his family were fortunate enough to be among the cabin passengers only because the government was footing the bill. They were a decided minority among the fortune hunters flocking to the Northwest in search of gold.[2]

Because of their unusual mission, the Vails, who were of the cut who lays up treasure in heaven rather than on earth, attracted considerable attention from their fellow passengers as well as from the press. Neither of the two interested groups seemed to put much stock in the family's curious mission to the heathen; one passenger wrote home that in his judgment, "sympathy and sentiment are wasted" on the Indians. A news item composed about James Vail's assignment expressed a similar opinion, closing with the wry comment, "We have little faith in the success of the enterprise."[3] But it was not only Vail's unusual calling that attracted notice to him; he was bringing with him persons rare to the wilderness, white women and children, and Electa, being single, respectable, and attractive, was especially noticeable. The family soon befriended one of the single males aboard, a gold seeker from Massachusetts named Francis Thompson, who had hired on as part of an exploration party for a large mining firm, and Thompson as well as two other passengers kept an account of the eventful trip up the Missouri to Fort Benton.

The outcome of this attempt to bring passengers and needed supplies all the way up the Missouri was of considerable significance to the continuing development of the Northwest. Steamers had been trying to accomplish the feat since the spring of 1859, but with little success, most giving up somewhere along the way due to shallow waters. The previous spring not a single steamer had reached its destination. One that had gotten as far as the mouth of the Milk River was lost when crew members, sneaking to the hold to steal whiskey, upset a candle and started a fire that exploded gunpowder in the cargo. All the passengers of the *Emilie* felt the excitement of the risky endeavor, but probably none more than the two sisters, Martha Vail and Electa Bryan, whose experiences up to that moment had been mainly limited to those connected with having been born and brought up on a farm in central Ohio. Any trip up the Missouri was a hazardous one, and it was necessary for the steamer to tie up every night to avoid running aground on shallows or becoming snagged on a bar. Another danger was severe winds that frequently drove the ship to one bank to wait out a storm. Passengers sometimes took advantage of an unscheduled stop to disembark and make a little side excursion ashore. On one such occasion the Vails' new friend, Francis Thompson, entertained the entire shore party by attempting to break a wild jackass into a gentleman's riding pony, but Thompson, not being much of a cowboy, was thrown and had to spend the next few days limping about his cabin.

The first sight of the immense herds of buffalo calmly feeding in the grassy valleys alongside brought nearly everyone onto the deck, and on rounding a bend in the river, the ship suddenly encountered directly in its pathway hundreds of the shaggy beasts swimming to the opposite bank, huge bulls and young calves diligently paddling in the wake formed by a mother's body. Captain La Barge quickly ordered that the ship be brought to a halt to prevent damaging its wheels on the massive black horns of the animals, and several sporting men, seizing on the opportunity to display their skills, rushed below to collect rifles and then shot game meat for the next meal, hoisting the heavy carcasses on board and dressing out one prized bull of nearly twelve hundred pounds. An animal lover on board tugged a young calf onto the deck, hoping to take it along as a pet, but Captain La Barge had to order it shot when it aggressively charged one of the passengers.

The trip up the Missouri had been compared to running a gauntlet through the unfriendly Indian villages situated on each bank, and at one point on their journey some braves who had been refused permission to come aboard commenced shooting arrows into the ship. The captain was forced to fire up the two small cannons on the forward deck in order to discourage any further attack. At other more peaceful villages, inhabitants took but little notice of the intruders, continuing about their daily chores as though they were not being scrutinized by the inquisitive whites. Passengers gazed on in amazement as an Indian widow, beneath the elevated platform bearing the body of a dead warrior, slashed herself and stood with blood dripping from her arms while she wailed the sorrow of losing a courageous husband. If Electa Bryan had not been such a staunch Christian, she could have interpreted this image of a widow's grief as a bad omen of what might lay in store for her. A second eerie sight came days later, the remnants of Fort Clark, now completely abandoned but littered with traces of the Mandan tribe literally destroyed by smallpox introduced by the whites: rotting and tumbled-down scaffolds, leg bones, and human skulls, more images of death to be contemplated by those less cheerful and optimistic than Electa Bryan.

Their route took the impatient gold seekers and lone missionary family through miles of badlands, stunted pine trees, and waxy-blossomed prickly pear; then, as the river that carried them narrowed and swiftened, the scenery became strangely beautiful: red sandstone cliffs carved by the wind into graceful, ornate towers, alternating with lush green bottomland where grizzly bears nibbled at tender roots; where elk, antelope, and mountain sheep grazed; and where wild roses and gooseberry bushes bloomed.

As they reached the swift rapids that marked the point other steamers had been unable to pass, the *Emilie* shuddered ominously, barely able to make the slightest forward progress, but valiantly struggling onward. Conquering the last of the rapids, the ship was greeted by a welcoming party of nearly one hundred Indians who had heard of the momentous event and gathered to escort the passengers and crew the rest of the journey. Francis Thompson marvelled at the "old battlescarred warriors," riding alongside them "in conscious dignity" and performing "masterly feats of horsemanship."[4]

On 17 June 1862, after spending more than a month on the river, the *Emilie* docked at Fort Benton, a small adobe fort huddled on one bank of the Upper Missouri at a break in the walls of protective, gray bluffs lining the river. Benton, an old fur trading post during the heyday of the trappers, was designated as the Blackfeet Indian agency at the 1855 signing of Lame Bull's Treaty, by which Indians were to permit safe passage through their lands in exchange for several tons of supplies. With the ongoing rush to the gold fields of the Clearwater regions, via the Missouri River and Mullan Road route, Fort Benton was rapidly developing into an important river port and supply center. Still, one of the Vails' fellow passengers was not duly impressed with what he saw when they disembarked, writing home that the fort was occupied by nothing more than Indians, half-breeds, horses, and wolf-dogs, and that any livery stable back home would surely be a more pleasant and desirable place to live.[5]

Anxious to reach their destination, James Vail and family, accompanied by Francis Thompson's group, left the foul-smelling fort and began a sixty-mile trek across the newly completed Mullan Road, nothing more than a rough trail heading westward from Benton, rising to barren clay bluffs and finally reaching grassy plains dotted with small lakes. On the second day the party arrived at the Indian mission, set at the rope guide ferry of the Sun River, and the family took a first look at their wilderness home. In late June the Sun was a wide, green-bordered river meandering through a broad valley that ascended in a series of plateaus on each side, like giant stairsteps to the distant blue mountains beyond. Herds of deer and elk rested on the river banks in the shade of cottonwood trees and others grazed far out on the surrounding plain as far as the eye could see. On the near bank of the Sun, entirely enclosed within the defense of a stake fence, sat several small farm buildings, all constructed of hewn cottonwood logs. The farm was notable only for being one of the few patches of cultivated earth in the new territory, its single industry being placer mining.

Thompson and companions continued on to the Pacific Coast, leaving behind the Vail family, armed with one small cannon and a considerable amount of faith, to commence a mission not unlike that of the Spaldings and Whitmans in Oregon country, and certainly no less difficult or dangerous.

SUN RIVER FARM

The first summer at the Indian farm may have been a period of disillusionment for its new manager for a variety of reasons. Though considerable land had been cultivated and several dwellings for the Indians constructed, the project did not show prospects of further advancement under his direction. The Blackfeet were hunters, known for their cleanliness and fine horsemanship, but were also feared for their savagery and warlike nature, so that those living within the area they roamed, even other Indian tribes, were in constant danger of attack. James Vail must have been continually haunted by the fate met by the Whitmans, who had been killed by Indians in 1847, his own staff inadequate to provide his family protection from similar attack. His assistants were only two: Joseph Swift, a teenage hired hand from Philadelphia, and Iron, an Indian assigned to provide meat since the Piegans considered the buffalo their exclusive property and would have taken offense at a white man disturbing the herds.[6]

Despite his worry over the precarious situation, a man as concerned with spiritual values as Vail would have found his contact with Indian culture a rewarding one. One of the Blackfeet religious ceremonies that most fascinated the white man was the annual ritual offering homage to the sun. According to the Blackfeet myth, Tailfeathers Woman was the first human being to communicate with the Divinity of the Sky, who commanded her to oversee the construction of sacred lodges to be used for intricate rituals. Then each year when the prairie grass turned deep green and the cow parsnips grew high, the members of the tribe would paint their faces, don headdress and bells, and perform a series of prescribed acts and prayers to the beat of the tom-toms in celebration of the renewal of life by the sun, the source of all power. The performance of the Sun Dance not only renewed the individual's spirituality in preparation for the next year, but also united him to the heritage received from his ancestors, just as the center pole of the sacred lodges linked earth and heaven into a cosmic whole. The Blackfeet tribes referred to their ceremony dedicated to the sun as experiencing vision. But though they had such close ties to the forces of nature, they followed a nomadic pattern of life and had an aversion to cultivating the soil, since doing so would lower them to the status of "diggers."

Another source of concern was the psychological pressure placed on the family, who suddenly found themselves — and so soon after the pleasant social life aboard the steamer — in the midst of a vast, uninhabited space where loneliness proved overwhelming. Keeping up good spirits under such conditions required ingenuity. The women tried to make the best of the situation, finding time to take the two children for outings in the government ambulance, but still the isolation was foreign to all of them. Martha and Electa, born at the tail end of a large family, were used to living among relatives — aunts, uncles, cousins, in-laws, nieces, and nephews. True, the last years at home had not been the most pleasant, but still they had never been lonely. Their father, James Bryan, in the company of relatives, had migrated in 1832 from Pennsylvania to Hancock County, Ohio, chopping down oak, elm, walnut, maple, hickory, sycamore, and wild cherry from dense forests, calling in neighbors for a log rolling and burning, and then commencing to farm the land. When his wife died, leaving him with small children, he married a second time to Mary Johnson, a native of Vermont, who became the mother of Martha and Electa. James was civic-minded, riding for miles to vote in the presidential election between Jackson and Clay and banding together with three other families to build a log schoolhouse and hire a teacher.[7] Both James and Mary were themselves educated people, who kept a library in their home and encouraged their children to attend the academy later established in town. While their father was healthy and their mother still alive, the Bryan children led an idyllic life. The farm provided nearly everything needed for both food and clothing: wool, grain, meat, milk, butter, eggs, fruit, and vegetables. The women regularly took to town as much as twenty pounds of butter and dozens of eggs to apply against their store bill for the few items required: crocks for food preparation, salt for preserving meat and cooking, sugar and syrup for sweetening, coffee and tea for rounding out a meal, paper and envelopes for writing home, nails for building and repairing, and tobacco for the men's evening leisure hours. But the major portion of the store bill was run up by the yards and yards of fabric needed to clothe a large family of girls — lots of calico, some muslin, a bit of silk and ribbon.

The Bryans' farm continued to do well. The livestock increased yearly — horses, cows, sheep, pigs, and chickens — and wheat and corn harvests were bountiful. There was no need for hired help, the two sons still at home worked the fields with their father, the women tending to yard and household chores. Other than the traveling shoemaker who boarded out in one home after another, making a new pair of shoes for each member of the family, the Bryans were nearly self-sufficient economically as well as socially. Their brand of family life met most of their needs for companionship. Though independent from the rest of society, they were quite dependent on each other; a younger member of the family, such as Electa, could develop a lifelong emotional dependency upon an older sibling. Those who married into such a family usually discovered they were not quite so essential as a member related by blood, one who had always been there.

The season of harmony in the Bryan household came to an abrupt end with the death of Mary Bryan, and James found himself alone with seven children to care for: Daniel, James Junior, Sarah, Mary, Martha Jane, Electa, and Cornelia. No longer well enough himself to work in the fields, James Senior gradually turned the farm over to Daniel and James Junior, both in their twenties. Though he never remarried, when Martha was eleven and Electa eight, their father brought to live with them a stepmother of a sort, a forty-six-year-old woman named Mary Ann, nearly the same name as their real mother.

As difficult as the family situation was during the first six years Mary Ann lived with the Bryans, it became worse when James Senior died. In the winter of 1855, his condition had deteriorated rapidly, and though a doctor was called in repeatedly, he died in early January, complicating matters by not leaving a will. His estate had accumulated debts against it during his long illness: a four-year doctor bill amounting to $65, and a general merchandise bill at the store of $13.99 above the value of butter and eggs delivered. In addition, there was the $10 owed for a coffin and services.[8]

James Junior was appointed executor of the estate, and trying to be fair to his common-law stepmother, he selected out first of all the household goods Mary Ann would need in rearing his two youngest half sisters, Electa and Cornelia. He set aside for her a parlor stove, a cooking stove with cooking utensils, four beds with bedding, a table and six chairs, six plates, six knives and forks, twelve spoons, one sugar dish, all the books, two spinning wheels, all the cloth and yarn, and several looking glasses.

In addition, he alloted her six hundred fifty pounds of pork, one barrel of salt, one hundred bushels of corn and wheat, one cow, one calf, eleven sheep, three herds of hogs, and $100, reminding again that the above-mentioned property was for the express purpose of Mary Ann's support of the two small children. The rest of the personal property, James disposed of at public auction to pay off debts against his father's estate.

Mary Ann, dissatisfied with her stepson's settlement, insisted she should have more, but the Bryan children disagreed, believing that since their father had never married her, she had no right to his real estate. Mary Ann went off to town in a huff, hired a lawyer, and sued the Bryan children for seizing their father's property. In the lengthy suit that followed, the court found in Mary Ann's favor, ruling she should be given, in addition to the personal property already granted her, one-third of the land and houses. Naturally, resentment ran so high that eventually the Bryan household completely dissolved.

On 9 April 1857, Martha married James Vail, also from Hancock County, and they set up housekeeping near his former home. The youngest Bryan daughter, Cornelia, came to live with Martha and James, and Electa also found a home with relatives. But Martha, not one to hold a grudge for long, soon permitted her stepmother to join the Vail household rather than being left at the farm alone.[9]

James Vail, a nineteen-year-old newlywed with an instant family of four to support, found a job teaching school. Soon after, he and Martha had their first child, a daughter whom Martha named for her mother, Mary Bryan. Harvey was born two years later.

Though within his first years of marriage James Vail had accumulated personal property valued at $400, a teacher's salary was insufficient to permit him to buy a house and land. When Reverend Reed, pastor of the Methodist church the Vails attended, received an appointment as Indian agent to the Dakota Territory, he offered James Vail a position managing the experimental farm. James and Martha, enthused at the prospects of doing missionary work in the wilderness, accepted his offer and commenced preparations for the journey west. It is quite possible that Electa was invited along not only to keep Martha company and help her with the children, but also because James hoped eventually to establish a school where she could teach Indian children. [10]

Neither the Vails nor Electa were complainers, and they had no intentions of giving up, but they could not have predicted the intense homesickness they would feel nor the hardships they would have to endure. Items that had been staples on the farm in Ohio — tea, sugar, salt — were now luxuries and had to be used sparingly, usually only when serving guests. It was for several good reasons that travelers to and from Fort Benton were received with such a warm welcome at the Vail farm.

THE COURTSHIP

In mid-September of the Vails' first year at Sun River, about the time the hot, dry season was finally drawing to a welcome close, Henry Plummer set out for Fort Benton, mulling over plans to leave the territories and the problems he had encountered there and return to the East. The prospects of the Civil War raging at home may have been more an incentive than a deterrent to a man who preferred action and constant opportunity to prove courage. Near Deer Lodge Valley, he and his companion, Charles Reeves, met the two brothers who are credited with discovering gold east of the Rockies, James and Granville Stuart, and the Stuarts jotted down the meeting in a diary they took turns keeping. "On our way to Hell Gate at Beaver Dam we met two fine looking young men. One of them said his name was Henry Plummer, the other was Charles Reeves. . . . They were from Elk City on Clearwater, and enquired about the mines at Gold Creek and at Beaverhead. They rode two good horses and had another packed with their blankets and provisions. We liked their looks and told them that we were going down to Hell Gate and would return to Gold Creek in a few days and asked them to return to Hell Gate with us and then we could all go up the Canyon together. They accepted our invitation." [11]

The first night back at Gold Creek, the men got up a friendly poker game in which James Stuart lost twenty-two dollars, though he did better the next night, losing only eighteen. Besides the poker losses, the Stuarts noted in their diary that they repaired Plummer's double-barreled shotgun, which he had broken off at the grip while crossing the mountains. Apparently uninterested in the scanty profits being made at Gold Creek, Plummer and Reeves moved on the morning of 21 September 1862 in the direction of the first major gold strike to be made on the eastern side of the Rockies, the Beaverhead mines, so-called because they were located on a tributary of that river. Though Reeves may have continued to Grasshopper Creek, Plummer and an old acquaintance from California named Jack Cleveland, who had been trailing behind, took the Mullan Road to Fort Benton, where they hoped to hire a mackinaw down the Missouri River. But on their arrival at the fort, they discovered that due to numerous reports that mackinaw passengers had suffered atrocities at the hands of Indians along the banks, boatmen were unwilling to attempt the trip. Plummer and Cleveland were stuck at Fort Benton where another steamer would not be arriving until the next spring.

Indian unrest had also caused alarm at the government farm, and fearing an attack on the palisade, James Vail rode to Fort Benton searching for men to assist him in defending his family. There he met Plummer and Cleveland and asked them to return with him to protect the farm until danger from the Indians subsided, offering them a small cabin inside the fort. [12]

At the farm, Electa Bryan and Henry Plummer met for the first time. Electa was shy and reserved, but Plummer, as well as Jack Cleveland, quickly took a romantic interest in her. Francis Thompson, in one passage of his reminiscences, refers to Electa as "pure," "unsophisticated," and "beautiful," though elsewhere he calls her only "pretty," a description that probably fits better. [13] After all, she was still single at age twenty in times when it was common for teenage girls, long since chosen for marriage, to be carrying small children in their arms.

Electa was now faced with deciding between the attentions of Plummer and Cleveland, who was supposedly crude and foul-mouthed. Plummer, on the other hand, is almost universally described as handsome, meticulously clean, soft-spoken, intelligent, and polished. He looked to be about 5' 11", and to weigh around 150 pounds, had gray-blue eyes, light brown hair that glinted reddish tints in the sunlight, and a slender, athletic build. It is needless to say which of the two men would be more attractive to a young Christian woman. In addition to Electa, the farmhand Joseph Swift was also completely taken with Plummer.

The setting could not have been more conducive to romance: a deceptively peaceful Indian summer, cottonwood leaves turning yellow and dropping one by one along the Sun River banks, and emotions of those inside the fort heightened by the imminent danger outside, making each moment of life seem precious. It soon became apparent to everyone that Plummer's interest in Electa was serious, and when he had an opportunity to speak to her alone, he told her about his past problems in Washington and California, explaining that he was a peaceful man by nature, but that he had been forced to kill men to save his own life. His confession did not stop Electa from falling in love with him.

The choice Electa and Plummer made at Sun River that fall reveals something about both of them. Electa was, as Thompson wrote, completely unsophisticated, in fact so much so that he did not consider her as a marriage partner for himself. Though Thompson had found her kind and likable in the many weeks he had spent with her on the steamer, he also realized she was not of the social background that would be suitable for a man with his career plans. Having spent her life on a farm tending livestock and laboring had left her with tastes a little too simple for him. The best dress in her wardrobe was one of brown calico which she had sewn herself. Even though she was educated, Thompson would not trust her as hostess to the guests he hoped to entertain in his home at some future date.

Plummer, even more worldly-wise than Thompson and considered an excellent judge of character, could not have failed to make the same observations about Electa, and the obvious question is why he did not follow the same line of reasoning regarding her suitability. Wherever Plummer had gone, beautiful women had been attracted to him, and he had formed relationships with some who, as Dimsdale described, wore "the finest clothes money can buy," dresses "worth from seven to eight hundred dollars" each.[14] Certainly in Plummer's mind Electa could not compete with such women, and he also had to be aware how important religion was in her life. Nevertheless, there is no reason to doubt that the very qualities that caused men such as Thompson to reject Electa were

Sun River Crossing, Montana. At the Vail Farm, located on the left bank
of the river, Plummer met and fell in love with Electa Bryan. (Photo by
Boswell, 1986)

precisely the very ones that drew Plummer to her — her wholesome-
ness and naivete. And surely he appreciated most of all her un-
shakeable belief in him. It is possible he felt no concern for what help
she would be in his future career because he was confident he could
succeed with or without her help, but more than likely, he saw in her
a potential to be whatever she chose to become. It would be safe to
say that Electa and Plummer had faith in each other.

Thompson believed Electa fell in love with Plummer only
because of her being "isolated in a palisaded log house with no companion of her own sex, excepting her married sister," and there is
some truth to his statement.[15] Though she was a loved sister and
aunt, firmly included in all activities of the Vail family, Electa was
somewhat of an outsider looking wistfully in, made more aware of
her aloneness and lack of fulfillment by helping Martha through the
experiences of motherhood, constantly observing the relationship
Martha and James shared. But this need for a relationship of her
own does not completely explain the feeling she developed for Plummer. She had undoubtedly had previous chances for marriage and

rejected them, and by every indication we are led to believe that Plummer was simply the man for whom she had been waiting. Apparently she felt no anxiety that he neither shared her strong religious convictions nor seemed to value close family ties as highly as she. There was something of the romantic in her nature, a flair for the exotic that made her believe she could never again love anyone else as much as the young desperado, who spoke so gently to her in an accent that sounded almost foreign to the ears of an Ohio farm girl. The trait which prompted her to love him so was the same one which had brought her all the way to this wilderness fraught with countless dangers. But despite her romantic tendencies, Electa's judgment of Plummer should not be taken lightly. She was not a starry-eyed adolescent, but a mature woman, sensitive and intelligent, and quite different from the average Victorian woman in her open-mindedness and acceptance. Also, Electa may have been the one person to hear what is lacking from any historical record: Henry Plummer's version of his life story. Her opinion deserves considerable weight in an evaluation of his character, and after listening to Plummer talk about his past, Electa firmly believed he was a good man.[16]

The courtship had taken place during a period of tense watching and waiting in the close environs of the fort, but with the approach of winter, James Vail concluded that danger had passed. Though he had to inform Cleveland and Plummer that he had not received expected funds from the Indian agent and therefore would not be able to give them any pay for their time, all parted as friends.

With thoughts of settling down on his mind, Plummer abandoned his plans to return to the East, instead turning back toward the location he considered the land of greatest opportunity, the new mines rumored to contain the "purest" gold in the world, the diggings on the Beaverhead tributary nicknamed Grasshopper Creek. Plummer was an experienced miner, known for the good luck he had had in California and Nevada, and naturally his hopes were high. Before leaving the Sun River farm, he promised Electa he would come back to marry her in the spring.

FIRST WINTER AT BANNACK

During weeks of being cooped up together on the Vail farm, Cleveland and Plummer had already begun to get on each other's nerves, and Electa's falling in love with Plummer rather than Cleveland had not improved their relationship any. Their trip to Bannack was not a comfortable one. Though the exact day of their arrival is unknown, Granville Stuart, who, since entertaining Plummer at Gold Creek had decided to open a butcher shop in Bannack, wrote in his diary that Plummer was living in Bannack by 23 November 1862.[17]

Fortunately for the upwards of four hundred men and forty women holed up in tents, wickiups, wagons, dugouts, and cabins, the first winter at Bannack turned out to be relatively mild — as far as weather goes. There was food, a Mormon freighter having unloaded ten wagons of supplies — bacon, beans, and black flour — and residents had wisely jerked some game meat. At the point snow and cold made further mining activity impossible for the time being, gold seekers had panned and sluiced over $700,000 from the banks and bars along the Grasshopper, and were lavishly spending their plentiful gold dust in the few available businesses. Impatient miners found an outlet for their restlessness by poring over the sparse books and newspapers being passed back and forth or by gathering in the saloons.[18]

Wilbur Sanders, later to become Montana's first senator, mentions the important role played by the saloons: They occupied a "large space in the social and public life of the camps to which nearly everyone was driven," he wrote. Most were "hospitably conducted by well-behaved attendants or proprietors, only a few of them contented to be known as bad."[19]

Of the "bad" saloons, the one guaranteeing the most action was the Elkhorn, so named because of the pair of huge antlers the owner Cyrus Skinner had purchased and tacked over the front door. Inside was a long, polished, dark wood bar, a few card tables, and, attached to one wall, two rows of bunks with grass-stuffed mattresses, usually occupied by customers. Skinner had arrived in Bannack with a record of five prison commitments behind him. From his native Ohio, he came west searching for land, but soon after his arrival took up with the rougher element. It was rumored that he had ridden with the well-known California bandit, Rattlesnake Dick. At any rate, he was convicted of grand larceny and sentenced to three years in San Quentin, from where he broke jail and took work as a laborer, only to be recaptured and sent back to San Quentin with ten years added to his previous sentence as punishment for the escape. Prison records describe him as 5' 9½" with hazel eyes and dark hair. On his left hand was tattooed an anchor and ring ensemble, on the left arm a woman with child done in blue ink, and on the right arm only a woman — all three adornments making for colorful bartending.[20]

When Skinner escaped prison for the final time, he headed for the new gold fields in the Clearwater area of Washington Territory, setting up as a saloonkeeper in Florence, but later joining the stampede to the Grasshopper. He may have been a little loud and overbearing, but he was a jovial host and not choosy about his customers, gladly welcoming plenty of the type Dimsdale characterized as "that brutal desperado whose formula of introduction to a western barroom is so well known in the mountains: 'Whoop! I'm from Pike County, Missouri. I'm ten feet high . . . I smell like a wolf, I drink water out of a brook like a horse. Look out, you ———— I'm going to turn loose.' "[21]

Skinner's rowdy clientele brought him, if not a good reputation, at least a good profit, which enabled him to latch on to one of the few available white women in the area, Nellie. And he believed in treating women with respect. Once while casually firing into a group seated around a campfire, whom he innocently assumed were only Indians, he nearly winged the very respectable Mrs. Biddle, who had just arrived in town with her husband. When informed of his near accident, Skinner apologized profusely, explaining he would not kill a woman for the world and offering to make it all right again by setting up drinks on the house. Dr. Biddle left his distressed wife, who was several months pregnant, sitting alone by the fire while he accepted the invitation.[22]

Plummer, though no stranger to Skinner's, preferred the more respectable and quieter saloon at the Goodrich Hotel, also frequented by Cleveland, who had the habit of getting a little high and boasting how he was out to kill Plummer, scornfully referring to him as his "meat." Plummer remained unconcerned over these threats for some time, but eventually hostilities between the two came to a head. Both Dimsdale and Nathaniel Langford related the incident surrounding the final quarrel, complete with direct quotations from the participants, though their information reached them from at least thirdhand, and we must keep this in mind when we read, as well as their general purpose in telling the story in the first place — to provide evidence that Plummer was a cold-blooded killer.[23]

One bitterly cold morning, Plummer had joined a group

huddled on the low benches around the big wood stove in the Goodrich saloon when Cleveland, who had already been drinking heavily and was armed, made an entrance. He swaggered to the bar, bragging in a loud voice that he was chief of the town and would gladly fight anybody who thought he was not. When Plummer let the remark pass, Cleveland began harassing Jeff Perkins about an overdue debt. Perkins insisted he had already paid back the money, but Cleveland continued needling him, handling his gun meaningfully from time to time to intimidate the unarmed Perkins. Plummer advised Cleveland to drop the matter as the debt was paid and he should be satisfied. Then, to prevent Cleveland from carrying out "his apparent design of shooting Perkins . . . Plummer fixed his eyes sternly upon him and in a calm tone told him to behave himself."

Cleveland grudgingly quieted down for the moment, but soon added, "in a defiant and threatening manner, with mingled profanity and epithet," that he was not afraid of anybody. Plummer jumped up. "I'm tired of this," he said, drawing his pistol and firing at the ceiling. A second shot struck Cleveland, who fell to his knees, pleading, "You won't shoot me when I'm down?"

"No," Plummer said, "get up." As Cleveland raised to his feet, he grasped wildly for his gun, but was too drunk to get it up, and Plummer quickly landed two more shots. Even a sober Cleveland would have been no match for Plummer, who "was the quickest hand with his revolver of any man in the mountains. He could draw the pistol and discharge the five loads in three seconds."[24]

During the shootout, the barber who kept a chair in one corner of the saloon and was accustomed to ignoring such distractions, continued shaving his customer without interruption. Though Cleveland still lay on the floor unattended, no one seemed interested in helping him. Finally Hank Crawford, the town butcher, took the wounded man home with him, coming back to Plummer later for Cleveland's blankets. When Plummer asked what Cleveland had said about the incident, Crawford reported that Cleveland refused to comment on the original trouble between him and Plummer, saying only that it was nobody's business. As for his own plight, he had stoically remarked, "Poor Jack has got no friends. He has got it, and I guess he can stand it."

Plummer responded that it was well for Cleveland that he had said nothing against him, "for if he had I would kill him in his bed." Cleveland died with no further help from Plummer, Crawford arranging burial.[25]

Though friends warned Plummer he was apt to be lynched for the shooting, no charges were brought against him, mainly because it was generally suspected that Cleveland had recently robbed and killed a young man named George Evans and therefore deserved to be shot.

Using Cleveland's case as a demonstration of the reliability of "what was generally suspected," note that Dimsdale pins the blame for George Evans's disappearance on Cleveland for the reason that the latter had no money before the murder and "was seen riding close to the place and the next day he had plenty."[26] So much for good, hard evidence. Granville Stuart wrote that he "suspected that Charles Reeves and William Graves (Whiskey Bill) committed this murder."[27] Actually it was never known for certain whether Evans was murdered. One day he had disappeared, and later a nude body was found in the general vicinity, but the body was never identified as Evans. Guilty or innocent of Evans's murder, Cleveland was still unpopular, and the community regarded his death lightly.

Though Bannack was located in Dakota territory, the town was completely isolated from any government issuing from the faraway capital at Yankton, where officials were scarcely aware of the new mining camp under their jurisdiction. Residents had their own safety to worry about rather than the safety of suspected miscreants. In order to survive, each had to defend himself as best he could. As Granville Stuart explained, "There was no safety for life or property only so far as each individual could, with his trusty rifle, protect his own."[28]

Langford concurred that "shooting of pistols and duelling were so common as . . . to excite no attention. Many bloody encounters . . . were regarded as very proper settlements of difficulties between the parties."[29] Both he and Dimsdale provide valuable information about their times when they stray from their obsession with proving Plummer "a very monster of iniquity." Dimsdale understood the gold camp mentality better than might be expected from an ailing, Christian schoolteacher. According to the "Mountain Code," as he called it, being called a "liar, thief, or a son of a b---h" was justification for instantly killing the insulter. Preserving a reputation for manhood required a response of immediate violence, using "whatever weapon is handiest—foot, fist, knife, revolver, or derringer." Westerners lived in an environment of constant excitement, and "in the moment of passion, they would slay all around them, but let the blood cool, and they would share their last dollar with the men whose life they sought a day or two before."[30]

Plummer's behavior during the Cleveland affair can evidently be chalked up as adherence to the Mountain Code. Cleveland used epithets that threatened his manhood, and Plummer responded with immediate violence. However, the killing of Cleveland was not to be written off so easily. The butcher, Hank Crawford, lived in fear that Plummer believed Cleveland had revealed secrets about him immediately before his death. Crawford was waiting for just the right moment to try to convince the miners' court to bring charges of murder against Plummer.

BANNACK'S FIRST CRIMINAL TRIAL

Crawford's opportunity to be free from the supposed threat of Plummer came a short time later. For the price of a few blankets, Charlie Reeves had bought a Sheep Eater (Bannock) wife from the Indians camped south of town, and when he abused her, she ran home to her father, who let her stay but refused to return Reeves's blankets. After engaging in an unsuccessful scuffle with the chief, Reeves gave it up and went to brood over a drink, came back and fired a few shots, and then accompanied by two friends, named Moore and Mitchell, returned to fire on the camp again. On the second attempt two whites and several Indians were wounded and one white and several Indians killed.

This incident gave rise to the charge made later in one of the pioneer's reminiscences that the road agents maliciously tried to stir up the Indians against the whites,[31] and rather than a feeling of concern over the loss of Indian lives there was a general fear of reprisal by the tribe for Reeves's attack. To discover the then current attitude toward the natives of the area one has only to consider public reaction to Colonel Patrick Connor's attack at the Bear River. As other writers have pointed out, Colonel Connor was lauded as a hero for surprising the same tribe assailed by Reeves at their winter quarters and slaughtering over two hundred members as they attempted to flee across the ice on the half-frozen river. Typical comments about the massacre were expressed by Emily Meredith, a "learned" and "very religious" woman who at the time was wintering in Bannack. Though she wrote home about her disappointment that when Colonel Connor had "destroyed" the Indians he had not "regained the mail" they had stolen, she indicated no concern about his killing innocent women and children.[32]

X. Beidler showed a similar disregard for Indian life in a story he related of his adventures as a packer: "An Indian came to my camp one evening looking pretty hard up, . . . I fed him." Next evening "he came into my camp again. I fed him supper again. . . . That Indian came back to my camp again — third time — then I got tired. We had some picks and shovels along and we dug a hole and place him and his horse into it after killing them."[33]

When citizens heard Reeves and Moore had stirred up trouble by assaulting the Indian camp over a personal problem and in the process being so careless as to injure and kill white men, they decided to take action. Reeves, Moore, and Mitchell fled in the direction of Rattlesnake Creek, and Plummer, hearing rumors that he was also to be charged for the murder of Cleveland, left with them. But those who went in their pursuit the next morning allowed themselves to get in the embarrassing position of being forced to negotiate with the suspects or be shot. After the two parties talked matters over sensibly, the four men agreed they would come back to town on the promise, undoubtedly at Plummer's insistence, of being given a fair trial. It would be a first for Bannack because up to this time the local courts had been used exclusively for settling disputes over mining rights.

On their return to Bannack, Plummer was immediately put on trial for killing Cleveland and found innocent before midnight. This prompt verdict provides a clue that the story of the shooting as reported by Dimsdale and Langford is not very accurate since Plummer's actions could scarcely be considered self-defense. Dimsdale wrote that "Plummer was tried and honorably acquitted on account of Cleveland's threats," and Langford added that several witnesses testified that Cleveland had threatened to shoot Plummer on sight.[34] However, a less well-known version of the Cleveland affair, as likely to be true as Dimsdale's since neither mentioned a source, stated that the shooting came about when Plummer tried to break up a conflict that had developed between Cleveland and another man, and that Cleveland, not Plummer, fired the first shot. At the trial Plummer testified before the miners' court that Cleveland had been trailing him ever since he had left California, threatening revenge for Plummer for once having testified in a case that resulted in Cleveland being sent to prison. This version better explains the prompt verdict of the jury and better coincides with Langford's statement that Cleveland entered the saloon on that fateful day with a threat to get even for something that had happened on the "other side" of the mountains. In addition, it explains Cleveland's reluctance to divulge to Hank Crawford the nature of the trouble between himself and Plummer, as well as making more plausible the two of them having been together at Benton, Sun River, and Bannack, though they were not friends.[35]

Since we have no eyewitness account of what transpired on that winter morning in the Goodrich saloon, we can only conclude that the jury heard evidence that convinced them Plummer had fired to save his own life and therefore acquitted him. But what we can glean from both Dimsdale and Langford's narratives of the affray is Plummer's habit of assuming responsibility for keeping order wherever he went, as well as his manner of handling himself. As Langford put it, Plummer was always "cool."[36]

The trial of Reeves, Moore, and Mitchell was held the day after Plummer's and drew so much advance attention that it was necessary to send up-canyon for unprejudiced jury members. One of those who volunteered for jury duty was Nathaniel Langford, who despite the below zero temperatures was attempting to build a sawmill. The trial took place in a large, overheated log building with the entire male population of the mining district in attendance and the overflow spilling out into the snowy street. Though on the night before lawyer William Rheem had promised to serve as prosecuting attorney, on the morning of the trial he surprised the court by announcing that he had switched over to the defense. The court was left without a prosecutor and had to enlist the services of Mr. Copley, even though, according to Dimsdale, his talents lay elsewhere. The assembled miners elected Mr. Hoyt as judge of the court and Hank Crawford as sheriff.

After hearing the evidence, the jury's decision was delayed for

Bannack's Skinner Saloon, noted for a dangerously rowdy clientele and a host who had a taste for tattoos and Greek Revival architecture. Accused by vigilantes of being a "roadster, fence, and spy" for Plummer's gang, Skinner was captured while standing in the doorway of his Hell Gate Saloon. Refusing to permit his "chère amie" Nellie to speak in his behalf, vigilantes hanged Skinner by torchlight from the nearest corral beam, with the words "I am innocent" on his lips. (Photo by Boswell, 1986)

quite some time by Langford's insistence on the death penalty for all three men, but eventually he agreed to a verdict of manslaughter with a punishment of confiscation of property and banishment, but only after the weather had warmed up some.

The new sheriff, Crawford, who claimed he had never fired a weapon at a man in his entire life, did not enjoy his duties and wanted to resign, but was persuaded to stay on. His first assignment was to sell the guns confiscated from the banished prisoners, and in so doing, he made the mistake of also selling the gun belonging to Plummer, who had been found innocent. In order to right this wrong, the miners ordered Crawford to retrieve all the arms and return them to their original owners, even though this left the sheriff to pay all expenses of the trial personally, including the board of the prisoners. When he demanded reimbursement for these bills as well

Interior of Skinner's Saloon, located on main street of Bannack, Montana.
(Photo by Boswell, 1986)

as the cost of caring for and burying Jack Cleveland, the miners'
court authorized him to seize Cleveland's horses, but he again ran
into trouble because Cleveland had had a partner with rights to half
of the herd. Throughout Crawford's problems, he and Plummer had
a series of disagreements, so "some of the boys," Dimsdale said,
"brought them together and they shook hands, Plummer declaring
that he desired his friendship."[37] Despite the frequent quarrels in the
mining camps, this practice of making friends all around afterwards
was quite common.

Quarrels and subsequent reconciliations continued as the long
cold winter wore on. Often the cause was no more than cabin fever
aggravated by alcohol, but another frequent source of strife were the
Civil War issues being decided on the battlefields back in the States.
During the final weeks of unsolicited idleness, even the most minor
of incidents could provoke a brawl. Buck Stinson, the barber who
rented corner space for his chair in Cyrus Skinner's saloon, once
reproved a man for speaking too crossly to a boy, and an argument
followed that progressed to blows. Though the clinch was quickly

broken up, Stinson and his adversary continued to seethe, walking the streets armed to the teeth until Plummer finally intervened, persuading Stinson to break down and apologize, thus putting an end to the feud.

Another dispute that came out of a card game at Skinner's had a more tragic ending. When a miner named Dick Sapp accused his professional opponent, Banfield, of filling a flush from the deck, the gambler drew on him. Others quieted Banfield and the game resumed, but in only a few minutes Sapp again protested he was being conned, and this time the gambler got off a shot at the unarmed man before others could intervene. Dr. Bissell quickly handed off his revolver to Sapp to make it a fair contest, and the two men dodged back and forth behind the posts holding up the roof, emptying their revolvers on each other without even once hitting the mark. They then switched to hand-to-hand combat, though still without injury to either party, until others broke them apart, suggesting they be friends and have a drink together. Before they could take the first sip, they heard a groan and, looking under the table, discovered that Toodles, a shepherd dog who also frequented the saloon for warmth and company, had been hit in the shooting melee and was dying. The next groan issued from the row of bunks along the wall, where they found that George Carrhart, a former legislator from Nevada, had also been hit. Dr. Bissell quickly put down his drink and lifted Carrhart to a table to examine him, reporting the wounded man could not possibly be saved. Moore and Reeves, who had been sleeping away their time until banishment, woke up and commenced firing at the two men who had killed their friend Carrhart, and Sapp ran from the saloon, catching a shot in the little finger. Banfield was struck in the leg and died later from lack of care of the wound. Sapp stayed at home the remainder of the night sulking over the unfairness of the incident and returned to Skinner's the next day backed up by a few friends who had volunteered to help him settle the score with Moore and Reeves. Though it was no easy task, Cyrus Skinner eventually took the fight out of both sides by offering drinks all around.

The habit of peacefully resolving such conflicts contributed to most of the residents making it safely through the first winter at Bannack, though there were some casualties and not just from hot tempers and gunplay, but from more impersonal killers such as pneumonia, typhoid, and mountain fever. When the ground became frozen too hard to chip out graves for victims, survivors sledded them to a temporary morgue built atop cemetery hill, a small stockade designed specifically to keep out hungry coyotes and wolves. The below-zero temperatures insured that bodies of the dead would be preserved until a thaw allowed for a decent burial. [38]

TRIUMPHANT SPRING OF 1863

Springtime meant chinook winds melting drifted snow and thawing frozen earth to a soggy muck, and maybe a courageous bluebird or two making a flashy, but absurdly early, appearance. And the miners busied themselves with more important matters than squabbling in the saloons. Those who had already acquired a claim immediately set to panning and sluicing, or slooshing, as it was commonly pronounced, while newcomers rushed to stake out the permitted one hundred feet, exploring new gulches up and down the Grasshopper. Some branched out much further, such as the Stuart expedition, which scouted the Yellowstone area, and its splinter group, which missed connections with the main party and ended up discovering the fabulous lodes in Alder Gulch, destined to surpass and eventually evacuate Bannack.

In March, the mining districts had become part of the newly formed Territory of Idaho, but the word had not yet reached those affected most by the decision. Many would not have cared about its implications anyhow since their intentions were to get rich quickly and go back home to the States. Henry Plummer did not fit into this latter category, though; he had made the West his home for eleven years and was interested in the future of the territory. He was among those searching out rich claims that spring; wealth would make an easier transition to the respectable life he planned to lead with Electa. With years of mining experience under his belt, the success he usually had could hardly be attributed to mere luck. In all the camps he had observed eager placer miners skimming off the loose gold and moving on, leaving that embedded in the quartz for those who came after. But there was a problem at Bannack in obtaining equipment for quartz mining, and hammering the outcroppings to a powder by hand, as some did, was slow and inefficient. After taking out claims on the Dacotah lode, Plummer and his partner solved the equipment problem by hiring a blacksmith to jimmyrig a water-powered stamp mill of wooden stems and metal shoes and dies cut from old wagon tires and forged together. Despite its crude construction, the little stamp mill successfully crushed out phenomenal amounts of gold for its owners. [39]

Plummer's mining endeavors worked out much better than his truce with Hank Crawford, which continued to suffer its ups and downs, Plummer ending each verbal skirmish with a request to drop hostilities and Crawford refusing out of distrust and fear. For a time, Plummer continued trying to be friendly, but finally suggested that if Crawford did not care to be friends, they could at least meet as in-hostile strangers. Crawford's associates, reporting they had seen Plummer lingering outside the butcher shop one night as though he might be watching Crawford, warned him to keep up his guard, and he followed their advice. [40]

Soon after, Plummer, no longer friendly but obviously angry, confronted Crawford about a rumor he had been spreading around camp that Plummer had intentions of courting an Indian woman named Catherine. Because of his engagement to Electa, Plummer was concerned about keeping a good reputation and challenged Crawford to a fistfight, but Crawford refused. Plummer then proposed a duel, and Crawford speedily sent word to his friend, Harry Phleger, that he needed help and wanted him to come to Peabody's saloon. When Plummer and friends arrived at Peabody's, Phleger greeted them cordially and invited them to have a drink, but all refused the offer. Turning to the one he believed most approachable, Deaf Dick, Crawford said in a raised voice, "Well, Dick, . . . you'll drink anyhow." When Deaf Dick retorted he would not drink with any coward, Crawford stepped forward to strike him, and Plummer handed his revolver to Dick, who was unarmed. Seeing Dick armed, Crawford handed off his own gun to Phleger, saying he supposed he was going to be shot now. Phleger wanted to know by whom, to which Crawford responded, "Plummer, I suppose." On hearing this, Phleger drew on the lot of Plummer's friends, and as Plummer wrestled with him in an attempt to get one of the guns, he was thrown by Phleger, who then kept the group covered as he and Crawford retreated out the door. Back at his room, Crawford was so worried over Plummer's skill with a weapon and his own ineptness that he broke down and cried himself to sleep, leaving Phleger to keep the watch alone the entire night.

After a few days, Plummer sent word to Crawford suggesting they drop the feud, but Crawford rejected the offer, saying to those who had brought the message, "He or I must die or leave the camp." Two days later Crawford found the chance he was waiting for when he spotted Plummer standing across the street with one foot resting on a wagon spoke and his gun lying across his knee. Egged on by others, Crawford fired with a double-barreled shotgun, a ball entering Plummer's arm at the right elbow, traveling down the arm and lodging in the wrist. The force of the blow knocked Plummer down. "Some son of a bitch has shot me!" he said to those who came to help him up. Though it would appear likely he would know it was Crawford who had fired the shot if the two men had been stalking each other for several days as Dimsdale and Langford reported, we have no better account to which to turn. With his right arm dangling uselessly, Plummer stood up, facing Crawford and calling him a coward. "Fire away," he told him, and Crawford did but missed and then fled as Plummer continued walking down to his cabin, holding his gun in his left hand. Running to the Wadams' cabin, Crawford asked to be admitted and hid himself behind flour sacks until dark.[41] When his brother brought him a horse, he left the territory, not wishing to be around to accept Plummer's invitation for a second meeting in two weeks.

The doctor who attended Plummer advised removing his right arm in order to save his life, but Plummer refused, saying he would rather die than live without his arm. The attempted surgery failed to locate the ball, and with friends standing by through tense days and nights, Plummer, his arm swollen to three times its normal size, lay with his life in danger. At last his fever broke and recovery began.

Hoffman Birney professes doubts that Dimsdale and Langford's accounts of the trouble between Plummer and Crawford, as told above, really get to the heart of the matter: "One is forced to ask if the true story of the events leading up to that encounter has ever been told." He bases his doubt on Plummer's general popularity at Bannack.[42] True, Plummer had had problems with Cleveland and Crawford, but despite this he had actually generated a favorable impression as a quiet, polite man ever since his arrival in Bannack. Rheem said that though Plummer "talked but little, when he did speak, it was always in a low tone and with a good choice of language,"[43] and even Langford admitted that Plummer "speedily became a general favorite" in Bannack partly because of "the advantages of a good early education" and "was oftener applied to for counsel and advice than any other resident."[44] Plummer was consulted about the typical problems of a new mining camp because of his years of experience on the frontier, but he was also sought out for personal help because, having no particular need to talk about himself, he made a good listener. And when people brought their problems to him, Langford wrote, he showed a "power of analysis that seldom failed."[45] Agreeing Plummer was a natural choice for sheriff, miners cast 307 out of 554 votes for him at the next election, a much larger majority than that received by other officers elected on the same day. On 24 May 1863, Plummer assumed his duties as sheriff of Bannack and the other surrounding mining districts. Hank Crawford's act would not be a very difficult one to follow.

Plummer commenced setting up his organization immediately. He was able to enlist some respected men as deputies: Smith Ball, Buzz Caven, and J. W. Dillingham. Others were not of such good reputation. Ned Ray, a known rough, was also a brave man and a good shot. Though Dimsdale claimed that Ray had escaped from San Quentin, prison records show that he was never an inmate there. Buck Stinson, who barbered at Skinner's saloon, was of no better reputation than Ray, despite being a married man. However, as many writers have pointed out, Plummer's choice of deputies was limited by the high danger and low compensation that went with the positions. Even the sheriff received no regular salary, but was paid only for specific services rendered: 25¢ for summoning witnesses and jurors, $1 for serving warrants, $2.50 for attending court trials, plus 25¢ per mile travel expenses.[46] More than anything else, sheriffing was a community service. Plummer's main income came from his mines.

In the six months since his departure from the Vails' farm, Henry Plummer had accomplished perhaps even more than he had hoped towards a life-style that would be acceptable to Electa. A news correspondent who had followed the gold rush to the Grasshopper dispatched a long article back to the *Sacramento Union*, capturing the excitement brought on by the gold fever sweeping the country.

> Before fall, Bannock will be second to no city north of Salt Lake. Over four hundred houses are built. . . . Several of the richest quartz lodes in the world have been opened, among which the "Dacotah" is averaging $20,000 to the ton, and in one day's crushing from the claim of

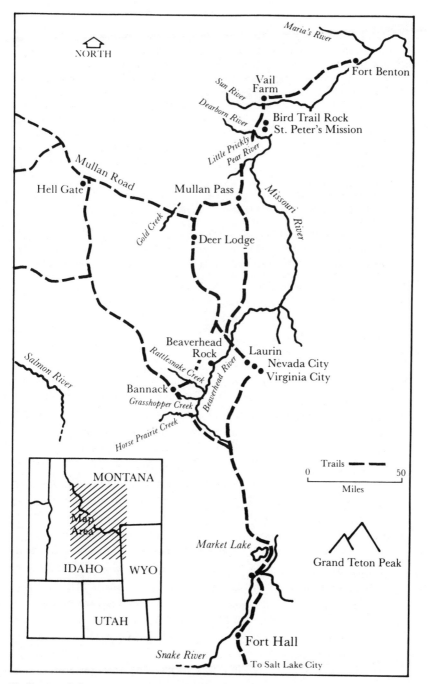

Trails to mining camps east of the Rocky Mountains.

Plumer and Ridgely I saw $3,800 in neat amalgam in the retort. The richest claim in Idaho Territory was discovered a few weeks since by a young man named E. Richardson. . . . In one day's crushing, with three sluices and four men there were $2,360 taken out, and on last Saturday they cleaned up in one afternoon's washing, $1,850. The proprietors have refused $25,000 for one half (25 feet) of the claim. The partners are E. Richardson, Henry Plumer (well known in Nevada), J. Cross and Cyrus Skinner. . . . The population is at present about 1,800, among whom are counted 147 ladies and 64 children. . . . Society in a new gold country! Scarcely a day passes without a train arriving. It is estimated that over 8,000 are on the way and will arrive before the middle of June. . . . No man stands higher in the estimation of the community than Henry Plumer.[47]

A quiet young man dogged by a bad reputation had ridden into Bannack one cold day in November, and by spring had taken the town by storm. He did not need a newspaper article to tell him that. After his election as sheriff, he filed legal record of the lot and cabin he had purchased and then headed north on the two-hundred-mile trip back to the Sun River for Electa.

THE WEDDING

It was not a good time to leave for Sun River. The flood season was just reaching its peak and the river crossing would be treacherous if not impossible. Henry Plummer was needed in Bannack, both to show his constituents that he intended to take his job seriously, and to give the growth taking place there a sense of direction. But Plummer showed a quite typical trait. He was a man of extreme patience, up to a point; then his repressed impatience exploded. He had obtained sufficient gold stakes to provide a more than comfortable living, and his claims in the Blue Wing area showed promise of silver. The delay in returning for Electa had been due to waiting for the sheriff's position, the badge of respectability he guessed the Vails would require, especially after hearing he had killed Cleveland.

Displaying his basic impatience with life, Plummer did not stay in Bannack as long as he should have after the election. His idea of an orderly world was one in which a person had peace of mind and was not bothered by anyone else. He liked setting the world in order and spent most of his time at it, in the calm, easy way he had of going about his job without offending others. As Langford observed, "he was quiet and modest, free from swagger."[48] Quiet and free from swagger, yes, but hardly modest, at least not in the sense of placing a moderate estimate on his own abilities and worth. He knew himself and was aware of his own skills and competencies, his quietness and reserve coming from his high degree of self-confidence. He expected, and eventually demanded, that others share the opinion he held of himself. Both Jack Cleveland and Hank Crawford had required his "demanding."

Though Plummer had felt a little contempt at Crawford's bungling of his official assignments, tasks Plummer could have handled quickly and efficiently, he was in general tolerant of inefficiency in others. But he would not allow Crawford to damage his reputation by spreading rumors about his personal life — not while he was engaged to Electa. All else failing with Crawford, Plummer had invited him to test who was the better man with fists. When Crawford refused, he had suggested pistols, offering, "You may draw it and cock it, and I'll not go for mine until you have done so, and uttered the word to fire." These were words spoken by a man who had confidence in his own skills.

When Crawford again refused, Plummer's patience ran out. "Pull your pistol and fight me like a man, or I'll give you but two hours to live, and then I'll shoot you down like a dog." At the end of the two hours the confrontation at Peabody's took place.[49]

Plummer had followed the same steps with both Crawford and Cleveland. He refused to waste his time holding ill-will and could not tolerate the threat to his own peace of mind when a grudge was festering against him. The Christian precept of not letting the sun set on one's wrath may have been impressed on him in childhood, or he may have acquired the peacemaking habit in the camp saloons. Whatever its source, he had become a professional at mending broken fences. If a person was not perceptive enough to see his good faith, he tried friendly persuasion for an incredibly long period, and then with the hard core finally had to issue a challenge, one in which he usually came out on top. Cleveland had trailed Plummer for weeks, harassing him, and taking advantage of his patience and near obsession for turning enemies into friends. Though Cleveland wanted to kill Plummer and was only holding off because Plummer was a better shot, he did not have the insight to realize Plummer's patience was wearing thin, not until Plummer informed him, in his characteristic terse understatement, "I'm tired of this."

Crawford was playing the same game, afraid of a confrontation and waiting for a safe way to get even. He first persuaded the miners' court to try Plummer for murder. When that did not work, he tried to get Phleger to do the job for him, and finally ended up shooting Plummer from behind. But Crawford had only appeared to get the better of the contest; actually it was Plummer who got what he wanted — the job of sheriff. And he was anxious to get started at it, to show what he could do with the position, but he also wanted Electa and was tired of waiting. He had been waiting all winter. In spite of high waters, he was confident he would find a way to cross the Sun River when he came to it.

The winter of 1862–63 had not been any easier at the government farm than in Bannack. Salt and spices needed to make food more palatable had dwindled to nothing and had to be omitted from dishes served. There was no appeal to Fort Benton, where supplies had also been exhausted by a much larger influx of newcomers than had been expected. Though newcomers survived the difficult winter on hopes of growing rich in the spring, the Vails had no such anticipation, having nothing to look forward to other than a recurrence of seasons like the one just spent. Not that they had lost faith in their project; they had not accepted it because they thought it would be easy.

In the months after Plummer left the farm, Martha grew concerned about his bad reputation and tried to persuade her younger sister to give up the idea of marrying him. But Electa stood firm. She was, as Thompson recognized, "infatuated," but it was more than that. Her waiting so long to choose a husband was partly due to a realization of her own worth, a worth that was confirmed by Plummer's strong desire for her. For all his self-confidence and strength, he needed her to give meaning to his life. Electa would not let Martha keep her from the happiness she saw ahead, but it was difficult to stand up to an older sister on whom she had been dependent since childhood and whose approval she had constantly sought. Martha was frustrated at not having her usual upper hand; and the struggle between the sisters, painful because of their love for each other, had reached a stalemate. Francis Thompson gives a fair account of events taking place at the farm on his return. Though he wrote many years later, he relied on diaries kept at the time, rarely letting his personal bias color the narrative.[50]

When Thompson reached the crossing, the Sun River was high with runoff from the mountains and unsafe for fording. He waited cautiously for several days on the bank opposite the farm. Seeing James Vail, he called to him, and Vail recognized him and went to the house to report his arrival to Martha, Electa, and Joseph Swift. Martha and Electa agreed the opinion of an impartial friend might solve their dilemma, and Electa promised she would accept Thompson's advice about her marriage plans.

Less than an hour after Thompson was finally able to ford the river, Martha cornered him, begging him to help settle the sisters' difference. Thompson listened to Martha's point of view first. She was a "most devoted Christian woman," he wrote, "and loved her sister most tenderly and felt that she was responsible for her future, as would a mother for her daughter."[51]

Thompson already shared Martha's doubts. On the trail, he had heard from men in a pack train about a young desperado named Henry Plummer, who was living in Bannack. The men said Plummer had killed a man in California, escaped from the state prison, killing a pursuing officer in the process, and then fled to Washington Territory, where he got in more difficulties and had to flee across the mountains to Fort Benton for a quick retreat down the Missouri River. Finding no boatman willing to risk being killed by Indians while running the river, he had gone to Bannack. The story Thompson had heard was a little different from the one Electa had heard from Plummer, but similar enough to cause Martha and Thompson grave concern.

From Joseph Swift, Thompson heard the same side of the argument he expected Electa to present. It was obvious to him how thoroughly Swift had been won over by Plummer during the months of the Indian scare. Though touched by Swift's love and admiration for Plummer, Thompson went to his interview with Electa filled with the same anxieties as Martha.

He began by warning Electa to reconsider, but nothing he could say seemed to sway her. Though she was shy, she expressed her feelings with a surprising candor and openness. "She said that she loved Mr. Plummer," Thompson wrote, "that she knew that he loved her, that she had the utmost faith in him, that the terrible stories of him were told by men not worthy of belief; that she could never be happy unless she married him."[52]

Realizing Electa shared the religious convictions of her sister, Thompson broke some news to her she had not yet heard. He told her the man she loved had killed Jack Cleveland just a few weeks after leaving the farm. Electa, remembering that Cleveland had also loved her, was shaken at his words and Thompson pursued his advantage by advising her that even if Plummer was justified in killing Cleveland, in the territory "it was generally the case that a man who killed another, died a like death."

His prediction of an ominous fate awaiting her future husband troubled Electa greatly, and Thompson capitalized on her distress by suggesting she take more time to make her decision. She should take the steamer from Fort Benton to the States, he said, and if by autumn she still loved Plummer, and he still loved her, then he could join her there and they could be married. Electa had promised to accept his arbitration, but instead, she replied only that she would consider his idea.

The Vails were anxiously waiting for the arrival of the *Shreveport*, the steamer Electa could take, because it would be carrying their employer, Reverend Reed, with their year's salary and the much-needed supplies. Thompson, who was awaiting the same ship to bring goods ordered for a general merchandise store he planned to open, was invited to stay at the farm until the *Shreveport* docked. Though the river was high, the spring season had been so dry that there was scarcely a blade of green grass in the entire valley. Provisions at the farm were scarce; the supply of sugar had run out, and since the cows had gone dry for lack of grass, there was no milk, cream, or butter. While on a hunting trip, Iron, the faithful Indian who had provided the farm with meat, had been killed by Bannocks, who had also stolen horses, saddles, blankets, and a gun belonging to the farm. The family was reduced to a diet of the game meat Vail and Thompson could provide—sometimes nothing more than prairie dogs—and corn meal ground in a hand mill. Though monotonous, there were a variety of ways to serve up the coarse meal: mush, johnnycakes, muffins, or Indian pudding.

Despite food shortages, the men took time out from hunting to go with the women and children for drives across the dry plains, and there was an unusual amount of activity at the farm. Travelers on the way to meet the overdue *Shreveport* stopped in daily, and the Indians frequently presented minor problems that had to be dealt with. On one such occasion, the Vails were visited by an Indian and his wife, who reported they were searching for a second wife who had run away with another man. The husband wanted to find her so he could punish her according to the law prescribed by his people. He had a choice of either killing her or cutting off her ears and nose and letting her live. Not long after the couple had left, the second wife walked in alone. Martha warned her of her danger, and after eating a few bites of food, the frightened Indian woman hurried off toward the safety of the mountains. Despite their own straits, Martha provided her with a ration of food to carry along as well as a blanket.

Meanwhile, Electa was still trying to reach a decision about marrying Plummer, and time was growing short since the steamer might arrive at any moment. Thompson said it was a long time before she finally gave in, agreeing to delay the wedding until fall. Martha was relieved when Electa half-heartedly began gathering her things together for the trip home.

On the first day of June, there appeared at the river crossing a priest from St. Peter's Mission, established by the Jesuits to serve the Blackfeet and located just ten miles off of the road between Sun River and Little Prickly Pear Creek. Like Thompson, the priest was leery of attempting to ford the roily waters, but not wanting to wait, he worked up his courage and spurred his horse forward. In midstream he was suddenly swept from his mount and dragged under by a strong current, nearly drowning before he finally made it to shore. His horse wisely swam back to the other side.

The next day, with Electa still planning to leave on the steamer, Plummer reached Sun crossing, and not waiting for safer waters, quickly crossed to the fortified farm. He had come to keep his promise to marry Electa, unaware she had had a change of heart.

Plummer was not at all what Thompson had been expecting, but "a good looking young man of twenty-seven, polite, and of good address," Thompson confided in his diary. He had "a straight nose and well-shaped chin" and "a well-cut mouth, indicating decision, firmness, and intelligence." His light gray eyes "seemed to be gazing through you." Thompson, impressed by Plummer's "dignity" and "brilliant conversation," wrote, "When I saw him I could but wonder if this could be the young desperado whom people so much feared." He made another important observation; Plummer "seemed devoted to Miss Bryan."[53]

On the very day of the arrival, Thompson noted that all of his "well intended advice was thrown to the wind and it was announced that the marriage would take place." With a few "quiet assurances," Plummer had calmed Electa's fears, and though Martha did not give up her objection to the marriage, she weakened at the news of Plummer's election as sheriff of Bannack and his substantial holdings in mining claims. As for Thompson, he was so favorably impressed by Plummer that he did not wonder at Electa's happiness over the coming marriage.

The wedding was to take place as soon as Reverend Reed arrived on the steamer, which was still expected daily, but day after day passed without its arrival. Plummer was impatient to hold the ceremony and return to his duties as sheriff, but the Vails, oblivious to his concerns, stubbornly persisted in their plan to wait for a minister of their faith. To pass the time, they suggested the entire group make an excursion to the Great Falls of the Missouri, about thirty miles distant. Though the trip would be a dangerous one, requiring passage through Indian country, the magnificent view was considered worth the risk. They set out, Plummer, Swift, and Thompson riding horseback alongside the ambulance wagon carrying James, Martha, Electa, Mary, and Harvey.

They reached Horseshoe Falls by dark without incident and camped there for the night, cautiously building their campfire in a ravine out of sight of Indians, who were especially tempted to attack small parties. On reaching the falls the next day, they were all duly impressed by the grandeur of the spectacle and then quickly started for home, hoping the return trip would prove as safe. Plummer and Swift, riding ahead as an advance warning party, reached the top of a hill and suddenly whirled around, riding back toward the wagon at full gallop. Suspecting an Indian attack, Thompson and Vail promptly prepared to defend the women and children, but as it turned out, the excitement had been caused by a herd of antelope that the young men rightfully thought Thompson might want to pursue with his rifle.

As they came in sight of the farm, grateful to be on sure ground again, they received a second alarm. The fort was completely surrounded by Indian ponies. Fearing it had been taken over, they had

St. Peter's Mission, Montana, which provided a priest, Father Minatre, to unite Plummer and Electa Bryan in marriage on 20 June 1863 at the Sun River Farm. (Photo by Boswell, 1986)

to make the difficult decision whether to abandon it and look else-where for shelter or advance and retake it if necessary. They decided in favor of advancing cautiously.

During their absence, a party of Flatheads had ridden in, and on observing their approach, the man left in charge had locked both front and back gates. But while some of the party kept him occupied at the front, others climbed over the back gate and let themselves in, demanding they be served food. While they were enjoying their new command, the Flatheads saw the advance party of the Vails drawing near the gate and quickly relinquished power. James Vail let them off with no more than a scolding.

Plummer had not intended to be gone from Bannack so long and was growing restless at the needless delay, the mission being only a few miles away. The next day after the excursion, he and Swift rode to Fort Benton for news of the dilatory ship, bringing back word that waters were too shallow for the *Shreveport* to reach its destination. Electa and the Vails now agreed to have the marriage performed by Father Minatre of St. Peter's. He was sent for and arrived on 20 June, family and visitors at the fort gathering in the best room for the wedding. Electa wore a brown calico dress, "modest and unassuming," and Plummer a blue suit foxed with buckskin. James Vail gave away the bride, Martha acted as matron of honor, and Plummer had asked Joseph Swift to be his best man, leaving only Thompson with no role to play. Fearing he might feel left out, Father Minatre invited Thompson to act as bridesmaid and he accepted. The ceremony was "long and formal."

The women had prepared a wedding breakfast of baked buffalo hump, considered a delicacy, and corn bread, and as soon as the meal was finished, the men hitched "four wild Indian ponies" to the ambulance wagon, and "the happy couple" left "for Bannack city, the new metropolis." Thompson added that "the poor sister, Mrs. Vail, was almost heartbroken."[54]

The couple began their first day of married life seated side by side on a buckboard. Their first problem would be crossing the swollen Sun River, and they would have to spend their wedding night camped under the open skies, probably near the trees along Dearborn River. The trip to Bannack, begun on 20 June, the culminating day of the spring floods, would take at least seven days through a route considered risky even in a large company of armed men. They followed a trail through a valley brown with dried grass and withered buffalo peas, passing between buttes and gradually rising to climb Bird Tail Divide. Descending, they entered Little Prickly Pear Canyon, colorful with violets and geraniums, but with the creek so high that the road John Mullan mapped out lay beneath water, and they were forced to cut their own path through miles of rocky terrain along the base of the steep cliffs. Then came another lower divide and a larger valley where Indians camped and ducks and hundreds of spindly-legged curlews waded in shallow ponds. Crossing the Rockies at Mullan Pass, they reached Deer Lodge, near where Plummer and the Stuart brothers had spent a few pleasurable evenings playing poker, and from there, on down the river, past Beaverhead Rock, the strange formation that Sacajawea had recognized as a landmark of her childhood home, and then over the hills to Bannack.

Plummer had gotten his bride safely back to Bannack, and they had also made it through their first week of married life.

MARRIED LIFE

For years after, early residents of Bannack recalled the day Sheriff Plummer rode into town with his new bride. Electa was sitting on the wagon seat beside him, smiling. Bannack was a typical mining boomtown — a single, dusty main street, set in a narrow canyon and lined by false-fronted buildings, the first such town Electa had ever seen. From the gulch where they entered, she could make out the mile-high town site stretched along the valley cut by a meandering creek. On its outskirts was a small camp of Shoshoni who ranged the area. The hills bordering the narrow valley were now dry and bare, except for sagebrush, all the cottonwood lining the creek and the pine and cedar that had been on the mountaintops having been cut down for cabins and wickiups. All about her was activity — prosperous tradesmen conversing on the uneven boardwalks before their businesses in voices loud enough to be heard above the violin music issuing from open saloon doors, and busy miners working the mountain opposite like ants swarming over an anthill — yet there was a certain orderliness to it all. On one side of Grasshopper Creek was a single street of residences, and on the other side a single street of businesses. These two sections of town were joined by a footbridge of no more than two unconnected logs slung across the water.

Main Street, strictly a male domain, boasted three hotels, three bakeries, three blacksmith shops, two stables, two meat markets, a grocery store, a restaurant, a brewery, a billiard hall, and four saloons. Though all of the businesses were built of logs, some had decorative false fronts adding a touch of class. Despite the isolated location and barren setting, the narrow canyon and neatly arranged settlement gave off an atmosphere of snugness and security, the completeness of a small world.

Plummer had purchased a town lot located just one block off Main Street, and he took Electa there to the small cabin in which she would be spending most of her time. Women rarely left home, not even for shopping or visiting neighbors. She soon learned that her husband's duties occupied nearly all of his time, but at first there was enough work setting up housekeeping to keep her busy also. The typical residence was a tiny one-room cabin built of rough logs still covered with bark and chinked between with mud. The floor was dirt, thickly padded with rye grass, over which an animal hide, fur side up, was lain and fastened down with wooden pegs. The roof,

Main street of Bannack in the 1860s.

made of willow poles, was caked with mud and coated with a top layer of shale to reduce the danger of fire from chimney sparks. Since the cabin had few if any windows, an open door by day and a candle or lantern by night provided lighting. Furnishings consisted of a stone fireplace for cooking, a crudely carpentered table and stools, and a bunk, on which rested a mattress stuffed with dry meadow grass. Notwithstanding the sparse household equipment, chores proceeded as usual: cleaning, sewing, ironing, and laundry, which was done in the same wooden tub used for bathing with water carried in a tin bucket from the Grasshopper.

The women were very resourceful about making home life enjoyable. Though they were forced to serve from tin plates and cups, they baked delicious meals, substituting ingredients as necessary from whatever limited supplies might be available. Always plentiful

(Photo courtesy of Montana Historical Society)

were wild meats such as antelope, deer, moose, mountain sheep, grouse, or sage hen. To make up for its many shortcomings, the cabin interior was usually decorated as cheerfully as possible: bare log walls covered with fabric, white muslin curtains hung at a single window, and bright calico prints tacked to crude shelves to convert them into cupboards. Electa, who was known as a woman who "delighted" in her home life, certainly made her cabin as inviting as any in town. [55] She was accustomed to brightening a home and doing household chores, but it was difficult for her to grow accustomed to performing them alone. Still, the women's lives were not one eternal round of housework since there was one social activity in Bannack in which they were included.

Dimsdale states that dancing was "the great amusement"[56] for all ages and both sexes, and Bannack's first cabin to have a wooden

Main street of Bannack, as seen from near Plummer's grave site in
Hangman's Gulch. To the left of the wickiup frame stands the supposed site
of the Plummers' home, now overgrown with sagebrush, but with founda-
tion logs of the cabin still visible. (Photo by Boswell, 1986)

floor was immediately borrowed to hold a dance, or ball as it was
called, complete with orchestra and dance programs. Granville
Stuart described these events as wholesome affairs that "all the
respectable people" enjoyed.

> "Best suits . . . long forgotten, were dragged out, aired and pressed, as
> best we could, and made ready for these festive occasions. A very few
> of the men who had their wives with them, sported white shirts with
> stiffly starched bosoms, but the majority wore flannel shirts with soft
> collars and neckties. These dances were very orderly; no man that was
> drinking was allowed in the hall. The young people danced the waltz,
> schottish, varsoviane, and polka, but the older ones stuck to the
> Virginia-reel and quadrille. There were usually about ten men to every
> woman at these balls so the women danced every dance."[57]

One of the fiddlers who provided the music for the dances was Buzz
Caven, one of Plummer's more respected deputies and the former
owner of the late Toodles, who had been accidentally killed during
the gunfight at Skinner's saloon.

Another early resident, Robert Kirkpatrick, also left an account of the dances at Bannack. "Little girls six and seven years of age danced regularly, and ten year old girls considered themselves young women in society." But he differs with Stuart about the orderliness of the crowd: "The musicians often got so drunk they could hardly keep their seats, and lots of the men half drunk in the ball room. The floor manager sometimes had to put men out of the hall for being drunk."[58]

Plummer, one of the best dancers in town, had attended the balls during the winter and spring prior to Electa's arrival. Sarah Wadams, fourteen years old at the time, claimed that before his marriage he had escorted her to "a number of dances" and that he was "pleasant and well mannered, never coming to a dance while intoxicated." Sarah remembered the music being provided by a horn, fiddle, and tambourine, or at other times by a banjo and bones, and supper being served after: "cold boiled meat, brought all the way from Johnnie Grant's ranch at Deer Lodge . . . served with bread and butter and pickles . . . and pie and cake, stewed dried fruit and tea."[59]

What is missing from all such recollections of the good times is any mention that Electa ever participated. Quite possibly she did not enter into the social life of the community. Throughout her entire life the only activities she is reported to have been involved in that took her outside the home are teaching school and attending church, neither institution existing in Bannack while she was there. She had probably expected the boomtown of Bannack to be something like her hometown of Findlay, Ohio, a proper, sedate farm village of some one hundred families, a Methodist church, a Presbyterian church, a county courthouse, two newspapers, an academy, a gristmill, and thirteen mercantiles—but not a single saloon.[60]

A NEW REPUTATION

Plummer's office, a room he rented at the back of a general store owned by George Chrisman, was no more than a block from the cabin where Electa spent so many hours alone. But the sheriff was rarely allowed the luxury of staying at his office. On the very day Plummer had arrived at Sun River for Electa, Bill Fairweather, like an unwilling pied piper, was toodling away to Alder Gulch hundreds of stampeders who deserted their Bannack claims to trail along behind him either on foot or on horseback to the richest strike in mining history. On his return, Plummer learned his district had been expanded by a distance of eighty miles from Bannack. Though he visited Alder Gulch regularly, he also appointed deputies to assist him there and to take charge during his absence. As mentioned earlier, there were few good men interested in risking their lives trying to keep in line the influx of roughs, desperados, and monte sharpers arriving daily from other gold camps, and Plummer was forced to accept whomever he could get. Yet since Langford attributed to him "a great executive ability" and "a power over men that was remarkable," he probably felt confident he could handle even the worst of his deputies.[61] Unfortunately he lost one of his best assistants, a man who could have been a great help in the difficult days ahead. While Plummer had been at the Vail farm waiting for Reverend Reed to arrive, a quarrel developed between his deputies in a brush shanty saloon at Nevada City, and the best of the lot, J. W. Dillingham, was shot. Charlie Forbes, Buck Stinson, and Haze Lyons were charged with the murder. Forbes was acquitted and the other two sentenced to hang, though they were both freed later by a popular vote instigated by interfering women. Dimsdale, not taking into account that Plummer was two hundred miles away waiting for his marriage at the time Dillingham was killed, credited the sheriff with giving the order to shoot.[62] Not only was Plummer out of town during the weeks before and after the deputies' disagreement, but no one would have benefitted more than he from the assistance and support of a good man such as Dillingham, especially in distant Virginia City.

As it was, Plummer was required to make frequent trips to Alder Gulch himself. Judge Pemberton recalls these trips, in particular one in which he "like to had a fight" with the sheriff. Having just recently opened a law practice in Virginia City, Pemberton was summoned to represent a client Plummer had arrested for theft, a "dark feller," as he described the defendant, "black, with a red shirt on, a dirty flannel shirt and black hair that stood out on end . . . the hardest looking rooster I ever seen in all my life." The young lawyer succeeded in getting the accused thief acquitted, receiving as payment his client's horse. But when he went to the stable to pick it up, he was informed he would have to pay a bill for the animal's keep, a sum of $19. Pemberton, informing the sheriff that it was not right for him to be charged since his client had been found innocent, refused to pay the livery bill. Plummer, though, insisted the new owner could not take the horse until the stable owner was paid. Threatening to initiate a lawsuit over the matter, Pemberton angrily commenced filling out the necessary paperwork, and Plummer, watching him for a time, then sauntered over. "Pemberton," he said, "you ain't got no use for that hoss."

"No, I ain't got no use for the hoss, but he's mine!" Pemberton answered.

"Well, wouldn't you rather have two hundred dollars in gold dust than that hoss?" When Pemberton admitted he would, Plummer had the horse auctioned in the street and bought it himself at a bid of $221. Thus Pemberton got his money for the acquittal of his client, the stable got its fee, and Plummer got a "mighty pretty hoss," but the real climax of Pemberton's tale is that the black defendant turned out to be none other than "the main roadster in the gang, a feller they called 'Brocky Pete,' " and the bay mare Plummer bought turned out to be "one of the best horses they had in the gang."[63]

Though the dialect attributed to Plummer above does not fit him, but rather its narrator, Judge Pemberton, a native of Tennessee, the anecdote is interesting for being one of the rare stories that shows Plummer in action at his job, as well as revealing that he had a weakness for a good horse. More important, Pemberton's added-on conclusion illustrates well the local practice of enhancing a commonplace recollection by linking it to Montana's most famous scandal. There was no Brocky Pete associated with the gang.

Another early resident who recalled one of Plummer's many visits to Alder Gulch is little Mollie Sheehan, who, though she did not see him herself, remembers listening to her parents discuss the sheriff after he had just left town, commenting to each other on "how picturesque he was in appearance, how gentle in manner."[64] Such trips to the camps lining Alder Gulch kept Plummer on the road for days at a time, but even when in Bannack, he had little free time for home life. Because he was so approachable, there was no loss considered too insignificant to be brought to the sheriff's attention, even the mysterious disappearance of a bedroll from its owner's wagon: "Met Henry Plummer just before getting to Rattlesnake," N. H.

Webster put down in his journal, "he was on horseback; I told him about losing my robe and overcoat there a few days before and he said he would try to find them for me; he is the sheriff of the country. He appears to be a very nice man, I like him very much."[65] Webster may have liked Plummer then, but later when the sheriff asked him to contribute $2.50 towards a jail he was erecting through subscription, Webster refused. Many citizens preferred the alternative of hanging prisoners to the expense of jailing and guarding them, especially since low-security confinement resulted in such frequent jailbreaks. Commenting on the sheriff's request, the editor of the journal marveled that Plummer did not immediately shoot Webster for refusing to contribute to his project.[66]

Plummer's constant involvement with his constituents left Electa alone, but in addition, she may have looked on certain aspects of her husband's work as distasteful, such as carrying out punishment for serious crime. When John Horan shot an old man named Keeler, Plummer had to arrest him and, after his being found guilty, have a gallows constructed for the execution. Before his execution date Horan escaped from his guards and had to be recaptured, and Judge Burchett, ignoring the prisoner's plea for a three-day postponement to allow time for the arrival of a priest who could hear confession, demanded the prisoner be hanged "damned quick." Plummer carried out the death sentence on the new gallows.[67]

There were some such unwelcome duties, yet Plummer was building up a good reputation in the mining districts, even his critics crediting him with being an efficient lawman. "It was generally believed," an early historian recorded, that Plummer "was making exhaustive efforts to protect the people and their property."[68] As for the problem of his former bad reputation, Hoffman Birney concludes that Plummer's "every action following his return to Bannack as a married man forces us to believe his reformation sincere. He forsook gambling as a profession, drank only occasionally and then very sparingly, deserted the saloons, paid strict attention to his official duties and had nothing to do with the rowdy element."[69] The resulting new reputation was such that several Masons expressed a desire to accept him as a member of their brotherhood as soon as a lodge was set up in Bannack.

Though Plummer was already "the law" in the area, in August he was presented the opportunity of being granted federal authori-

Bannack Jail on the bank of Grasshopper Creek, built in 1863 by Sheriff Plummer through funds he raised from private donations. To the front and right of the jail stands the building that housed Chrisman's store, where the sheriff kept an office. (Photo by Boswell, 1985)

zation for his work when Marshall D. S. Payne rode to Bannack, requesting the nomination of a candidate for deputy U.S. marshall of eastern Idaho and promising Langford his nominee would be appointed. Langford took up the matter with the thirty members of the Union League, of which he was president, and they voted unanimously for Plummer. But Langford, showing the knack for aggravating others (later prompting one Ed French to shoot him in the eye), refused to make the nomination to Marshall Payne. On learning Langford was trying to block his approval as deputy marshall, Plummer invited Langford to sit down on an ox-shoeing frame with him and discuss the situation. Though a man of few words, in the ensuing conversation Plummer uttered more than a few "oaths and epithets," telling Langford, "You'll be sorry for this before the matter ends. I've always been your friend, but from this time on, I'm your enemy."[70] Langford gave the impression that Plummer's nomination for deputy marshall rested solely in his hands and that he was able to prevent Plummer's consideration; however, Wilbur

Sanders disagreed, maintaining that Plummer "was a candidate for United States Marshal of the new territory with respectable but limited support."[71] Likewise, Beidler claimed that Plummer's application was forwarded by Idaho territorial authorities to Washington for consideration. There is further evidence to believe this was the case.[72]

One question that has never been satisfactorily answered about this period of Plummer's life is how he was getting along with Electa. Those who interviewed early citizens of Bannack report the gossip of bitter arguments between the newly married couple, angry words loud enough to be heard in the street. Though such reports may be baseless, the adjustment period of their marriage could well have included strong disagreements, especially since both partners held such high expectations of the other. Rumors that Plummer, though courteous and patient at work, was irritable at home may hold some credibility. It would not be unusual for a tired man to be snappish after a difficult day. Still, Plummer could not have rated all that low as a husband; he was known for wanting to make up differences, even having apologized to Crawford during their difficulties. And he was reputed to be a generous man. As for Electa, Langford found her as "loving as a child."[73] There may have been some initial disappointments and some serious problems, but not likely any conflicts sufficient to destroy their love so soon.

Their two main problems were her strong attachment to family and his love for a low-paying job that required him to spend even more days away from home supervising work at distant mining claims that provided the couple's real income. Of necessity his claims were widely scattered due to rules limiting an individual's holdings to one hundred feet at each discovery site. And each claim had to be worked continuously; otherwise ownership rights were forfeited and the claim could be jumped, making it necessary that owners keep careful check to insure miners hired to work a claim stuck close to the property.

There were enjoyable experiences in Bannack for those with a companion, sitting on the doorstep on a warm evening or walking to a mountain meadow to pick wild flowers or hear meadowlarks; but Electa was always alone, and it was impossible she could continue to survive such loneliness when she had never yet been weaned from her older sister. Plummer, who had left home and family at an early age to make his way on his own, probably could not understand such a dependence as Electa had for Martha, just as she failed to understand the importance he placed on his career.

There is no written evidence of how her love fared for him under these difficult circumstances, but he made a statement that reveals her importance to him. "Now that I am married and have something to live for, and hold an official position," he told Langford, "I will show you that I can be a good man among good men."[74] Plummer's admitted reliance on Electa to give meaning to his life left him vulnerable to the usual dangers of placing the source of motivation outside of oneself.

THE SEPARATION

Since the *Shreveport* still had not put into port and there were therefore still no supplies or salaries, the Fourth of July 1863 was not a day of celebration at the Indian farm. The steady diet of unsweetened coffee, wild meat, and cornmeal was getting old. James Vail and Francis Thompson tried to brighten spirits by loading up the fort cannon and firing a salute of patriotism, but they lamented having no fireworks to go along with it. Mary and Harvey may have appreciated the bit of excitement provided by the cannon blast, but Martha, still despondent over Electa's marriage, declined to participate.[75]

An even more serious problem facing the family was that the Indians were daily becoming more troublesome. A small band who had spent a night camped at the farm moved on towards St. Peter's Mission, where it was discovered soon after that all the horses had been stolen, and travelers on their way to meet the steamer brought in news of a massacre in Little Prickly Pear Canyon. Though no bodies were found, one portion of the trail was littered with remnants of the victims' possessions, among them letters an unknown young man had received from a little girl back in Wisconsin.

Travelling at night so as not to be spotted by Indians, Vail left Martha and the children in the care of Francis Thompson and Joseph Swift and rode to Benton for news of the long overdue ship, only to be told it was not coming at all. Waters of the Missouri were too low for it to be run to its head, and the captain of the ship had ordered the goods unloaded on the river bank and returned to St.

Louis, abandoning disgruntled passengers to a two-hundred-mile hike to reach their destination. A few early stragglers had arrived at Benton on 3 July, reporting that Reverend Reed should not be expected and that no further steamers would be attempting the journey that year. The Vails were in quite a predicament.

Francis Thompson was sympathetic at their distress, but he was worrying over his own problems in trying to rescue his abandoned goods, and Joseph Swift, who had worked on the farm for an entire year without wages, understandably did not want to sign on for a second year. As a substitute for wages, Vail offered six of the farm's oxen, which Swift accepted and then promptly hired on to assist Thompson in setting up as a merchant. The two of them departed for gold country with intentions of locating a store site, leaving the Vail family alone at the farm to meet their crisis as best they could.

Thompson rode a sort of chariot he had put together from scraps left at the fort — wheels, an axle, a dry goods box, and strips of buffalo hide to bind it all together — a contraption James Vail had nicknamed Thompson's "go-devil." Following behind on horseback came Joseph Swift, herding the oxen Vail had given him. After making camp their first night on the trail, the prospective merchants each leaned back against a tree and commenced recording the day's events in their respective diaries, Thompson noting that the strange picture the two of them presented "may have struck some stray Blackfoot as a literary institution."[76]

At Deer Lodge, Swift sold his oxen at such a good profit that Thompson invited him to invest as a partner in the projected business, to which Swift agreed. The following night they camped at Cariboo, where they enjoyed a supper of beaver tail and bread.

After considering possible sites at Bannack and the several towns along Alder Gulch, they selected the two buildings that the Stuart brothers had vacated on Main Street in Bannack, and with their pooled resources, bought a team and headed for Benton to pick up the merchandise dropped by the steamer somewhere downstream. At the Sun River crossing, they found James, Martha, and children in the same straits as before, game meat and dried corn still barely holding out. Swift drove on with the team, leaving Thompson to take a short rest at the farm before pushing on.

On 22 August, Thompson made a last appearance at the Vails', alone in his go-devil and bound for Bannack. On reaching the Deer

Lodge area, he was warned not to attempt Indian country alone and therefore offered his services as a guide to a party of men from Lewiston: Lowry, Romaine, Zachery, Page, Yeager, Wagner, Marshland, and Doc Howard, who claimed to be a graduate of Yale medical school. The Lewiston party turned out to be pleasant company, treating Thompson as their guest by inviting him to eat the delicious meals prepared by their cook, Red Yeager, and tending his horse for him throughout the trip. En route they overtook a heavily loaded pack train owned by a wealthy trader named Magruder, who was headed for Virginia City to take advantage of the high prices his goods would command there. Though Thompson stayed at Bannack, his travelling companions caught up to Magruder and hired on as his employees, clerking in his Virginia City store during the day and sleeping in a back room at night. More will be heard of Magruder and Doc Howard's party later.

One of the first persons Thompson ran into on the streets of Bannack was Sheriff Plummer, but when Thompson informed him about the party he had just escorted to town, Plummer seemed disgusted with him. "Thompson, those men are cut throats and robbers," he said. "Hell will be to pay now!" Thompson protested that the men had been very agreeable and that they had also spoken very highly of Plummer. "They speak well of me for they don't dare do otherwise," the sheriff answered. [77]

Thompson also learned from Plummer that the Vails had temporarily left the farm and followed after Electa, reaching Bannack a few days prior and moving into a cabin on Yankee Flat, where the Plummers were taking their meals with them. When Thompson stopped by to see Martha, she invited him to join them as a boarder, suggesting terms Thompson found reasonable, and he accepted for both himself and Joseph Swift, who was still on the trail with the load of merchandise.

The second day after Thompson's arrival in Bannack, while conversing with Electa, she surprised him with the news that "Mr. Plummer was away from home so much attending to his duties as sheriff, that she with his consent had concluded to go to her home in Iowa, and he was to meet her there in the fall."[78] Her announcement surprised not only Thompson, but the rest of the townspeople, who could not help wondering what her real reasons for going were and advancing individual theories of explanation. Some said Plummer was sending her away because she got in his way, but others thought she was leaving voluntarily because she did not trust him any longer and he had been cruel to her. Though she had said she was lonely and wanted to visit her family, it was also suspected this could be a delicate way of expressing that she was expecting a child and wanted to be near a family doctor for the birth.

The most logical explanation for the separation is the reason Electa gave Thompson. She had been open and honest with him in expressing her most private emotions back at the farm, leaving no justification for thinking her secretive or deceptive on this occasion. She wanted to go home, as she had told him, because her husband was always gone and she was left alone. The Vails would soon be returning to the farm when the matter of supplies was concluded, and Electa had had enough of the lonely days in the small cabin, waiting for her husband to come back from some mine where he had been called to give an opinion on whether its owners were discarding precious silver in the piles of tailings, or counting the days it might take to locate a herd of lost or stolen horses. The diary of an early miner, John Grannis, makes clear the endless days residents spent in tracking down strayed livestock, and as sheriff, Plummer was expected to join in the search.

Electa, who had probably never before spent an entire night alone, could not have slept very comfortably alone in a town where men had to go armed. But what is puzzling about her words to Thompson is that her husband was to join her in the fall. It was already fall. She may have intended for him to follow after her in a few weeks, or she may have been referring to fall of the next year, which would have been a lengthy separation for the couple. Also, she made no mention of them later returning to Bannack, and was apparently requesting Plummer to give up his career in the West altogether. As for her reason for leaving so soon, she had no control over the time schedule of her departure, there being no regular stage to Salt Lake City at the time, so that the next one out could also be the last one for the year.

Any doubts about whether Plummer still loved Electa after her decision to leave him are put to rest by the scene of her departure from Bannack. When the stage pulled out on 2 September 1863, with Electa aboard, Plummer was riding alongside! And he continued to accompany her in that manner for several days.

Bannack's Goodrich Hotel, where Plummer took up residence after Electa returned to the East. (Photo courtesy of Montana Historical Society)

The trip to Salt Lake City was far from comfortable. Thompson, who had once taken the same route, complained that the coach was

> simply a box wagon without springs of any kind, drawn by two mules. The company had no ranches upon the route, but every thirty or forty miles some man was stationed who put up a little wakiup and guarded a few animals, if the Indians kindly left any, so that a change might possibly be made if the team could go no further. Passengers had to furnish their own provisions and do their own cooking. The season was usually dry, feed for stock very scarce, and all the animals were weak and scrawny. . . . Alkali dust . . . found its way into everything, baggage, clothing, ears, eyes and nostrils.

A coating of dust always had to be scraped from any food carried along in order to make it edible. If there were delays, drivers tried to make up the lost time by travelling at night, but usually fell asleep, leaving the mules to stray from the road and passengers to dismount and "grope around on the ground to find the trail." The one advantage to the open air wagon was the opportunity it provided to view the picturesque scenery along the way — Red Rock Canyon, Market Lake, and most impressive, the majestic Teton peaks.[79]

At Eagle Rock ferry on the Snake River, the Plummers crossed paths with a wagon train headed back in the direction from which they had just come. It was carrying the new chief justice sent to the territory by President Lincoln, and the meeting turned out to be a momentous one because the justice formed an opinion of Plummer that colored his thinking throughout all their future relations.

Sidney Edgerton, a former congressman from Ohio, had brought with him his wife, Mary, two sons, a small daughter, and thirteen-year-old Mattie, the eldest. Besides the immediate family, there was a niece, Lucia Darling, and a nephew, Wilbur Sanders, who had brought his wife, two children, and a hired girl. The final member of the party was Henry Tilden, an ailing fifteen-year-old from their hometown in Ohio, whom Edgerton had agreed to bring along as his ward in hopes a change of climate might improve the boy's health.

On meeting Plummer at the ferry, all of the Edgertons took an immediate liking to him, but their opinion was just as quickly reversed after talking with a wagon master who had also stopped his freight train at the ferry. The wagon master had heard rumors about the sheriff's former notoriety and, Mattie wrote, "proceeded to enlighten us regarding Plummer, knowledge that left us no doubt of his character and prepared Father and Wilbur to be on guard against this noted desperado." Mattie found the sheriff fascinating; it was the first time she had seen an authentic "bad man, one who was quick on the draw." Henry Tilden, the other adolescent in the party, took a similar interest in the "bad man."[80]

From this fateful meeting on the Snake River comes the only existing physical description of Electa. Though she did not speak to the family, Mattie did take notice of her. "She stayed in the wagon but she was pointed out to us as the wife of the Sheriff of Bannack. . . . Mrs. Plummer was a small woman, I remember. I guess you would call her a blonde. She had big grey eyes and her hair was brown, soft and fluffy."[81]

After the encounter with the Edgertons, Henry Plummer's days were numbered — one hundred twenty-six to be exact. It is not known at what point on Electa's journey Plummer finally left her

Sidney Edgerton, first governor of Territory of Montana. (Photo courtesy of Montana Historical Society)

and turned back, but wherever and whenever, it was the last time they were to see each other. Plummer must have ridden home feeling that her love for him was a "diminished thing" since the days of Sun River.

THE EDGERTONS

The Edgerton women, who had left behind their fine china and damask chairs and donned silk masks to prevent damage to their complexions as they crossed the plains, were not especially enthusiastic when they climbed the last hill and stood looking down at the town Electa Plummer had just abandoned. Lucia Darling, noticing first the conspicuous gallows, found the view less than inspiring. So did young Mattie Edgerton. "I think there was not one of us who did not feel a keen sense of disappointment at the prospect," she wrote. "Not a ray of sunlight enlivened the scene. The grey clouds above and around us made the bare mountains and the log cabins between them look extremely forbidding." Hattie Sanders agreed that Bannack was "most unattractive and disappointing," and Mary made the general dejection unanimous, writing home to her twin sister, "It is a great country. There are two things that it abounds in, hills or mountains and sage bushes."[82]

Despite their dislike of the town, the families needed shelter for the approaching winter and, at a sheriff's auction Plummer conducted Edgerton purchased as a home a building on Main Street that had previously served as a store. Wilbur Sanders was not so fortunate, finding for his family only a single room, one-half of a two-room cabin located on Yankee Flat. Mary and Hattie immediately pitched in to convert the two rude cabins into cozy homes, using a combination of the limited supplies available and their own ingenuity. And Mary was pleasantly surprised at the peacefulness of their new environment: "I think the town is very quiet and orderly for such a mining town—much more so than I expected to find it."[83]

Mattie recalled how their first night in town they had to fortify themselves with the promise they would be leaving the place in spring, and "with this comforting thought," she wrote, "we were lulled to sleep by the sound of falling waters from the sluice boxes on the mountain." A second image stuck in Mattie's mind over the years: "Miners . . . lived on the mountain sides in dugouts above the two flumes carrying water to the canyon below. After dark we could see their lights shine out like mammoth fireflies from the doors when they were opened."[84]

Mary covered the peeling bark of the log walls with clean white sheets she had brought across the plains and, rejecting the two crude stone fireplaces as being unsuitable for cooking, had the portable sheet-iron stove carried in from the wagon. Though her table may have been "made by some one who could handle a saw and a hammer but evidently had not mastered the plane,"[85] the meals she served on it more than made up for the poor craftsmanship. She sometimes spent an entire day baking, shuttling in and out of the tiny oven loaves of bread, soda biscuits, veal potpie, bread pudding, cake, gingersnaps, and mince pies made from dried apples and wild currants but as delicious as any she had baked back home.

Mary Edgerton, like Electa Plummer, was an educated woman forced to live in the rough settlement because her husband saw the potential for a promising career there, and both women were devoted Christians who had been cautioned against marrying a man of no religious faith by their families, families to which they were bound by strong, permanent ties. Edgerton left Mary alone in this wilderness, sometimes for several months at a time, even while she was expecting their sixth child. But Mary complained little, even though she never did develop a love for their mountain home and would have been happy to leave it at a moment's notice. Her suppressed dissatisfaction with her life comes through in her frequent letters home, in which she made long lists of items she wanted her sister to send her because they were cheaper at home than on the frontier. When she wrote a thanks for the numerous gifts sent, a note of ingratitude always crept in: "I hardly know how to thank you for all the many *presents* that you sent us. You ask how my dresses fit? They are rather large and long for me, but I can remedy that easily. I like them very much. The girls' hats are the oddest-looking hats I ever saw. I presume you wrote how to trim them, but the letters are back in that other trunk."[86]

Mary was quite concerned about the influence their present environment might have on her children: "I should hardly like to send them to school here, if there was one, for they would learn so many *bad* things that would injure them more than all the good they would learn. Most of the boys here swear as soon as they can talk. Our boys have not got any of those habits yet . . . Wright . . . and Sidney have the reputation of being the best boys in town."[87] Bad as conditions might have been during Mary's time in Bannack, they had improved considerably in the few months since Electa had left. There was now a preacher of sorts, a regular religious service, and a choir, and Lucia was attending a class to learn German. In addition, Lucia was making plans for setting up a school of her own, having been a teacher in Ohio. She also lent her support to the choir, unlike Mary, who declined to accompany her niece and daughter to meetings conducted by the "good but ignorant man" in a house where "dogs and cats strolled in and out among the congregation."[88] Though Mary sent the smaller children to Sunday school, where Lucia was one of the teachers, she kept the family as close to home as possible, allowing only a few excursions to gather wild flowers or berries and a single trip to visit the mines and stamp mill. Dances were also forbidden, except for one special ball Mattie and Lucia attended to stop sharp criticism that the family was snobbish.

Despite a touch of gold fever spread to her by her husband and fanned by her own dreams of luxury — "If the new . . . claim . . . turns out anything . . . we shall be able to have all the glassware that we need a year from now" — Mary ran her household with spartan frugality. "Have been without milk most of the time we have been here; when I do get any, have to pay 25¢ a quart. I get along very well without it." She closed each new request to her sister with, "It will save us a great deal to have them sent to us." Later she took advantage of the high prices in the area by selling some of the pots and pans that her sister had provided.[89]

Being a respectable woman who kept off the streets of Bannack did not mean Mary was lonely. Homesick for family, yes, but never lonely since all the politically ambitious residents of the camp frequented her home. Francis Thompson, who never mentioned giving a single present to the two Vail children, presented the Edgerton children with a cradle and padded chair on one of his frequent visits. Mary naively wrote home about how good people were to them, providing them with sugar-cured hams, moose meat, antelope quarters, and a very special gift from Mr. Gridley to her — a gold pin worth $25.

Mary rarely mentioned her niece, Hattie Sanders, and never wrote of the Vails, who were the Sanders's neighbors. And whereas

the Vails had dedicated the last year trying to become involved with
the Indians, Mary's family found they must waste a good deal of
their time trying to avoid the tribe camped just beyond the flat. They
made pests of themselves by pressing their noses to a window and
peering inside or by tapping on the door to beg for food. Mattie
reported they took to locking the door when they saw the "disgusting
looking creatures" approaching. In a letter written for Pauline, the
younger Edgerton daughter, Mary enumerated some of the Indians'
habits that she found so offensive: "They pick off all the dead
chickens and pigs and all the old bones and bits of meat that the hogs
don't get and carry them up to their wickeyups, and cook and eat
them. Do you think you would like to eat such dirty stuff? I know I
shouldn't. I don't like to have them come into the house, they are so
dirty."[90]

Later, when Indians killed ten white woodcutters near Fort
Benton, Mary came to regard them as more than just a nuisance,
and Edgerton dropped his former ideas about "noble red savages"
and wired Washington for troops. When no help appeared, he and
Sanders attempted to enlist a local militia but attracted little interest
from the miners. Still fearing war would break out, Mary confided
to her sister at home that she hoped Edgerton would not have to go,
"but *I do want to have* the Indians killed."[91]

As it turned out, Indian hostilities cooled rather than heated,
and the expected war did not develop. However, there were new
problems to take the place of the old—white robbers. Later in October, two armed men, wrapped in blankets and wearing hoods over
their heads, held up and robbed the four passengers and driver of the
Peabody stage just a few miles out of Rattlesnake ranch. Passengers
and driver held differing opinions on who the culprits were. This incident was followed by isolated reports of the robbery of individuals
travelling alone—even those carrying no money who were warned to
come better prepared next time.

Though Edgerton had never bothered to make the difficult trip
to Lewiston to be sworn in as justice, he had not come across the
plains to sit on the sidelines. He and Sanders held several serious
discussions about the crime problem in the area, agreeing it was in-
appropriate that the one man with any authority in the district was a
person of bad reputation. But Plummer was quite firmly entrenched
in his position; he was, as Sanders put it, "the acknowledged civic

magnate" of the "entire country."[92] Not only did he have more than half of his term as sheriff yet to serve, it was quite possible he would be selected as the deputy U.S. marshall of the territory east of the Rockies. Any effort to oust him in a manner acceptable to the populace could not be taken on by lone individuals, but would require the concerted effort of leading citizens, many of whom were already wavering between an allegiance to the new representative from Washington and a prior loyalty to Plummer.

Francis Thompson, who had the dubious distinction of guiding the first band of cutthroats into Bannack, had also made the mistake of informing them he had a large shipment of goods en route. Sheriff Plummer told him he could expect trouble from his close involvement with them and advised him not to open the door of his store after dark without first finding out who was knocking. He also helped Thompson stack goods boxes around his bunk at the back of the store to form a barricade, leaving a porthole to shoot through in case of attack while he was sleeping. Though Thompson slept in his store, both he and Joseph Swift continued to eat at the Vails, as did Plummer.

Through this daily contact, Thompson claimed to have developed a love for Plummer, who was always so "gentlemanly and polite."[93] Thompson realized that Plummer's work required him to be out of town frequently, but he made the observation that sometimes when Plummer missed a meal, a robbery also occurred. He did not mention his suspicions to his younger partner, who "loved Plummer like a brother." Joseph Swift had confided to Mattie Edgerton that Plummer was his close friend, who had been very influential in keeping him out of trouble, steering him away from the saloons and gambling houses when he noticed him there. "Joe," he would say, leading him out, "this is no place for you."[94]

In addition to Swift, the sheriff had other staunch supporters, including his sister-in-law, who had come to respect him through the closer contact. In fact, Mattie Edgerton thought that most people who came in contact with the sheriff liked him, though her own father did not share their feelings.[95] Edgerton was not especially well liked himself, Sanders lamenting how people who did not get to know his uncle well generally did not like him. Besides Edgerton and Sanders, there were others who disliked Plummer, mainly a group of their intimate friends and mostly fellow Republicans. Their dislike was based on his former reputation. Among this group of Edgerton's friends were Langford, himself rather unpopular in the area and later to be rejected by the Senate as a candidate for governor, and Sam Hauser, the "capitalist," as he was called, who had arrived on the *Emilie* with the Vails and Thompson and was later appointed a governor of Montana. Also Thompson, now a crony of Edgerton, who spent long hours at the store chatting, was coming around to the unsworn justice's way of thinking.

In the middle of November an incident occurred involving Edgerton's ward, Henry Tilden, that caused floating suspicions to crystallize. When Sam Hauser got on the Virginia City coach with a sack containing $14,000 in gold dust that he and Langford planned to take to the States, he noted with alarm that Sheriff Plummer was also a passenger. The day was bitterly cold, and Plummer made Hauser the gift of a scarf to warm him on the long trip. Hauser, already nervous at sharing the coach with a man of Plummer's reputation, interpreted the scarf as a device to mark him as a person carrying money and experienced the greatest uneasiness throughout the journey. But the coach passed safely through Rattlesnake Canyon, and Hauser breathed a huge sigh of relief as they rolled up at the Goodrich Hotel.

Because he still entertained doubts about Plummer's character, Hauser decided to ask him publicly to guard his sack of gold in some safe place. "That's all right," Plummer told him, "I'll take the gold and return it to you."[96] He deposited it with George Chrisman for the night, returning it to Hauser the next day. As Hauser and Langford were preparing to leave for Salt Lake with a Mormon freighter that night, a series of loud shrieks came from the direction of Horse Prairie Hill, but Hauser and Langford continued on their way, leaving others to investigate the source of the outbreak.

Those who went to the rescue discovered the cries to be emanating from young Henry Tilden, who had taken a tumble into a ditch and had his horse fall on top of him. The boy was not so much hurt as frightened out of his wits from an earlier experience, and he hurried on to the Sanders's cabin to tell his story. Hattie Sanders listened to Tilden's strange tale and took him to the Edgertons, who had already heard his cries at the time of the accident. Mattie remembered him telling how three masked horsemen on Horse Prairie had "ordered him to hold up his hands while they searched him. Finding nothing in his pockets but a comb, and a picture of his girl, they let him go, and he went without delay, speeding toward Bannack." Then Mattie stated he concluded his story with the surprising words, "One of the men I know was Henry Plummer."[97]

Sanders and Edgerton, both lawyers, were skeptical of Tilden's story and the next day questioned him carefully as to how he was able to identify Plummer. Tilden told them it was his revolver and overcoat. The lawyers reminded him that being able to distinguish one pistol from another in a town where so many went armed was unlikely, especially in the dark. However, they were both impressed by his mention of the overcoat since it had a distinctive red lining, and they could think of no one in town, other than Plummer, who had such a coat. Mattie and Lucia, who were listening closely and were frightened at what they had just heard, were warned not to breathe a word. Tilden, Mattie, and Lucia were not the only ones frightened; both Edgerton and Sanders decided to keep secret the information they had just heard rather than risk their lives by repeating Tilden's charges.

Meanwhile Langford and Hauser, well on their way, had set up camp for the night, stashing the heavy sack of gold dust out of sight. Langford, unable to sleep because of the cold, spent most of the night wandering around, and at one point spotted four masked men lurking outside camp. He could not identify them because of their masks and the darkness, but when they saw him, they rode away. Strangely enough Langford did not report seeing the masked men to anyone in the freight train so they could be on guard, and the party proceeded on to Salt Lake without further difficulty.[98]

As soon as the sheriff heard about Henry Tilden's story of a robbery, he came to the express office where the boy worked to question him. Out of his fear of Plummer, Tilden denied recognizing any of the robbers, but he was so frightened by the questioning that, according to Mattie, "every night after closing hours he ran the whole distance to his boarding place."[99]

Mattie's earlier interest in Plummer was piqued by Tilden's claims, and the sheriff was now confirmed in her mind as the bad man he was rumored to be. She waited daily just to observe him crossing the log footbridge near her house as he went to and from the Vails' house, noting he was always immaculately clean and wearing such fine clothes she could not imagine where he had bought them.

Mattie was not the only person in town watching Plummer closely. The next Sunday when her father stopped to visit Thompson at his store, he was surprised when his friend quickly locked the door behind him and then made a check of each window to be sure they could speak in private. "Judge," he asked, "who is doing this robbing?" When Edgerton commenced to expound his theory, Thompson interrupted him. "Plummer!" he said. Edgerton then confided to Thompson that Henry Tilden had recognized Plummer as one of the men who had held him up.

Now that Thompson no longer trusted the sheriff, breaking bread with him daily became an awkward experience, but he continued to eat with the Vail family, always keeping his ears open to learn as much as possible about Plummer's activities. Within only a short time, a new suspicion arose. Since Plummer habitually sent money to his widowed mother in the East, he was frequently on the lookout for a traveler who would act as carrier. On hearing of Edgerton's planned trip to Washington, D.C., the sheriff inquired about the exact date so he could send a package along. Edgerton, fearing he was being set up for a robbery, quickly cancelled his departure, deciding to postpone the trip until something could be worked out to make travelling conditions in the area safer.

THANKSGIVING DINNER

As Thanksgiving drew near, the Vails decided to hold a holiday dinner and invite in other families in town to celebrate with them. Plummer, who was meeting the expenses, showed considerable class by ordering from Salt Lake City a forty-pound turkey at the cost of $40 in gold, as well as an assortment of fine wines.

When Martha Vail and Plummer came to deliver the invitation to Lucia Darling and the Edgertons, Mattie made good advantage of an opportunity to observe the sheriff at close range. "Plummer seated himself in a chair, which he tilted back against the wall, and hung his hat, which he had removed, over his knee. It was unusual at that time," she added, "for the average miner to take off his hat as a concession to good manners when entering a house. I have no recollection of hearing him speak, but I noted that he seemed ill at ease. . . . Possibly he, being aware of my scrutiny, felt additional embarrassment."[100]

The Edgertons accepted Mrs. Vail's invitation, partly because the entire community respected her but also because they were afraid to offend Plummer. The Sanderses accepted for the same reasons, and both families showed up decked out in their finest: Hattie, Wilbur, Lucia, Mary, and Sidney, who had put on a white shirt for the first time since his arrival in the territory. If James Vail was present, none of the guests was impressed enough to mention him, regarding Plummer as the head of the Vail household. Mary thought their host was a "very feminine-looking man," but wrote home about the "excellent supper. . . . I tasted butter for the first time since we came here and it was a treat."[101]

Hattie found the entire evening "memorable," describing the meal Martha had prepared as "one of the most sumptious dinners I ever attended . . . everything that money could buy was served, delicately cooked and with all the style that would characterize a banquet at 'Sharry's.' " As for Plummer, she described him as "slender, graceful and mild of speech. He had pleasing manners and fine address, a fair complexion, sandy hair and blue eyes — the last person whom one would select as a daring highwayman and murderer." Her theory about the Plummers' separation was that Electa was a "splendid Christian woman," and her husband had sent her away because he felt that "he was not fit to live with her." She could not help believing that his feelings for Electa were sincere, and "this was his finest trait."[102]

If reliable, Hattie's explanation would resolve the question of the problem existing between Plummer and his wife; however, it contradicts what Electa had told Thompson, that it was her own idea to leave and that her husband had given his consent. Another difficulty in accepting Hattie's idea is that she wrote her account thirty-four years after the events, and the numerous errors she makes in the brief paragraphs about the Vails reveal a very limited acquaintance with the family. Still, Hattie was Martha's nearest neighbor, and though her wording may not be exact, it is likely she, at some point at least, received the impression from Mrs. Vail that Plummer was unfit to live with her younger sister because of his past.

During the critical days of his attempt to live down a bad name, Plummer did not need any reinforcement of former doubts about his character, and certainly not from within his own family. But Martha was probably only repeating feelings Plummer had expressed about his relationship with his wife, a marked change from a few months earlier when he had quietly assured Electa that he was a good man who lacked nothing more than her to make a success of his life, or when he had told Langford, "Now that I am married and have something to live for, and hold an official position . . . there is a new life before me, and I want you to believe that I am not unfitted to fill it with credit to myself and benefit to the community."[103]

Electa's departure had evidently caused Plummer some self-doubts. She had wanted to go home, would not stay in the West another day with him, not even after Martha arrived. Possibly her older sister only made things worse with an I-told-you-so attitude about the way her marriage was turning out. Electa had made difficult decisions about the relationship twice, and now it was Plummer's turn to wrestle with the same decision. If he was not her moral equal, it would be unwise to give up a position he valued highly to resume their marriage in the East, especially since the "official position" gave him a sense of worth and his wife made him aware of his unworthiness. Martha, who claimed to feel as responsible for her younger sister as if she were her mother, undoubtedly inserted herself in the issue. Though slightly inaccurate, Hattie Sanders's memoirs may present a fairly precise picture of the emotional conflicts taking place in the Vail household that Thanksgiving.

But overlooking whatever problems they may have been experiencing, the members of the Vail family united to make a pleasant evening for all. Their efforts were not wasted on the guests, Sanders also giving a glowing account of the feast and the eastern polish of the host. As reported to his daughter-in-law, "An assembly of the most prominent citizens" was present to enjoy "delicacies that had never before graced festal board in Bannack. Plummer was the soul of hospitality upon that occasion. His easy flow of conversation . . . the well modulated voice which entertained with compliment and jest . . . his elegant manners, his gracious attention to his guests made him an ideal host."[104]

But Sanders and Edgerton were already making plans for their host's future, and "every man present knew that Plummer was doomed." There were several reasons they were anxious to be rid of him. From the first they had believed him a "desperado," and with the new knowledge Tilden revealed, they feared their lives might be in danger, so much so that Plummer's every action, including a re-

quest so simple as carrying a package back East for him, was interpreted as part of a robbery plot.

They also feared Plummer in a political sense. He belonged to
the opposition party, a party Edgerton equated with treason. Unlike
Plummer, Edgerton was known for the intolerance of his political
beliefs, a main factor in his difficulties in the territory. He passed a
similar prejudice on to Mattie, who had the pleasure and excitement
of her first dance "spoiled" when someone asked her if she were
serious about her dancing partner, who "had good looks, intelligence and pleasing manners. All this," she explained, "could not
make me overlook the damning fact that he was a Democrat."[105]
Plummer was also a Democrat, as experienced and skilled in politics
as he was at prospecting for gold and silver, and a dangerous
political opponent because his low-key, easy manner appealed to the
masses.

On the other hand, both Sanders and Edgerton, conscious of
their own moral and social superiority, had a tendency to look down
at the miners, who in turn were bored by the long-winded and stuffy
lawyer's talk. The uncle and nephew had left Ohio and come to the
territory to satisfy political ambition, and they recognized Plummer
as a man with whom they would have to contend, a man Sanders
thought was "in many respects the most conspicuous citizen of
Eastern Idaho."[106] In a political confrontation with Plummer, the
two lawyers could easily have come out on the short end. They
would not be sorry to see him gone.

BRAVE NEW PROSECUTOR

Wilbur Sanders, a teetotaler who embarrassed his cousin Mattie by
singing too loudly in church, had come West to serve as his uncle's
secretary.[107] He was not quite the social equal of the Edgertons,
Sidney having been a congressman who had taken his wife to
Washington to hobnob with political celebrities and Mary being a
sister to the founder of Oberlin College, which Sanders had not attended though he did not mind letting people think he had. Sanders
showed due respect for his uncle, recognizing him as the pathway to
political success, and in turn Edgerton recognized his nephew's
potential, calling on him frequently for counsel and trusting important errands to him. On the morning of the day Hauser and Lang-

ford were preparing to leave for Salt Lake and Henry Tilden for Horse Prairie, Edgerton had summoned his secretary for a special mission. A cavalcade of "bold riders" on the best horses to be found in the country, Sanders reported, were galloping the streets of Bannack from one saloon to another, displaying their "perfect horsemanship," and Plummer was among them. In Sanders's eyes at least, it was no credit to the sheriff that he fit in so well with the flashy riders; road agents were known for loving horses, riding them well, and stealing them. Since miners commonly requested Plummer to accompany them to a new silver strike to evaluate the ore, promising him a claim near the discovery for his trouble, on seeing the party of horsemen, Edgerton promptly detected it might be an expedition to a silver mine and dispatched Sanders as an emissary to the group. [108]

As Sanders related, he looked across the street, saw Plummer sitting on his horse, and went over to ask where he was going. Plummer replied he was on his way to take possession of a herd of horses quartered by the Parish ranch on Blacktail-Deer Creek, Parish being near death and several citizens having expressed a fear that his wife, a member of the local Indian tribe, might take the livestock and return with her people to the other side of the mountain. Sanders insisted he was certain the horsemen had other intentions, namely staking quartz claims, but Plummer answered he knew nothing about them. When Sanders persisted, Plummer said, "All right get your horse and come along," but adding he doubted there would be any claim staking done, which Sanders again refuted. The conversation continued on in the same vein until Plummer at last agreed — if Sanders did not care to come along — to stake a claim in his behalf should the opportunity arise. Satisfied he had carried out his uncle's wishes, Sanders returned to his office. But Edgerton soon appeared in the doorway with Francis Thompson and Leonard Gridley at his side and urged Sanders to catch up to the Plummer party and ride along with them. "I volunteered to do so at their request," he wrote, "and I went for my blankets and revolver while they proceeded to find me a horse."

When Sanders was ready to leave, he discovered his uncle had procured not a horse, but a "diminutive mule" that balked at climbing the slope to cemetery hill, much to the amusement of those who soon gathered in the street below to watch Gridley struggling to coax the pair to the summit. After half an hour, Sanders and Gridley's combined patience outlasted that of the mule, and all reached the top, only to discover there was no trace of the silver party's trail. In the approaching darkness, Sanders traveled in the direction of the Rattlesnake Station, but when a snow squall contributed to the mule's unwillingness, he was forced to dismount and drive it ahead of him the final eight miles. At the station, he found no news of the ten members of the Plummer party. Accepting the invitation of the bartender, Red Yeager, to share the grass mattress spread before a fire burning on the hearth, Sanders, who conceded that silver fever made strange bedfellows, crawled in next to a suspected horsethief, Bill Bunton, and fell asleep. Though Parish's doctor, who was sleeping in one corner, was too "stupefied by intoxication" to be disturbed, the others were wakened three times, twice by the boisterous arrival of Jack Gallagher and once by Gridley, whom Hattie had sent to rescue Sanders. Back at Edgerton's cabin, Sanders heard the tale of Tilden's holdup, and the pieces of the puzzle began to fall into place; Plummer had not been at the Rattlesnake Station on the previous night because he was on Horse Prairie robbing Henry Tilden.

Within a matter of weeks another robbery occurred. On its second day out of Virginia City, the Salt Lake mail stage overtook a strange band of three men, each wearing a blue and green blanket entirely covering the body and a mask pulled over the head with holes cut for eyes and nose and mounted on a horse similarly disguised, blanketed from ears to tail, leaving only eyes, muzzle, and legs exposed. Though two of the passengers were relieved of a total of $500, the robbers missed the money in the mailbags as well as that on the driver, who had been commissioned sums by several persons. Those aboard suspected George Ives of being the ringleader.

In addition to accumulating mining claims and worrying over the robberies, Edgerton was at the time burdened with the more important task of pushing for creation of a new territory in eastern Idaho. During the week before Christmas he sent his nephew to Alder Gulch to enlist support. While Sanders was still there, a wounded grouse led a hunter to the frozen body of Nick Tiebolt, a young man who had been missing for some time. Outraged citizens quickly banded together to arrest the suspects, and Sanders offered to prosecute them.

The main suspect was George Ives, who had been part of the Stuart expedition to the Yellowstone but now worked at boarding horses, mules, and oxen teams that pulled the long supply trains to the gulch. He was a tall, blonde, good-looking young man and an excellent horseman, who owned a fine horse, though he had the uncouth habit of leading it behind him into every store or saloon he patronized. But when mounted on his steed, he presented an impressive sight, Sanders said, sitting his saddle "like a swan on a billowy lake." Plummer had already stated that he suspected Ives of being responsible for the Salt Lake stage robbery, and Sanders, confident Ives was guilty on all counts, viewed the coming trial as a critical struggle between the forces of law and order and those of crime, or as he quite significantly added, if necessary there would be "order without law,"[109] a rather strange stance for a lawyer.

The murder victim had disappeared after being sent to pick up a mule team from Ives, and when the corpse, which was badly pecked by magpies on the shoulders and back, was brought into Virginia in a wagon and left on public view, those who examined it were incensed by signs that Tiebolt had been dragged into the brush while still alive. Marks of a small lariat scarred his neck and scraps of sagebrush were clasped in his left hand. Emotions ran high, both among those indignant over the crime and those clamoring for Ives's acquittal.

The trial was held on the snowpacked street of Nevada, where two large wagons were pulled, one to provide seats for the prisoner and his lawyers, the other for witnesses. Near the wagons a blazing bonfire was built from a stack of wood borrowed from a resident who had the bad luck of being absent at the time. Benches loaned from a nearby hurdy-gurdy hall were arranged in a neat semicircle around the fire to form a jury box, and a line of guards armed with shotguns separated the jurors from the nearly one thousand onlookers, who occasionally interrupted proceedings with suggestions and catcalls or simply wandered off, when lawyers' speeches grew monotonous, for a quick trip to a barbershop, restaurant, or saloon.

Sanders did not win any friends on the opening day, combining legal jargon with high-flown language in speeches that just plain lasted too long and calling Buzz Caven, Plummer's deputy in Virginia, a coward and belittling the list of jurors Caven presented because one happened to be a professional gambler. Sanders therefore "had no desire to make their acquaintance." As assistant, Sanders accepted another lawyer mining in the area, Charles Bagg, whom he described as a "stubby, hairy" man, "of dilapidated garb, whose bootlegs did not have sufficient fiber to stand up, and into one of which he had vainly essayed to tuck one of the legs of his pantaloons."[110] Though according to Francis Thompson, a staunch temperance man, Bagg had the great failing of being "an infernal nuisance" when he was drunk (which was all too frequently), the ragged little lawyer balanced the prosecution team in more ways than one. He and Sanders succeeded in getting one suspect, Long John, to testify that Tiebolt had paid Ives his bill from a buckskin purse full of gold dust, then mounted one mule, and rode off leading the other. For a moment, Ives stood watching him leave and then suggested that they kill him for his money. The group tossed a coin, the lot falling to Ives himself, who rode after Tiebolt, called to him to turn around (since he thought it would be cowardly to shoot him in the back), and fired, hitting him in the head. Ives took the purse, Long John said, left the body where it lay, and brought the mules back to camp. A second witness Sanders might have used was not called upon, a Dr. Glick, whom Langford claims had knowledge that Ives belonged to an organized gang. Glick did testify for the *defense* later in the trials. Sanders wrote that he also had other witnesses who could have given information about Ives's connection to the stagecoach robbery, but he chose not to use them either, relying solely on Long John's testimony.

The trial lasted three days, the prisoners being bound in logging chains, locked up, and guarded each night. One of the miners who spent a night on guard duty recorded the event in his diary, revealing the miners' weariness of listening to speeches and arguments between the attorneys: "After pacing the heavy watches of the night away morning dawned clear and pleasant," John Grannis wrote. "The court came at an early hour and was called to order by Judge Byham. The lawyers were given until 3 o'clock to get through and submit the case to the jury."[111] And the lawyers met their three o'clock deadline, the judge sending the jury off to a store to deliberate and leaving the audience to shift from one frozen foot to the other in the waning winter sunlight, unwilling to give up their places before hearing the verdict. Within half an hour, the jury returned with a written report, but the decision was not unanimous.

One juror felt he must vote his conscience, believing, though George Ives was probably guilty of other robberies, the prosecution had not proven him guilty of Tiebolt's murder.

Unwilling to permit a single juror to spoil his victory, Sanders jumped to the witness wagon and motioned that the assembled crowd ignore the lone dissenting vote and accept the decision of the majority of the jury. His motion carried. Next he moved that Ives be hanged immediately, which also carried. Seeing that Sanders was in control of the crowd, Ives, though bound in chains, slowly made his way over to the prosecutor and took his hand, requesting him to put off the execution until morning. Before Sanders could answer, a guard who had been following events from a perch on the dirt roof of a cabin called down, "Sanders, ask him how long he gave the Dutchman!" But Sanders did not need the help of Beidler, the guard who stood a few inches shorter than the muzzle of his shotgun, to make up his mind. He had already decided to proceed with the hanging, and he made a third motion which also carried: that the court take possession of Ives's property to pay the expenses of board for the three prisoners and the nearly one hundred guards employed throughout the trial. When the defense lawyer protested it was bad enough to kill an innocent man without using his property to pay the expenses of his killers, Sanders responded it was not unusual for the defendant to pay costs after a death sentence, and "if a lawyer was not aware of that fact . . . he should go to a law school instead of a law office." Surrounded by guards, Ives was led to an unfinished log building and placed on a gum boot box under a dangling rope. As Beidler placed the noose around his neck, the judge asked for final words. Just before the box was pushed from under him, Ives said, "I am innocent of this crime; Alex Carter killed the Dutchman."

Sanders, congratulated for his initiative and courage, was escorted back to Virginia under a large guard that remained with him through the entire week. The next day Long John was set free in reward for his testimony, and the third prisoner, George Hilderman, whom Sanders described as "an old, weak, foolish man," was sentenced to banishment on the grounds of being a conspirator to the murder, Sanders informing the audience that it was the "duty of any person finding him in the settlements after New Year's to shoot him on sight." On hearing his sentence, the old man broke down, protesting he had no way of leaving and did not know where to go, but the only response to his plea was a shout from someone in the crowd advising him to go to hell.

Hilderman, known in the area as "the Great American Pie Biter," had earned the title because of his huge teeth and broad jaws which could spread wide enough to squeeze in seven layers of apple pie. Langford added that the old man was "somewhat imbecile," once having lost a bet after being tricked into biting into a layer of pies that still had tin plates inserted between them and not being able to ascertain why he was not successful in biting through the stack.[112] In his dilemma at being banished without a horse and supplies, Hilderman applied for help to Plummer. He furnished him with a pony and sufficient provisions to leave the area.

At the conclusion of the trials, five men, who concluded that prosecuting the criminal element of the community was going to be too slow and expensive, met in the back room of a Virginia store to adopt a quicker and cheaper method of dispensing justice. Surrounded by darkness, the five members raised their hands as Sanders administered the oath of the newly formed Vigilance Committee, patterned after the San Francisco model, swearing to be true to each other, to reveal no secrets, and to violate no laws of right. The appropriate atmosphere for the formation of this committee had been set by some shocking news that had just reached Virginia City.[113] The pack train of merchant Lloyd Magruder, which had left town early in the fall, had not arrived at its intended destination in the Lewiston area. Some of Magruder's friends felt certain that he had been robbed and killed somewhere along the mountainous Indian trail that wound its way to the western side of the Rockies. The main suspects were themselves members of the Magruder party, the band of "cutthroats" Francis Thompson ushered into Bannack the previous summer. The resulting outrage aroused in Virginia City over the suspected atrocity provided some additional backing for the vigilance movement.

At the beginning of the Tiebolt murder trial, due to the ambience of mob control pervading the proceedings, defense attorneys had dispatched George Lane to Bannack to carry the news to Plummer. But Bannack had already heard about the unauthorized posse that had arrested the suspects and stood guard over the trial, the story of their actions being augmented by rumors that the next intended victims were the law officers at Bannack. Accordingly, a road barrier had been set up outside Bannack, and Lane may not have been able to get through to Plummer. Even if his message did reach the sheriff, there may not have been sufficient time to ride to Alder Gulch before the trials ended. For whatever reason, Plummer did not interfere in the trials, leaving Sanders to carry the day.

VIGILANTES IN ACTION

George Ives's final words were an accusation of Alex Carter, and the newly formed Vigilance Committee wasted no time in going after the accused. As Dimsdale and Langford told the story, on 23 December, a party of twenty-four men left Virginia, being informed on their arrival at Deer Lodge Creek, that Carter was lying dead drunk at the Cottonwood station after being thrown out of a dance held the night before. But when they reached the station, they discovered that Carter and friends had escaped after receiving a letter of warning from Red Yeager. The vigilantes' informant as to Carter's whereabouts had been none other than Yeager himself, the cook for the group Thompson had escorted into Bannack as well as Sanders's sleeping partner at the Rattlesnake Station on 14 November. For his "criminal interference" with justice by delivering the letter, the group determined to arrest Yeager. He was captured in a wickiup at Rattlesnake and brought back to Dempsey's ranch for questioning.[114]

Yeager, a good-natured, wiry man about 5' 5" tall with fiery red hair and whiskers, admitted delivering the warning, but accused George Brown, the barkeep at Dempsey's, of writing the letter. When Brown confessed to composing the message, the vigilantes took a vote—unanimous in favor of hanging both Yeager and Brown. At this point, one member of the vigilance group decided he wanted out before things went any further, but others discouraged him by raising their shotguns, pointing them in his direction, and cocking the hammers. Dimsdale said the waverer "concluded to stay."[115]

Fearing to return to town with their two prisoners, the vigilantes took them no further than Laurin's ranch, a few miles down creek from Nevada City, and permitted them to lie down in the corner of the barroom for some sleep. At ten o'clock they were wakened. Yeager sat up, informing his captors he realized his time had come and would therefore tell them all about the gang and die happy if he could only live to see others hang who deserved it more than he. "I don't say this to get off," he assured them. "I don't want to get off."

When the leader urged him to list off the names of the gang so they could be written down, Yeager cooperated. Henry Plummer was the chief; Bill Bunton, second in command; George Brown, secretary; Ned Ray, council room keeper at Bannack City; and the rest, roadsters: Sam Bunton, Cyrus Skinner, George Shears, Frank Parish, Haze Lyons, Bill Hunter, George Ives, Stephen Marshland, Dutch John Wagner, Alex Carter, Whiskey Bill Graves, Johnny Cooper, Buck Stinson, Mexican Frank, Bob Zachary, Boone Helm, Clubfoot George Lane, Billy Terwilliger, and Gad Moore.

Yeager explained that the gang was organized similar to the vigilantes, with captains, lieutenants, and oaths, and that its purpose was to rob, without taking life if possible. Members took an oath to be true to each other and to perform the services required of their respective positions. Those who revealed any of the secrets or disobeyed orders were to be hunted down and killed. To recognize each other they wore mustaches, chin whiskers, and scarves tied in a sailor knot and used the password, "innocent." Though he was a member of the band, Yeager said, he was not a murderer.

After jotting down the list of members, the group, including X. Beidler, the little guard who had served as George Ives's executioner, gathered up lanterns and stools and marched the condemned through the snow to a stand of large cottonwood trees on the riverbank behind Laurin's ranch. As they approached the place of execution, Brown began to pray for his Indian wife and children back in Minnesota, but Yeager reminded him, "Brown, if you had thought of this three years ago, you would not be here now, or give these boys this trouble." Ropes were tied to the tree limbs and one stool placed on top of the other. Brown went first, saying only, "God Almighty, save my soul."

Yeager calmly climbed onto the two stools for his turn, and looking down at the men below him, suggested again, "I wish you would chain me and not hang me until after I have seen those punished who are guiltier than I." When the vigilantes showed no inclination to delay his execution, he shook hands all around. "Goodbye, boys," he said, "you're on a good undertaking. God bless you." Then he fell from the stools. Notes describing their crimes were pinned to the backs of the victims, and the bodies were left dangling from the tree for several days as an example.

As the vigilantes returned to Nevada City, they were dreading the expected confrontation with citizens aroused by their captain having taken justice into his own hands. But all were relieved to find their fellow members fully organized and in power. Despite the freezing weather, the executive committee insisted members go after those on Yeager's list immediately, and four men, among them X. Beidler, were sent to Bannack to carry out the execution of Sheriff Henry Plummer and his two deputies, Buck Stinson and Ned Ray.

Bannack was already in the midst of a problem involving an individual's refusing to submit to the authority of elected officials: Neil Howie had just brought in a prisoner, and on meeting Plummer, had informed the sheriff that he had Dutch John in custody. When Plummer asked what the charge was against him, Howie responded that he was certain John had attempted to rob the Moody wagon train. "Well, I suppose you are willing he should be tried by the civil authorities," Plummer said. "This new way our people have of hanging men without law or evidence isn't exactly the thing. It's time a stop was put to it."[116] Nevertheless, Howie refused to release his prisoner, instead hiding him in a cabin on Yankee Flat.

When Beidler's delegation got to town, however, it was discovered that despite Howie's act of rebellion, forming a branch at Bannack was not going to be as easy as had been expected, and the enlistment of members was temporarily abandoned for that night. The next day Mattie Edgerton heard her father and Sanders discussing the best way to take Plummer, and their conversation gives insight into Sanders's way of thinking: "Wilbur, at first suggested that someone warn Plummer of his danger, and when he went to the stable for his horse have men concealed there to shoot him. On due consideration this seemed to appear more unlawful than previous hangings, and the idea was abandoned."[117] At length Edgerton and Sanders hit on the idea of forming three companies, a separate one for each man to be arrested. Mattie worried over the safety of the men who would be capturing the desperados, feeling certain some would be killed.

THE HANGING

Sunday morning dawned with temperatures far below zero and snow covering the ground, and "an unusual silence seemed to brood over the little settlement," Thompson recalled.[118] Though James Vail was out of town, Martha prepared breakfast as usual for her children and boarders. Plummer, who had left the cabin he and Electa had shared and moved into a room at the Goodrich Hotel, had been "ailing for several days" and was spending much of his time at Martha's home resting. He was feeling well enough, though, to come to the Sunday breakfast table to join the family, Joseph Swift, and Thompson.

For Thompson, the meal was a constant struggle for self-mastery. He knew the vigilantes planned to hang Plummer that evening, and he was tempted to warn him so he could escape. As he ate, he kept remembering how Plummer had helped him from time to time, and his conscience bothered him, but when he recalled the murder of the Magruder party, he felt a conflicting emotion. From the first he had wondered how Plummer knew that Doc Howard and his friends were criminals, and he could not help thinking there might be a connection somehow between them and Plummer. As Thompson viewed his moral predicament, the choice lay between his love for one man and his duty to the community. The decision was made easier, however, by realizing it would be dangerous to interfere with the vigilantes' plan. He kept quiet. Leaving the Vails, he went to open his store, where Edgerton soon joined him, drew up a chair in front of the stove, and began chatting. Outside the street was nearly empty—Buck Stinson, making his rounds, poked his head in the door once and Ned Ray dropped in for a few minutes. Thompson thought both deputies seemed "very nervous and anxious to know what was taking place."[119] At supper Plummer was still sick and could eat but little and then lay down on the lounge. About eight o'clock Thompson went to the Edgerton's cabin where he was told Sunday night choir practice, usually held at Hattie's home, had been cancelled. Mary did not want her daughter and niece anywhere in the vicinity of Yankee Flat, not with the Vail cabin being located there. Thompson sat with Mary's family the rest of the evening, waiting and listening.

Things were not going according to plan. A vigilante group was supposed to have been formed already upon Beidler's arrival with the letter of execution, the advance planning indicating intentions of killing Plummer may well have existed even before Yeager's alleged confession, probably since the time of the Ives's trial as had been rumored in Bannack. Due to the lack of enthusiasm among Bannack citizens on the first night, Dimsdale wrote, "It was resolved to spend the following day in enlisting members, though no great progress was made after all."[120] As both Thompson and Mattie acknowledged, Plummer "had attracted many friends," and "plenty of people in town . . . did not believe he was the leader of the road agents."[121] In order to persuade those reluctant to take arms against an elected official, Henry Tilden was produced to testify of Plummer's involvement in crime. A final impetus was given by the rumor that three horses intended for the escape of the sheriff and his deputies were being brought into town. Up to the last moment, men off the street were hastily recruited for the three arrest parties by shoving loaded shotguns into hesitant hands and insisting, more than once if necessary, that they come along.

At about ten o'clock, Thompson and the Edgertons heard the creak of snow on the path that passed their home, fifty to seventy-five men splitting into three squads after crossing the bridge. Buck Stinson, still wearing the suit he had put on to take his wife to church, was taken at the cabin where the couple boarded, and Ned Ray was found on a gambling table where he had passed out. The group who came for Plummer quietly surrounded the Vail cabin. Plummer, still feeling ill, lay on Martha's lounge, unarmed. When the knock came at the door, she answered and saw a "well known citizen" who asked for Plummer. He got up and came to the door without a weapon, supposedly an unusual thing for him to do, and then putting on his coat, joined the group waiting outside. Martha was alarmed, but Plummer calmed her, saying the men only wanted to talk to him about Dutch John. He walked across to Sanders's cabin and knocked at the door. Though Sanders was inside, he had hoped to avoid a final encounter with Plummer and quickly extinguished his lantern. Plummer now spoke to the assembled men, who faltered in their purpose, halting outside the cabin. Realizing a crisis had developed and that he must appear, Sanders stepped out, quickly giving a military command: "Company! forward march!" The group obeyed, but Plummer had recognized Sanders's voice and

Bannack's Hangman's Gulch, site of the execution of Sheriff Henry Plummer and his two deputies on 10 January 1864. (Photo by Boswell, 1985)

spoke to him. "You men know us better than this." Sanders stood firm in his resolve. As they walked, the three prisoners protested their innocence, and Plummer asked that they be given a trial. He was undisputably a brave man, but it was a bravery derived from overcoming fear of losing a life whose value he keenly recognized.

There had to be a first moment of terror when he knew they would not listen to reason, that they really intended to hang him. The armed men quickly formed a circle around the gallows to hold back the gathering crowd as they waited for Tilden to run to the Edgertons for more rope. Plummer spoke of his wife, wanted to see his sister-in-law, and asked for time to settle his business affairs, but his requests were not considered. Ray's turn came first. As Madam Hall, sobbing loudly, tried to force her way through the barricade of armed men to reach her lover, Ray was hoisted up and dropped, and she was roughly escorted back to her cabin. Stinson was next. Plummer, walking around nervously inside the circle of vigilantes, was becoming "awfully alarmed." At first no one approached him. "Now came a moment of suspense," Thompson says. "Under the gallows which he had erected and used as an officer of the law in sustaining good government, stood a nice clean looking young man, only twenty-seven years of age, of pleasing and affable manners and of good ability."[122] Joseph Swift, belatedly learning of what was taking place, rushed to the scene, fighting his way up to Plummer and pleading that he be spared until he "had to be forcibly removed." Swift then "threw himself on the ground at the outskirts of the crowd and wept like a child." Seeing him, Plummer pulled off his scarf and tossed it in Swift's direction. "Give this to Joe," he said.[123] Stinson and Ray had "discharged volley after volley of oaths and epithets," but Plummer now stood quietly as his arms were pinioned. "Give a man time to pray," he told them, but they would have none of it, and so he made a final request, "Give me a high drop, boys." They did.

Watching Plummer leave with the large group of armed men, Martha Vail had become frightened and ran to the Edgertons, "hysterically calling" for Francis Thompson. Mattie remembers seeing her "weeping bitterly" as Thompson and Mary tried to calm her by repeating what Plummer had told her—the sheriff was only wanted in town to discuss Dutch John's arrest.[124] When they had quieted Martha, Thompson escorted her back to her cabin, staying

Bannack's Meade Hotel. Built in 1875 as a county courthouse and later converted to a hotel, the brick structure stands on the original site of the temporary morgue of Plummer and his deputies. The hotel's owner, Amede Bessette, wrote that the last man hanged by the vigilantes at Bannack, who was named Rawley, was probably innocent. (Photo by Boswell, 1985)

Meade Hotel interior. (Photo by Boswell, 1985)

with her and pacifying her as best he could for what seemed to him like an endless time. Finally an unidentified man appeared in front of the cabin with the message, "It's all over!"

Thompson now had to tell Martha what had really happened. On hearing the truth, she fainted and he ran next door for Hattie, bringing her to tend Martha so he could leave. If Martha had been permitted to follow after Plummer, the hanging might have been prevented. On a previous occasion, the trial of Stinson, the miners had shown a weakness for the tears of respectable women and reversed the decision.

For an hour, armed guards paced about the scene of the execution, then dispersed, leaving the bodies hanging on the gallows for the night. The next day the frozen corpses were carried to an unfinished building. Plummer's scarf was never given to Joseph Swift.

Mrs. Stinson and Sarah Wadams came to the makeshift morgue to retrieve Buck's gold wedding band, finding the hand frozen so solid they had to cut off his fingers to extract the ring.[125] Since Ned Ray had been dressed in buckskin at the time of his arrest, Madam Hall was permitted to take his body to her cabin for burial preparation. Martha did not come for Plummer.

Witnesses remember seeing all of the men laid out: "In the lower part of a two-story log house not yet completed, lay on the floor, frozen solid, the bodies of the three . . . side by side, with each a deep groove in the neck showing the marks of rope strand spirals; clad in their Sunday clothes, newly shaved."[126] A pencil drawing made of the hanging, the only representation of Plummer known to exist, shows him clean shaven and clad in "Sunday clothes" at the time he was taken.[127] Using Plummer's own funds, Thompson arranged for the burial, though Plummer was not allowed a plot on cemetery hill.

In the spring, at least according to X. Beidler, a document arrived in the dying town of Bannack approving the application that Plummer had forwarded to Washington to be the first U.S. marshall of Idaho territory east of the Rockies.[128]

THE MOB AND MORE HANGINGS

Following the hanging of the sheriff and his two deputies, the vigilantes sought out "the Greaser," so called because he was the

only Mexican in town. Though Joe Pizanthia had not been impli-
cated with the road agent gang, Langford said the armed party went
"with a view of investigating his career in the Territory."[129] They
had heard he had recently been involved in a brawl and was holed
up somewhere recuperating from a chest wound. One of Plummer's
more respected deputies, Smith Ball, who had joined in the search,
pushed open the door of the cabin where "the Greaser" was hiding,
and received a shot in the leg. The man behind Smith Ball was hit in
the chest and died immediately. Deputy Ball tied a handkerchief
over his wound and joined others in firing into the cabin, the general
shooting becoming so wild that stray bullets whizzed through the
door and window of Thompson's store, located in front of the cabin.
Looking out, Thompson spotted Edgerton, a Henry rifle in his
hands, standing among the excited group.[130]

When the Mexican did not surrender, the crowd asked Edgerton for the loan of the howitzer cannon stored in his cabin and he
consented. Mattie watched the men, "white-faced and trembling,"
drag the gun and shells from under her father's bed.[131] They returned to the besieged cabin, towing the little brass cannon behind
them with a rope, and, after appropriating a box from Thompson's
store for a mount, shelled Pizanthia's hideout until it exploded. The
suspect could now be seen lying on the dirt floor, crushed beneath
the fallen door, and Smith Ball fired into the body until his revolver
was empty. Removing the rope from the cannon, they slipped it over
Pizanthia's head and he was dragged to a pole and strung up. Pizanthia, still half alive, was then riddled with more than a hundred
bullets. Setting fire to the debris of the cabin, they tossed the body
into the flames in way of a funeral since none present cared to bury
the suspected criminal.

Not wishing to admit to his family that he had been among the
crowd, Edgerton returned home with a more acceptable explanation. Mattie said he told them he "had witnessed the scene from
the hill above," then turned on his heel and gone home since "he
thought it about time for the Chief Justice to be elsewhere."[132]

In his chapter entitled "The Execution of 'The Greaser,' "
Dimsdale condoned the mob's actions as "prompt and really
necessary severity," adding that had the punishment been left to
"outsiders, the penalty would have been cruel and disgusting in the
highest degree."[133]

Pizanthia's killing is usually represented as the single instance in which things got out of control, but apparently the situation in Bannack was unstable and disorderly from the moment of Plummer's execution. Directly after the hanging of the sheriff and his deputies, hotel owner Bill Goodrich ran to Chrisman's store and grabbed Plummer's double-barreled shotgun, supposedly "the envy of every miner in the camp," as payment for his hotel bill, then "rushed into the street thronged with excited people and brandishing the gun above his head, shouted so all could hear: 'The gun is mine! The gun is mine! It cost me $275 and I mean to keep it.' "[134]

The excitement in the streets had not died down by morning; the curious were flocking in to see the bodies dangling from the small pine-tree frame in the gulch a few hundred yards off Main Street. One witness wrote, "I would not believe it until I saw for myself and he (McMurtry) accompanied me. Said it was not safe for me to go alone."[135]

It was in this chaotic setting that Pizanthia's execution had taken place. The next score to be settled was with Dutch John, suspected of attempting to rob the Moody wagon train, and the vigilantes voted for his immediate hanging. John was taken to the same building where two of the bodies had lain for two days — Stinson still on the floor but Plummer now on the bench, their hands tied behind them. By lantern light, a rope was thrown over a beam and a barrel placed under it. Dutch John told them he had never seen a man hanged before and wondered if it would take long to die. He was assured that it would be very short and he would not suffer much pain.[136]

Back at Virginia City, the committee ordered that five more of the gang be rounded up — Haze Lyons, Boone Helm, Jack Gallagher, Frank Parish, and Clubfoot George Lane — and their death sentences carried out, X. Beidler acting as hangman. Dimsdale's statement that all five confessed to their crimes during questioning is contradicted by a witness. John Grannis, the same miner who had stood guard all night during the Ives trial, wrote in his diary the night after the joint hanging: "Obeying a notice of the vigilance committee I went to Virginia this morning . . . I was on guard all day and saw them hung. The five was hung in a row. All of them maintained their innocence to the last."[137]

Within the next few days, Stephen Marshland, Billy Bunton,

Cyrus Skinner, Alex Carter, Johnny Cooper, George Shears, Bob Zachary, Bill Graves, and Bill Hunter were all hanged. Though Dimsdale assured the deaths were quick, easy, and "without seeming pain," eyewitnesses again presented a more realistic picture. In way of example, George Bruffey, who watched the hanging of five men at Virginia City, noted that Frank Parish, so crippled he had to be helped on to the box placed underneath his intended noose, "struggled hard" in dying.[138] Another reassurance Dimsdale occasionally gave, which tends to put additional strain on his credibility, is that the gang members had some sort of death wish, and when informed of their doom, "appeared perfectly satisfied."[139] A more realistic interpretation is that despite their bad reputations, the victims of the vigilantes showed considerable courage in facing death.

No one can say for certain that all of these men were guilty as charged. Undoubtedly most had bad names, ranging in degree of notoriety from exconvict, former insane asylum inmate, squawman, and Secessionist to cripple. The general belief is that all deserved what they got, historian K. Ross Toole expressing the consensus opinion that no evidence exists that any of the victims were innocent.[140] The problem with such a statement is that the process is supposed to work the other way—evidence is required to prove guilt, not innocence.

The final hanging at Bannack took place at the end of 1864, the victim being R. C. Rawley, who had made the blunder of expressing an opinion that the committee members were "strangling --'s" and that they had hanged some "good men." The Vigilance Committee, according to Dimsdale, could not allow such conduct to "remain unpunished" and investigated the Rawley case. They were able to uncover belated evidence that he had actually helped the gang and would in the future again "connect himself with some new gang of thieves, and as it was more than suspected that such an organization was contemplated, it was determined to put a sudden end to all such doings, by making an example of Rawley. . . . They arrested him at night . . . without the knowledge of a single soul except his actual captors. . . . The first intelligence concerning his fate was obtained from the sight of his dead body, swinging in the wind on the following morning." Dimsdale concluded his account of the episode with, "The effect of the execution was magical. Not another step was taken to organize crime in Bannack, and it has remained in comparative peace and perfect security ever since."[141]

But an early pioneer named Amede Bessette, who knew this final Bannack victim well, disagreed with Dimsdale that Rawley, or, as he spelled the name, Reighly, had any intentions of connecting himself to a gang of thieves. Though likable enough, Bessette wrote, Reighly was only a "little, harmless, educated fool," who would not have had the courage to join the road agents, nor would they have wanted him in their band since, after suffering the misfortune of freezing both feet and having them amputated, he was left to hobble about on two wooden pegs. On hearing one morning just at daybreak that a man was "frozen stiff at the end of a rope," Bessette walked out to the gallows, describing the sight that met his eyes as follows: "I saw Reighly at the end of a rope. Below his shoulder his coat was torn about six inches square and the piece hung down: Four or five inches to the left of the center of his back another piece of his coat was torn in the shape of a flat-iron. In both places the white lining of his thin coat could be seen. His pants were torn in a half dozen places. Two bones in place of human feet projected from the legs of his pants. His tongue hung about an inch out of his mouth." Though Bessette hastened to add that his purpose was not to speak ill of the Vigilance Committee, he stated he believed that in this particular case "an honest mistake was made."[142] Mistake or not, the awesome sight of Rawley's body swinging in the morning gloom had the desired effects of stemming further criticism of the vigilantes and preventing further attempts to defend Plummer in fact up to the present day.

RESTORATION OF ORDER

By February 1864, Plummer's gang was eradicated, the reign of terror was ended, and law and order prevailed, or so Dimsdale, Langford, Sanders, and others would have us believe. Pemberton, the young lawyer who acted as court reporter at Ives's trial and later became a judge, stated that "after Plummer was hung, life and property were safe. It was said that a man might lay a sack of gold dust down on the sidewalk and it would be there till the buckskin rotted off, before anyone touched it."[143]

Actually, travelling with gold dust was still unsafe, as Edgerton realized when he asked his wife to quilt gold ingots into the lining of his coat so they would not be detected if he were detained while on

Boot Hill, Virginia City, Montana. Though vigilantes reported that the five men whose graves are pictured above confessed their guilt, witnesses to

his way to Washington. Though the vigilantes' dogged persistence in tracking down anyone suspected of crime persuaded those with a propensity for obtaining their gold the easy way to lie low for a while, road agent activity soon continued — and on a larger scale than before. Alex Toponce, a freighter operating between Virginia City and Salt Lake, wrote in his reminiscences about ten road agents holding up and killing all but one passenger on a Wells Fargo stage

the joint hanging wrote that all five maintained their innocence to the end. (Photo by Boswell, 1985)

in 1865,[144] and James Miller noted in his diary, during July of the same year, that twenty road agents had just held up a stage, killing four people.[145] *The Montana Post* contained articles in 1865 that expressed great concern over the continuing road agent problem, and it is interesting to note that the attacks after January 1864 showed more earmarks of being performed by a gang, by the large number of robbers and better organization, than those committed during

Plummer's time. Those usually involved no more than two or three persons.

The Vigilance Committee was kept busy punishing robbers and road agents for several years after February 1864, not disbanding until years later when the press and courts chastised them for conducting their own "reign of terror." Citizens posted a public notice warning them that future hanging would be retaliated five to one.

Before evaluating the evidence against Plummer, it is appropriate to take a closer look at the credentials of his executioners, those credited with ushering in the so-called era of safety. The contention that the vigilantes enjoyed popular support becomes a moot point when we realize that their method of enlisting members was at times identical to their method of punishing those they considered guilty. The son of Alexander Davis, a judge of the miners' court, wrote that when his father was "importuned" to join the vigilante organization, he "politely refused to do so, informing the members that his principles would not permit him to be a party to executions that did not have the sanction of a court and jury. The members, miffed at his seeming censure of their actions, apprised him that he had the choice of joining the Vigilantes, leaving the region or being hung."[146]

Though Sanders assured historian H. H. Bancroft that the organization was made up of "the best people in the community,"[147] a lawyer would be hard put to defend the morality of some of their tenets. While the executive committee was responsible for "any criminal act," the governing bylaws stated that "the only punishment that shall be inflicted by this Committee is DEATH" thus making no attempt to equate punishment to severity of crime.[148] Alex Toponce claimed that when Mrs. Slade protested her husband's execution on charges of being disorderly, Captain Williams of the vigilance organization threatened her with the same fate as her husband if she did not quiet down. Even Bill Fairweather, discoverer of gold in Alder Gulch, narrowly escaped being hanged for his vociferous insistence that there had been a miscarriage of justice in Slade's instance. There is also the example of a Mason, fearing for his life after being falsely accused of a crime, who came to the brotherhood for protection. But those who were not Masons had no such protection to turn to. Being suspected of any crime left a citizen in a panic for his life, a situation comparable to the Salem witch trials, except that in Massachusetts the accused was at least tried in a public court.

Their practice of impounding the property of those they hanged left the vigilantes open to charges of being motivated by personal profit, no matter how petty, from the death of their victims. There is the taint of booty to Captain Pitts ordering the roundup of the late Johnny Cooper's horses, or in Beidler's coveting Dutch John's bead leggins and pocketing the knife he found on the corpse of Nick Tiebolt, explaining to those who saw him that he recognized the knife as one Tom Baume had loaned to Nick a year ago.

In cases where a victim had considerable wealth, such as Cyrus Skinner or Henry Plummer, the issue of appropriating the property of the deceased became more important. Laying claim to a suspect's mining interests to pay "expenses" could prove a strong temptation, especially in a country where gold fever infected even the most stalwart citizens. Edgerton, for one, left the territory with over seventy-five claims to his credit.[149] Small wonder rumors such as the following sprung up later: "Plummer's body had hardly frozen in the cold night air before a wagon train pulled out with oak kegs filled with raw gold. It had been loaded from three cabins of first-rank citizens, previously poor as church mice, but wealthy after that hour. On returning to Bannack the freighters told everything. Vigilante leaders ran some of them out of the country and threatened to hang others if they did not shut up."[150]

A third problem that should be mentioned is that the executioners did not follow the procedure they had set up in their bylaws. Captains and their companies were supposed to arrest a suspect and then present proof to the executive committee whose duty it was to make final judgment. Bylaws stated specifically that the supreme ruler was to reside in Virginia City. Yet the captains rarely made the required trip back to Virginia City with their prisoners, preferring instead to take advantage of the nearest corral beam or cottonwood limb.

Dr. Smurr, who explored the basic philosophy behind the vigilance movement, pointed out the vigilantes' distrust of the jury system as represented by the miners' courts. They favored instead an organization governed by a small body and one supreme leader, who had the "duty to legislate for the good of the whole Committee," again quoting bylaws. Members were to carry out orders blindly, lawyers were not permitted to speak for the defendant, and there was no appeal to a higher court. Smurr also cited instances in which quick justice resulted in the death of innocent men. He attributed the broken pledges to prisoners who had been promised they would be taken back to Virginia City for judgment to individual captains and their companies who were "anxious to inflict summary punishment."[151]

Among the "anxious" was X. Beidler, who, frustrated in other lines of trade, "concluded to quit prospecting for gold and prospect for human fiends," and he was always present when a grave needed to be dug, a makeshift scaffold rigged, or a rope adjusted around a neck, and not just for the excitement, but in his own words: "I'll be paid, you bet."[152] Before Alex Carter was hanged, he one day happened to meet Beidler on the street, and Carter's manner of greeting the enthusiastic vigilante seems, though crude, quite appropriate. Carter, looking down from the height of his magnificent horse whom he'd named Stonewall Jackson, asked Beidler, "You grave-digging, scaffold-building s-- of a b----, what are you doing here? Do you want to hang somebody?"[153] Granted that the committee may have been formed by citizens of lofty ideals for the purpose of making a safe community, in practice it became difficult to control the actions of members at the lower levels, and Smurr's reference to the "blood-lust of enraged mobs" is perhaps a fair description of their motivation as evidenced during the execution of Joe Pizanthia.[154]

In Plummer's case, most of the aforementioned weaknesses of the Vigilance Committee came into play. His extensive holdings in gold and silver mines were at the disposal of the committee upon his death with no obligation on its part to release information as to the distribution of his property. Also, the mob instinct was evoked in the very act of overthrowing a figure of authority. And last, he was not examined and allowed to reply after his arrest as others were, namely Yeager, Brown, and the five in Virginia City. If the prescribed procedures of the committee had been followed, Plummer would have been arrested and brought to Virginia City, after which the governing body would have determined his guilt or innocence. But Plummer's guilt was decided some time before the formation of the vigilance organization. It had been decided by the Thanksgiving supper, perhaps even as early as the meeting on the Snake River when the wagon master spoke of Plummer's reputation as a desperado to Edgerton and Sanders, men steeped in rigid notions of traditional respectability and willing to accept rumor as truth.

Since the vigilantes relied on Dimsdale to present their case against Plummer and since his book was the only major account to appear near the time of the actual events, we will turn to it for an examination of the evidence. The first question to be answered is just how extensive was the "reign of terror" over which Plummer supposedly presided.

Dimsdale, who also blamed the road agent organization for scores of killings never detected, set the figure of documented murders at one hundred two and listed and described each case:[155]

> Lloyd Magruder and four men travelling with him were robbed and murdered by Doc Howard and party.
> Nick Tiebolt was robbed and killed by George Ives.
> George Evans disappeared and was presumed robbed and murdered.
> A Mormon was presumed to have been robbed and murdered on the road to Salt Lake City.

Thus the total number of persons murdered in connection with a robbery during Plummer's months in Bannack comes to six, with two more presumed.

In addition, nine robberies occurred in which no killings took place:

> In October 1863, the Peabody coach was robbed.
> In November 1863, the Oliver coach was robbed.
> Anton Holter was robbed of a few greenbacks and shot at by George Ives.
> Mr. and Mrs. Davenport were robbed while eating their lunch on Rattlesnake Creek, though Mrs. Davenport's money was returned.
> The house of Le Grau, baker and blacksmith at Bannack, was broken into and robbed, though the money was hidden too well for thieves to locate.
> Dutch Fred was robbed of $5.
> Henry Tilden was robbed of $10 on Horse Prairie. (Those who heard Tilden relate the incident say he had no money on him at the time.)

"Another man" was robbed of $2 or $3 a few miles from Nevada.
Wagner and Marshland attempted to rob the Moody train, but
     failed.

During this same period, twelve killings also occurred that were
not connected to robberies:

Five Indians were shot in two different fracases with whites, and a
     Frenchman named Brissette was killed when he ran to the tepee
     being fired on.
Banfield was shot in the melee following his gunfight with Sapp and
     died later from improper care of the wound.
Plummer shot Cleveland in the Goodrich saloon.
Stinson and Lyons shot Dillingham in a wickiup saloon in Virginia
     City.
Ives killed "a man" near Cold Spring ranch in broad daylight.

Two of the twelve killings mentioned above were not attributed to
the gang:

Banfield or Sapp accidentally shot Carrhart during their conflict over
     the poker game.
Horan murdered Keeler and was hanged for it.

To summarize, during the nearly fourteen months Plummer
lived at Bannack, eleven robberies occurred in the mining districts
east of the Rockies and two more were presumed; five Indians were
killed and thirteen whites, with two more whites presumed. Dimsdale's figure of one hundred two is obviously an exaggeration. If he,
Wilbur Sanders, or any of their informants had known of more
crimes, they would have been included in the book in gory detail.
Actually, considering the thousands rushing into the area and the
resulting tumultuous times, the crime statistics are not as high as
would be expected.

Regardless of crimes that undoubtedly went undetected or
unreported, those mentioned in the paragraphs above are the ones
that the vigilantes knew of and accordingly reported to Dimsdale for
his book and the ones that they held Plummer responsible for as
head of the organization.

The evidence to support their belief in Plummer's guilt for the
above crimes was also reported to Dimsdale, mainly through
Sanders, who also assumed the task of proofreading the finished
book for accuracy. Relying solely on this book for the charges
against Plummer would eliminate any additional evidence presented

by Langford, who wrote twenty-six years later and therefore included many stories that grew up after the fact. Actually, any time Langford or any other writer produces evidence against Plummer that Dimsdale did not include, it is suspect. Dimsdale, with Sanders's help, prepared the book as carefully as a legal case to include all evidence that would persuade the population that Plummer was guilty and that the vigilantes were justified in assuming power because of his corrupt administration.

A prime example of suspect evidence that is not included in Dimsdale's book is the garbled account Alex Toponce gave of the three hangings at Bannack. Toponce claimed that he refused Buck Stinson permission to serve a warrant on a member of his freighting party, after which Beidler, Fetherstun, and Howie pursued Stinson, House, and Barnes, overtaking and hanging them in a cabin on Rattlesnake Creek. "It was reported," he said, "that they hung all three of them right there, each one on a corner of the cabin, and had one corner to spare. They found a constitution and by-laws of the society on Stinson and a list of the members, 139 in all. In the morning they went on to Bannack and arrested Ed Plummer, the Sheriff, and hung him and two other white men, members of the gang, and a young Mexican."[156] If such documents as Toponce mentioned had been found on Stinson, Dimsdale and Sanders would have made good use of them, certainly including them in the book.

Though Dimsdale must be the primary reference, we will continue to supplement his work with additional information supplied by other writers for the sake of comparison and to provide details that help evaluate the case as presented by the vigilantes' spokesman.

Drawbacks in using Dimsdale as a main source have already been mentioned, the bias and exaggeration, part of which arises from the century of change separating us from Dimsdale. He was a Victorian moralist setting down a lesson about Good and Evil and the eventual triumph of the former. He saw Plummer not as a man but as a symbol, a "very demon" who committed "outrages against the laws of God and man." Any good qualities Plummer appeared to have were mere deception to cover up his "true colors."[157] Dimsdale must therefore alter his story to fit this pattern. Logically, a purely evil man would not display such traits as courage and dignity in facing death. Plummer "begged for his life," Dimsdale wrote, "falling on his knees, with tears and sighs declared to God that he was too wicked to die. He confessed his numerous murders and crimes, and seemed almost frantic at the prospect of death."[158]

An eyewitness named E. J. Porter, who claimed to be one of the hanging party, contradicted the above passage, stating that Plummer, Stinson, and Ray "all proclaimed their innocence, saying that they had not done anything to be hung for."[159] A second witness, also more believable than Dimsdale because he had nothing to prove, gave an account of the hanging to his friend, J. Holleman, who prepared a statement that was sent to H. H. Bancroft. Though Holleman wrote that he considered the sheriff guilty, he added, "I do not believe Plummer begged for his life. I heard at the time that he did but a friend of mine who was at Bannack at the time told me there was nothing to it."[160] Statements such as the one Holleman reported—terse comments hastily jotted down in letter or diary—help to put Dimsdale back in perspective. With need for this balance in mind, we can proceed to examine the testimony of the first witness Dimsdale presented against Plummer.

FIRST WITNESS FOR THE PROSECUTION

Ignoring such bandwagon witnesses as N. H. Webster, who after the hangings concluded that the sheriff's road agents must have stolen his missing buffalo robe and overcoat, we will take a look at the accuser who started the ball rolling. In her history, Helen Sanders credited Henry Tilden with providing the first proof of Plummer's guilt: "The real character of Henry Plummer, who had led a life of crime in California, had been long suspected by a few, but the first proof of his complicity with the Road Agents was the story told by Henry Tilden, the lad who crossed the plains with Governor Edgerton."[161]

As Dimsdale described the incident, "Henry Tilden . . . reported that he had been robbed by three men—one of whom was Plummer—between Horse Prairie and Bannack." On the next page he added that $10 was taken from Tilden.[162]

Since Mattie Edgerton claimed to have heard Tilden tell his story twice, we will quote her remarks in full to get the details:

> At nightfall loud shrieks were heard from the Horse Prairie Hill. They proved later to have emanated from Henry Tilden, who had

been sent to Horse Prairie by Father and Wilbur to drive in some cattle for butchering. On his way back he was met by three masked horsemen who ordered him to hold up his hands while they searched him. Finding nothing in his pockets but a comb, and a picture of his girl, they let him go, and he went without delay, speeding toward Bannack. As he topped the hill above town his horse stepped into a ditch and threw him. This was too much. He made night vocal with his shouts for help.

Standing at our back door, I heard him and wondered who it could be calling so loudly. More frightened than hurt, he went at once to Wilbur's house, where he related his experiences of the day to Cousin Hattie. She brought him over to our house, where he repeated his story, concluding with the declaration, "One of the men I know was Henry Plummer."

The next day, Wilbur having returned from Alder Gulch, Henry came again to our house and was questioned by both Father and Wilbur. "How do you know one of the robbers was Plummer?" he was asked.

"Because he had on that overcoat of his he always wears, lined with red. Then he came into the Express Office (Henry worked there) day before yesterday to get a revolver he had sent for."

"That revolver proves nothing," was the reply, "but the overcoat is convincing. No one else in town has one like it." Then Wilbur said to Lucia and me, who were in the room and attentive listeners, "Girls, never breathe a word of what you have heard, or our lives will not be safe." I can testify that we kept quiet, as did Father and Wilbur, except once, later to be mentioned when Father took a man into his confidence. . . . A few days later Plummer came into the office to ask Henry if he had any idea who any of the holdup men were. Naturally, Henry protested his ignorance, but he was terribly frightened. Every night after closing hours he ran the whole distance to his boarding place.[163]

In another article, Mattie added that the robbers "neither advised him or killed him," meaning by "advised" that they didn't threaten Tilden for travelling "without enough cash to make it worth while to rob" him.[164]

Wilbur Sanders, who together with Edgerton, questioned Henry Tilden the day after his ordeal, left an account similar to Mattie's, but different enough to require its inclusion:

I had sent Henry S. Tilden, a young man who had accompanied me from Ohio to Bannack, to Horse Prairie to get some cattle which had been left there in the fall and drive them to town. About 9 or 10 o'clock in the evening he had made his appearance at my house on

Yankee Flat, and related to my wife his experience of the day and evening. . . . About half way between Horse Prairie and Bannack he saw
in the distance, in front of him, several horsemen, and, upon approaching them in the road, they commanded him to halt, dismount
and throw up his hands. Some of them dismounted and presented their
revolvers at him, while one of them proceeded to search his pockets for
money, with a result somewhat discouraging, whereupon they proceeded to say to him that they did not wish his money, that they did not
desire him to say what had been his experience that night, and, if he
did, notwithstanding this request and notice, he need not hope to
escape death at their hands. . . . They permitted him to remount his
horse and proceed on his way. He was a boy of fifteen or sixteen sum-
mers, thoroughly frightened by this episode. . . . His journey into
town was rapid, riding across Yankee Flat at a gallop, his horse
stumbled and threw him upon the ground, and for a time he was insen-
sible, but upon recovering consciousness he proceeded on foot to the
residence of Mr. Edgerton and told the family what had occurred to
him and who several of the party were that had stopped him in the
highway in the manner described. He then came to my house, repeated
the story, and my wife accompanied him to the residence of Mr.
Edgerton, where several of the neighbors were called and consulted.
. . . Upon my return to Bannack I was disinclined to believe that
young Tilden's identification of Plummer as the principal actor in the
attempted robbery was correct, but the young man was of undoubted
integrity, and he was certain that if the identification of individual faces
was a possible thing, he there saw and knew Henry Plummer.[165]

Comparing the accounts of the two cousins, we notice that
Sanders said the men threatened Tilden's life and Mattie said they
did not. Also, Mattie thought Tilden identified Plummer by his gun
and coat lining, the men being masked, yet Sanders stated Tilden
identified him by his face. This leaves the question of whether Mattie was mistaken in thinking the men wore masks, or whether
Sanders meant Tilden could identify Plummer's face even though it
was masked. The latter seems unlikely since the masks worn on
other robberies were sacks that completely covered the head, holes
being cut for eyes and nostrils. Evidently the cousins disagreed
about whether Tilden said the men wore masks. Since no actual robbery took place, the issue of disguises is important to establish some
surreptitious intent.

If Sanders's version is correct and Tilden was stopped and
searched by three unmasked men who told him they did not want his
money and then let him go, the incident need not necessarily be in-

terpreted as an attempted robbery, but could have been only a precautionary measure by the men to ascertain whether the approaching stranger was armed.

On the other hand, Mattie's version described an attempted robbery, but left identification of any of the masked men doubtful, especially since the event occurred shortly before nine o'clock on a November night. Francis Thompson agreed with Mattie, claiming that Edgerton told him the men were masked.[166]

Helen Sanders's history is correct in stressing the important relationship between the attempted robbery of Tilden and an assessment of Plummer's guilt. Tilden is the only person on record, either in Montana, Idaho, California, or Nevada, who claimed to have witnessed Plummer's involvement in a robbery. Wilbur Sanders took advantage of this singular testimony to convince those who still had doubts about Plummer's guilt after the four vigilantes had brought the news of Yeager's testimony and Dutch John had confirmed it. Langford says Tilden's testimony was the clincher: "And when it was determined on the afternoon of January 10, 1864, that Plummer should be hanged, Tilden was sent for and related his story in detail, which convinced all who heard it, of Plummer's guilt."[167]

Wilbur Sanders confessed that he was at first disinclined to believe that Tilden's identification of Plummer was indeed correct. Sanders's disbelief is easy to understand. Who would want to rob Henry Tilden since he had no money? Tilden could not have been mistaken for part of the Langford-Hauser party because he was riding toward Bannack rather than away from it. Even if someone had attempted to rob the boy, it was not likely to be Plummer, who had ridden off earlier that day in the opposite direction, with Sanders following him on the mule, and had returned from the same direction in which he left, the east side of town, not the south, where Tilden was accosted. Also, of what use would it be to Plummer to have an entire band of men under his direction, as Sanders suspected, if he had to participate in the holdups himself, thus risking being recognized?

But Sanders eventually disregarded such objections and accepted Tilden's word because "the young man was of undoubted integrity." Therefore, Sanders concluded, Plummer could have made a long, circuitous doubling back after he left Bannack that day and a second one when he returned that night. It was the only way to fit Plummer's departure and return into Tilden's story.

Sanders warned Mattie, Lucia, and Tilden not to tell anyone that Plummer had been recognized or their lives would not be safe. Tilden felt the weight of the fear, as did all of the Edgerton clan.

Langford however remained fearless. Though he and Sam Hauser supposedly suspected Plummer, they made their plans to carry $14,000 in gold dust to Salt Lake in full earshot of his deputy. At camp the first night, Langford claimed to have seen the same three robbers Tilden saw, first from a distance of about four hundred feet. "In the dim moonlight" he could make out three men, whose "features were concealed by loosely flowing masks." On seeing him, they fled, but he followed, noiselessly wading a stream and crawling through thirty feet of willow thicket to an opening beyond. "Not fifty feet distant from where I was lying, stood four masked men. One of them had been holding the horses — four in number — while the others were taking observations of our camp. After a brief consultation, they hurriedly mounted their horses and rode rapidly off towards Bannack."[168] Langford's story appears to confirm Mattie's contention that Tilden's robbers wore masks, but the fact that he did not return to camp to warn others of the danger has raised doubts about his having seen prowlers at all that night. Mattie credited Langford with a lively imagination.[169]

The night of 14 November 1863 reads like a scene from *Midsummer Night's Dream*, with Sanders, Plummer, Langford, and Tilden wandering through the mists, bumping into each other, or at least trying to, but despite all the fears, accidents, and accusations, no robberies took place that night. Nothing was stolen from Tilden nor from Langford and Hauser, who continued on their five-hundred-mile trek unmolested, reaching Salt Lake City with their gold intact, even though Plummer had stashed it for them the night before and knew their trip plans.

The question still remains whether Henry Tilden saw Plummer on Horse Prairie on the night of 14 November. We have no reason to doubt Sanders's judgment of the boy's honesty. Tilden was a timid adolescent, reportedly sick with consumption and separated from his family. He had come to a new land with people who did not take him into their home but had no qualms about using him to run unpleasant errands. The entire Edgerton group had been deeply impressed at their first meeting with Plummer, the only figure of authority in the strange country, who seemed so likable but was actually a "bad man." Only two days before the robbery, Plummer had come to the express office, where Tilden worked, to pick up a revolver he had ordered. When Sanders sent the boy out alone on a stormy night to accomplish an impossible mission, he had given up and returned, meeting three men who pointed guns at him and searched him; the face Tilden saw, masked or not, was that of Henry Plummer. After that traumatic night there were days of silent fear for Tilden, until at last he told the vigilantes who had robbed him and ran to the Edgerton house for rope to end the life that threatened his. We have no report of what Tilden told the vigilante group, but considering his fear of Plummer, he would not have wanted to live in the same town with the accused after having revealed his secret. His testimony would determine whether Plummer lived or was immediately hanged, and Tilden convinced those assembled that he had been able to identify Plummer that night.

The validity of his story is quite another matter. If the men were not masked, it may have been only Tilden's fear at being out alone on a dark night that caused him to interpret an encounter with armed men as an attempted robbery, even after being told by the men that they did not want his money.

On the other hand, if the men were masked, as the majority opinion seems to be, identifying any of them after 8:00 P.M. on a November night would be doubtful since as early as 8 September, the sun was setting at 6:30 P.M. Though it is likely Tilden would connect any assailant with Plummer, the first "bad man" he had known, and the gun might appear to be the same one picked up at the express office two days before, it would not have been possible to distinguish one gun from another, see the lining of a coat that a man was wearing, or perceive its color as red in the darkness. For all of these reasons—the boy's distraught emotional state, the disguises, and the darkness—positive identification would have been impossible.

Plummer was neither informed of Tilden's accusation against him nor asked of his whereabouts on the night in question, but had he been given the opportunity, he could have explained that he and about a dozen other well-known residents of the area spent the time rounding up a herd of horses that they feared the Indians planned to drive to the other side of the mountain. Both Sanders and Edgerton saw the party depart and return, and in a direction opposite from Horse Prairie. It was with good reason that Sanders doubted the truth of Henry Tilden's claim to have recognized Plummer among his assailants.

RED YEAGER'S TESTIMONY AGAINST PLUMMER

While Tilden received credit for first associating Plummer with a robbery, Yeager was the first to claim personal knowledge that crime in the area was organized and Henry Plummer the organizer. Dimsdale quoted Yeager as saying, "I know all about the gang." Judging by the similarity of verbiage, Dimsdale's informant was Beidler, who claimed to have heard Yeager's testimony firsthand, though it should be pointed out that Judge Alexander Davis left an account that differs considerably from Beidler's. "Red confessed," Beidler said, describing the execution of Yeager and Brown. "We hung both of these men at Lorrains's on a cottonwood tree. Brown begged for mercy and died praying. Yager shook hands with us and his last words were: 'Good-bye. God bless you. You are on a good undertaking.' Then we went on to Bannack to get Plummer, Stinson and Ray."[170]

The Bannack vigilantes may have needed Henry Tilden as a second witness before they were convinced of Plummer's guilt, but not Beidler; he was apparently satisfied with only one accuser. In regards to this small amount of proof the vigilantes required, George Bruffey, in his reminiscences, claimed that Carter and three others were hanged even before Yeager had confessed they were members of a gang. Perhaps Bruffey has only tangled the sequence, but his charge brings up a relevant point: the activities of the vigilantes were secret; we do not know when the individual hangings took place nor what men said before they were hanged. We know only what the vigilantes chose to report afterwards.

In the vigilante account of the big breakthrough, that is, the discovery that a gang existed, there is something rather bizarre about Yeager's reported behavior. In Alexander Davis's account, Yeager breaks down completely during interrogation, but Beidler and Dimsdale staunchly insist on Yeager's courage and calmness up to the end, which tends to lend more credibility to his confession.

Still there seems to be some inconsistency of behavior in Beidler's account when Yeager claims he was not a murderer but a messenger, yet he good-naturedly accepts the death penalty, shaking hands all around with his killers and asking a blessing on them. Yeager was apparently trying to ingratiate himself with his captors: "I agree to it all," he said when they preached to him about the lawlessness in the area. Then when Brown begged for mercy, Yeager commented, "Brown, if you had thought of this three years ago, you would not be here now, or give these boys this trouble." Yeager protested too much that he was not trying to buy his life by giving wanted information: "I don't say this to get off. I don't want to get off." But his testimony was obviously influenced by a desire to say what those who held his life in their hands wanted to hear.

According to Beidler, Yeager claimed there was a gang and named twenty-four members, not one hundred thirty-nine as Toponce recorded. Beidler did not list the assigned duties of each member, the childish offices Dimsdale earnestly reported—a stool pigeon, a spy, a fence, a horsethief, and as secretary, George Brown, though we are told of only one letter he composed in this official capacity: "Get up and dust, and lie low for black ducks," the message that foiled the vigilantes, though it is so brief it hardly needed to be committed to paper. Yeager should have been able to remember the essence of the message on his own. Neither did Beidler mention the robber band having a code of dress, an oath, or a password, the famous "innocent" appearing to have been of Dimsdale's origin. And Dimsdale put the password to good use in his book, explaining away any victim's last insistence of innocence as being nothing more than the password. As for wearing moustache and chin whiskers for mutual identification, the pencil sketch of the hanging of Plummer, Stinson, and Ray shows all three clean shaven, and Mollie Sheehan also described George Ives as "smooth shaven."[171]

Assuming Beidler's account of Yeager's confession is true (though we would not be the first to call Beidler a liar—Alva Noyes's grandmother did), there are still several problems with the testimony. First, it is not in Yeager's words; however, assuming that Beidler and Dimsdale captured the general meaning, we still do not know if what he said was true, or if he even believed it was true. It would have been possible that the lawless element of the community counted on Sheriff Plummer's sympathy in the event they should be caught. After all, he was a man with a record himself, and circulating rumors of his supposed support of contemplated robberies would help to bolster timid accomplices enlisted to do the dirty work. In other words, it would have been possible for Yeager to repeat such a rumor, either because he believed it himself or because he thought it would save his life.

What we really need to know from Yeager (and what Beidler does not tell us) is whether he witnessed Plummer operating as the chief of the road agents or whether it was something he had only heard. Without knowing which was the case, we cannot determine the value of his information. However, if the vigilantes actually had in their possession a witness who could give concrete details of the sheriff planning and directing crime in his own district, it is likely this living proof of the corruption of the existing justice system, from top to bottom, would have been paraded before the entire community like a trophy. Instead, the witness was immediately destroyed.

Perhaps Yeager was not preserved because his testimony consisted mainly of words put into his mouth, or his so-called confession may have been no more than saying "yes" to questions put to him. There is reason to believe that Sanders was looking for an aye-sayer from the time of the Ives trial. A biographer of the colonel states that Ives secretly informed Sanders after the trial that Plummer was the head of the gang. [172] Yet Sanders himself, when he wrote up the trial in detail, made no mention of receiving such information from Ives. However, the rumor was spread and can be found in the writings of others; it may be the result of Sanders's search for just such a statement as that attributed to Yeager, to set in motion the removal of Plummer. In stronger language, the idea of a gang with Plummer at its head may have come originally from Sanders rather than Yeager.

It is doubtful that Yeager belonged to any organized gang. As Calloway has already pointed out in his book on the subject, the vigilantes took Long John, key witness against George Ives, along with them to identify road agents; yet when the party ran into Yeager, fiery red beard and all, Long John did not even recognize him. [173]

Yeager did not come up with a single concrete detail regarding the planning of any robbery, and anyone who takes time to examine the individual robberies case by case will notice a decided lack of intelligent planning. As mentioned earlier, Langford and Hauser's wagon train carrying $14,000 in gold dust got through without even an attempted attack. And George Ives's trial proved that Nick Tiebolt's robbery and murder were instigated on a spur-of-the-moment whim after Tiebolt made the mistake of flashing a heavy poke. At the trial, the key informant made no mention of Ives having to split the take with headquarters.

The Moody wagon train, a real prize, carrying over $75,000 in gold and $1,500 in greenback and accordingly guarded by well-armed men anticipating attack, was taken on by only two men: Marshland and Dutch John, who were still making last-minute plans in earshot of the wagon party. Marshland was too timid to carry out the first attempt, and the second was so badly botched that rather than the robbers making off with the booty, the freighters ended up holding a mock trial to determine who got Marshland's possessions — a horse, gun, and twenty pounds of tea stolen from the Mormons.

The robbery and killing of the Magruder party was more successful. Langford correctly identified Howard as the "arch and bloody instigator of the brutal tragedy," but Dimsdale attributed this crime to Plummer also, and such historians as Helen Sanders have accepted his word as fact. Information about this robbery and murder came from Billy Page, who was at the scene and later offered up testimony. Page described the incidents in explicit detail but he did not state that the crime was planned beforehand, explaining instead that Howard told him one day on the trail "that Magruder had a great deal of money, and they meant to have it." Page's testimony at the trial as taken down by a reporter for *The Golden Age* and reprinted by other papers is there for those who wish to read it, only there is no mention of Plummer or a gang being involved in the crime in any way.[174]

Most of the robberies attributed to the gang were not of wagon trains, but much smaller affairs such as the two holdups of stage passengers or some minor losses suffered by individuals travelling alone. No information exists that can link these isolated robberies together into a single chain, in fact the more we read of them the less we think they were connected by the planning of a leader who directed the roughs. No details exist of groups sharing information, working together, or dividing loot. In his book on the gold frontier, Dan Cushman expresses the same opinion, that judging by results no masterminding took place. "Men were robbed and brutally murdered by their own party," he writes. "Other robberies were hastily got up affairs, ill-planned and bungled."

Cushman, speaking of how from the earliest days of the gold camps miners and merchants carrying gold used to slip out of town quietly as a precautionary measure, offers the following explanation for the origin of the notion that the road agents were organized: "Virginia was believed to be full of spies who watched for rich shipments of gold. At a later date this was built up into a legend of intricate organizations with spies, couriers who were ready to go flying along the trails at a moment's notice, bands of highwaymen with military chains of command, special handshakes, knotted neckties, passwords, and a single mastermind."[175]

Dimsdale, Langford, and Sanders passed down the above legend, describing an elaborate network of spies stationed throughout the territory, who gathered and disseminated intelligence on every ounce of gold transported. Members were well heeled and horses well trained, Red Yeager having killed two mounts in delivering Brown's letter of warning to Alex Carter and party. That the vigilantes used the legend to arouse fear and thus rally support can be detected in the speech Charles Bagg gave after the hanging of the Virginia City five. Bagg, who was Sanders's assisting prosecutor at the Ives trial, commenced by stating his remarks were intended for the benefit of any persons who might question what had just taken place: "The men were convicted by evidence of their own confederates in crime, for there were one hundred men who'd been murdered between the mines and Salt Lake for their gold dust within the past twelve months, and these road agents had said the pirates' flag would wave over the town before Spring."[176]

The mention of the pirates flying their flag over Virginia City is evidently a reference to the rumor that Plummer had a grandiose plan to unite all the displaced southern rebels into a military organization that would take over the government of the entire West. Bagg's speech had the desired effect of inspiring fear in at least one listener, George Bruffey, who thought to himself, "Who would have ever known what became of me if I had been killed by these men since few of my associates knew where I was from?"

Another person who naively accepted the exaggerations and rumors of brutality being spread about the road agent organization was Mary Edgerton, who wrote home justifying the shelling, hanging, shooting, and burning of young Joe Pizanthia, who was not even charged with being a gang member: "You may think that was hard, but the house had been the headquarters for all those villains for a long time. . . . During the past year they have committed about one hundred murders. . . . The victims were murdered and robbed and their bodies, some of them, cut into pieces and put under the ice, others burned, and others buried."[177] Likewise, Wilbur Sanders wrote about Nick Tiebolt's mutilated body, not mentioning in the same sentence, as George Bruffey did, that the condition of the corpse was due to magpies having pecked on the back and shoulders.[178]

Any organization of the roughs and robbers into a gang seems to be just what Cushman labels it: a legend, fanned and spread by those who wanted to replace the existing system of justice with one under their own control rather than the electorate's. Red Yeager's testimony, as presented by either Dimsdale or Beidler, provided no detail that could be used as evidence to the contrary.

The critical issue in accepting Yeager's supposed confession becomes not so much what he actually said and whether it was true, as if he made a confession at all. As has been noted earlier, the vigilantes claimed that Plummer, Stinson, Ray, Parish, Gallagher, Lane, Helm, and Lyons all confessed to their guilt, yet eyewitnesses reported that each of the eight men professed his innocence up to the last. We cannot trust the executioners' prepared accounts of the final statements of their victims. To determine whether Yeager confessed we have only the word of the vigilantes upon which to rely, and in such instances the vigilantes have not proven to be reliable witnesses.

DUTCH JOHN'S CONFESSION

There is no record of the testimony given by Dutch John, accused of attempting to rob the Moody train. Dimsdale was tight-lipped about what the prisoner actually said, but he claimed it was a "long statement, corroborating Red's confession in all important particulars." We do know, however, that the confession was extracted with great difficulty, seven or eight "parties" making a try and giving up. Finally, a "literary gentleman," probably Sanders, informed the prisoner that he was going to be hanged, upon which John burst into tears and made a statement, according to Dimsdale, "evidently hoping that it might be held to be of sufficient importance to induce them to spare his life."[179] The literary gentleman did not bother to take down the statement or write a summary of it later; all we are told is that it backed up Yeager's confession. The problem with both confessions is that they were made under the duress of waiting to be hanged and with the hope of saying something of "sufficient importance" for the vigilantes to reward them by sparing their lives. It was certainly not an appropriate time for John to inform the vigilantes they had made a mistake in assuming there was a gang, that he had planned the robbery himself.

Mattie Edgerton explained Dutch John's reason for making his final statement, and again we must rely on the vigilantes as to whether he actually confessed to anything. "I shall always believe that the price of his confession was to have been his life," Mattie said, "but there being no penitentiary where he could be imprisoned, hanging seemed to be the only alternative, and he well merited the death sentence."[180] John's surprise on being read the death sentence the Vigilance Committee issued indicated that he had indeed expected his statement to purchase his life.

It is not known whether Dutch John's confession made mention of Plummer, but at any rate it had no bearing on Plummer's death sentence, which had already been issued by the Virginia City vigilantes before Beidler came to Bannack and before Tilden testified to the assembled group. John's corroboration was used only to convince the Bannack people, who were skeptical of what Yeager had said, but evidently it was insufficient and Sanders had to bring in Tilden. Backed by Edgerton as chief justice, Sanders could have insisted that all witnesses against Plummer, a man of official position, be brought into court so they could testify under oath and before the public, but he chose not to. Tilden, Yeager, and Dutch John were all witnesses for the prosecution who did not have to undergo cross-examination by the defense, yet none of the three were able to provide one piece of concrete evidence that connected Plummer to a single robbery or murder. Small wonder the two lawyers did not take their case to court.

We are not the first to conclude that there is no real evidence against Plummer. Dan Cushman has already expressed the opinion, though he bases his findings not so much on the sources we have quoted as on conversations he held with pioneers of the area while residing in Beaverhead County. "Plummer, by the context of his career, deserved what he got," Cushman writes, "but the charges set forth would never have stood up in court. Aside from hearsay, inflated in the passage of time, no actual proof exists that Plummer profited by a dollar from road agentry, or planned a robbery. His record was against him. He was destined for a gunman's grave or the hangman's noose ever since his early days in California."[181]

We will look at these early days in California to which Cushman refers, but before doing so we should make it clear that our purpose in writing is not to prove Plummer innocent of the charges for which he was hanged in Montana. Innocence is assumed until guilt has been proven. Our purpose is to reveal what kind of man Plummer was, and before leaving Montana, we need to summarize what can be learned about him from his experiences while sheriff of Bannack.

THE SHERIFF OF BANNACK, MONTANA

As Cushman indicates, most of what is written about Plummer is hearsay that has been inflated through the years. Articles have been published about the rich hordes of gold he stashed away, caves full of sparkling nuggets waiting to be discovered, but there were no big hauls made by anyone during Plummer's administration. The only successful robbery was of the Magruder party, who left town with $14,000; twenty-six years later when Langford wrote, the amount had swollen to $24,000. Doc Howard spent some of the Magruder plunder in making the escape and deposited the balance in the San Francisco mint, from which it was returned to Magruder's widow after Howard's execution. The other robberies were only small amounts taken from individuals. Actually, the miners of Bannack and Alder Gulch, who worked for about $7 a day ($10 if underground) lost more money to the Main Street agents, who charged them $18 each for a pick and shovel, 90¢ for a tin cup, $5 for a frying pan, $6 for a kettle, 55¢ a pound for flour, $1 a pound for salt, and $3 a pound for butter, than they ever lost to road agents. Merchants and suppliers came away from the gold camps with fortunes, not miners, road agents, or lawmen. Any wealth Plummer accumulated came from his mining claims, whose maintenance and supervision were costly and time-consuming and whose profits were well earned.

Plummer was not a robber chief, gunslinger, or a dual personality. What he really was he has not been remembered for: he was simply a lawman and by all reports a very good one. He brought to the Beaverhead diggings the reputation of a dangerous man as well as experience in civilizing frontier towns, both of which were valuable to him in setting up a system of popular justice in the mining districts. And that is exactly what he did, set up an operating form of justice in a lawless territory. It was he, not the vigilantes, who brought law and order to the area. By taking individual subscriptions, in amounts as small as $2.50, he raised funds to build the first jail, thus offering an alternative to banishing or immediately killing a criminal suspect. Convincing early residents of the desirability of such an alternative was no easy task, since many of them strongly objected to the expense involved in building and maintaining such a facility. In addition, Plummer appointed immediately following his election a network of deputies throughout the mining camps to support the work of the miners' courts.

We have only to compare conditions in Bannack on his arrival in the winter of 1862 to the situation one year later. Before Plummer came, the miners' court had limited itself to settling mining disputes, and its first criminal trial was at his insistence — his own acquittal in the Cleveland case. In fact, the legal structure Sanders used in prosecuting George Ives was the democratic system that Plummer advocated and supported. Though, as Dr. Smurr has pointed out, the vigilantes did not have faith in the popular jury system, Plummer did. Opposing the "new way" being taken by the vigilantes, Plummer took the conservative route, sticking with the tried system that had been adapted to the peculiarities of the social environment. And in some instances, the miners' courts receive good marks for the justice they rendered. One of the interesting contributions made by this experiment in popular justice was the habit of allowing the audience to participate in the proceedings by making suggestions or criticisms or demanding that the lawyers put an end to useless wrangling and get on with the business at hand. Probably the most valuable deviation from standard legal practice, as far as possible application to modern problems, was that of restraining both pros-

ecuting and defense lawyers from attempting to sway an unsophisticated jury. As Sanders pointed out in his account of the Ives
trial, before his arrival to the area, lawyers tried to remain as neutral
as possible in order to allow the jury to contemplate the evidence
presented with an open mind. Sanders, however, objected to the
practice and quickly set new precedents.

Even Plummer's accusers praised the executive ability he
showed during this period, building a jail, directing his deputies,
and assisting any person who asked for his help or advice. But of
course their praise does not come from completely innocent motives.
First of all, they had no other choice because his abilities were well
known at the time, or, as Plummer would have it, because they did
not "dare do otherwise." Their compliments were also part of the
propaganda spread to convince the populace that Plummer possessed the potential to organize and keep in line every restless bummer and hardened rough who happened to wander into the area,
which brings up the issue of the possible corruption in his administration. The question to be asked is whether he was tough
enough to withstand pressure from his old associates on the other
side of the mountains. Considering the amount of fear he inspired,
we could guess that he was if he chose to be. He saw a career ahead
of him in the kind of work he liked, and he had no reason to allow old
friendships to destroy his chances. Actually, the charges that he was
soft on criminals probably grew out of certain personal traits rather
peculiar in his profession — a gentleness, a respect and courtesy even
for those charged with offenses, and a relaxed manner of operating,
pursuing his duties without vindictiveness or urgency to punish.

Judge Rheem, who worked with the sheriff at Bannack, noticed
another peculiarity about him that may have made some of his constituents a little uneasy. Langford referred to it as Plummer's "pres-
cient knowledge of his fellows," but Rheem was more blunt in
describing Plummer's "cold, glassy" eyes that "seemed to be gazing
through you at some object beyond, as though you were
transparent." Rheem was also suspicious of Plummer's constant
control of voice and facial expression: "No impulse of anger or surprise ever raised his voice above that of wary monotone."[182] The
judge was correct in suspecting that deeper emotions lay beneath the
calm. Cleveland stirred them up and did not live to regret it.

Thompson also reported seeing Plummer lose his cool on one

occasion: Mattie Edgerton and some girl friends had come to Thompson's store. "I was busy weighing the young ladies," he wrote,

> when the door opened and Plummer came in. We were all talking and laughing, when a young man . . . walked in. Immediately both men began to fumble for their arms, and I saw that there was to be trouble. As they approached each other both began cursing and the young ladies fled shrieking to the street. I ran between the two men facing Plummer and put my two hands against his shoulders which hindered him from quickly getting at his heavy sheath knife. His opponent was unable to release his pistol in time to shoot, as I had crowded Plummer to the rear door of the store where he made a lunge by my face with his knife, but was unable to reach his victim. I threw open the rear door and pushed Plummer out and his opponent vanished by the front door and was hustled out of town by Oliver & Co. If I ever understood the quarrel between the two men I do not recall it, but Plummer afterward apologized for beginning a quarrel in my store, and more especially when ladies were present, but said that I saved the rascal's life."[183]

The incident Thompson reported coupled with the bad reputation Plummer brought to town arouses suspicions of a tendency to violence, just as it did at the time. We need to open the doors to his past to take a closer look at previous incidents that brought about the reputation which followed him from California.

CALIFORNIA, NEVADA, and IDAHO

SAILING TO THE LAND OF PROMISE

On the day James Marshall dipped his hand in the tailrace of Sutter's sawmill and scooped out the first gold nugget, Henry Plummer was only fifteen years old. When he was but nineteen and the state of California not yet two, Plummer left home and family and joined the rush west. Following the mail route that had been established by the government, he sailed from New York harbor on a steamer bound for Panama. The goals he sought in California were both health and wealth; he had apparently contracted tuberculosis while very young, and at the time going west was commonly considered a good remedy for delicate health. After a few days at sea, the mail steamer entered the zones of "genial warmth" those crowded aboard had been looking forward to, and on the eighth day they caught their first glimpse of a tropical shore: "With what infinite delight did the first comers to the tropics land on this shore, skirted with palms and bananas!" wrote one passenger. "Lolling negroes, chattering monkeys, croaking papagayos, piles of cocoanuts, plantains, oranges, and pineapples, thatched shanties, stagnant ditches, clouds of mosquitos — all greeted us at once." The small port of Aspinwall in Navy Bay, in which they disembarked, was actually nothing more than a "miserable collection of huts" set in a jungle swamp, where busy washerwomen wrung out their laundry and dangled it to dry on the arms of statues of Columbus and the Indian princess who first greeted him on his arrival to the new world.[1]

Leaving Aspinwall, the enormous party of gold hunters crossed the forty-eight-mile stretch of mosquito-infested jungle of the isthmus on muleback. After four days they reached the city of Panama, "squalid and poor," with its roughly cobbled streets and adobe huts thatched over with palm leaves, though in the distance they could discern the outlines of once magnificent brick and stone buildings, now overgrown with a tangle of vines and trees, that had formerly housed the ancient city that had been sacked into ruin by the British buccaneer Sir Henry Morgan.

At the Grand Hotel, filled to nearly bursting, the travelers waited for the *Golden Gate*, the steamer that would take them to their destination, passing the time by visiting the dusty street markets during the heat of the day and strolling along the seawall promenade in the evening. When on 8 May the ship arrived, all were disappointed to learn that the second leg of their journey would be as uncomfortable as the first. Before the feverish influx to gold country, steamers had provided their passengers with all the luxuries of a pleasure cruise: fine china, gourmet meals, and solicitous service. But such niceties became impossible under the present overcrowded conditions. The *Golden Gate* had space for seven hundred fifty persons, but on Plummer's voyage, one thousand fifty first-class passengers and five hundred eight steerage passengers were jammed aboard, forcing the majority to live and sleep on the deck and resulting in what the captain described as a "pandemonium of drunkenness and riot, from her departure until her arrival," actually a rather fitting introduction into what lay ahead at the gold fields. On their third day out came the first casualty. One of the ship firemen, a native of Ireland, died of what the ship doctor diagnosed as congestion of the brain. On the seventh day, they put into port at Acapulco, allowing the ship to take on water and the passengers to go ashore to buy fresh fruit. When after fourteen hours they again set sail, they followed close alongside a wild shoreline backed by high mountain peaks. The second day from Acapulco another death occurred on board, a passenger from New York who had come down with dysentery. For the final days of the journey, they encountered strong headwinds that delayed them, not arriving until 21 May 1852 after twelve days at sea, in the harbor of San Francisco, already clogged with other members of the Gold Rush Fleet.[2] Beyond the harbor they could see a range of lofty mountains looming up out of the fog. Plummer had at last reached the land of golden opportunity.

Perhaps it was not quite what he had been expecting throughout the long trip. The three barren hills on which the town was built slanted down to a series of muddy flats curving around the bay. There hundreds of tents and canvas sheds were randomly scattered, and on a slope directly in front of their ship stood a plaza, where a low, adobe-brick customhouse sprawled, flying a weathered stars and stripes in the fierce wind. The business section was littered with boxes of dry goods stacked in front of half-finished buildings and jammed with people of all races and nationalities, scurrying in every direction and pushing to be next to step onto the planks sunk in the deep mire in the street. The majority of the places of business were drinking houses, but also well represented were gambling dens, equipped with the usual monte and faro tables, and bawdy houses, decked out with gaudy furnishings and expensive baubles. There were also more than one hundred restaurants where the ship passenger, weary of the tiresome sea diet, could order a glass of fresh milk and an excellent cut of prime beef, or, if the budget allowed, some of the more cosmopolitan delights such as oysters and roast duck.

Though when Plummer arrived the gold rush was reaching its peak and the town was badly overcrowded, he was able to find a room at 48 Bush Street. Shortly after, he located work as an accounts clerk at a business at 128 Montgomery, very convenient to his rooming house.[3] However, it was not long until he was ready to make his way to the source of the wealth he had heard so much about and booked passage on a steamer up the Sacramento River bound for the mines at Nevada City, touted as one of the richest diggings in California and also lamented as one of the roughest.

Plummer had spent his childhood and youth in the secure atmosphere of a stable, prosperous family of New England, but his young manhood was now to be spent in the gold camp society. Wild, transitory, and completely lacking in stabilizing influence, the closest thing to home life for the majority of gold seekers was the camaraderie found in the saloons and the goal of the adventurers gathered from all corners of the earth was becoming rich. He was receptive to his new environment in which each man was a law unto himself, quickly noting all the signs of manhood recognized by his peers: cursing, drinking, gambling, and most important, instantly defending oneself against insult or threat of violence from others.

GOLD IN CALIFORNIA

The first evidence that Plummer was living in Nevada City comes in 1853, a notice in the newspaper that a letter was waiting for him at the post office. The letter addressed to Henry Plumer, his correctly spelled name, arrived in the mail on 1 July and was promptly picked up.[4] Plummer's first occupation in the area was ranching and mining with a partner from the state of Maine, the Robinson and Plummer ranch being located three miles northeast of Nevada City in the Wilson Valley along the road to the mining camp of Washington. In September the two partners placed an advertisement in the *Nevada City Journal* announcing that "a large, bay ox, marked with a triangular figure on the right hip" had strayed into their corral and requesting the rightful owner to come and claim his property.[5]

Plummer and Robinson, like many others in the area, were having good success with the mine. Nevada City had followed the typical growth pattern of the mining camps, first attracting placer miners in the autumn of 1849 along Deer Creek, where reportedly large hunks of gold could be hacked out of the banks with no more than a pocket knife. According to old-timers, in these early days "gold dust could be safely left in the rockers at the diggings, or at the cabins, and crime of every kind was extremely rare. Almost the only offences against the public were brawls caused by liquor, usually bloodless."[6] But as word of the rich outcroppings spread, growth became so rapid that within a year more than ten thousand miners had flocked in, and along the worn mule trails leading up from Deer Creek a picturesque little town developed—a Wells Fargo office, a few general merchandise stores, and a Methodist church of planed-lumber built on the narrow streets winding their way up to a few cabins perched on the sides or tops of seven wooded hills.

In spring of 1851, a problem cropped up that was to continue to plague the community from time to time for several years to come. A fire broke out downtown and destroyed nearly every house of business before it could be extinguished. Then in the fall of 1852, twelve of the buildings that had been rebuilt in the "wooden town" following the devastation were again consumed by fire, and winter brought a new threat—famine—as heavy rains made roads to Nevada City impassable, provisions barely holding out until new supplies could be brought in.

The following year, with creek beds and banks gradually becoming panned out, miners commenced burrowing hundreds of "coyote holes" in search of the gold embedded in veins beneath the surface, quartz mining coming into full swing within a few months with its resulting around-the-clock, deafening clatter of stamp mills crushing down tons of ore to a fine powder and setting free minute amounts of precious metal.

Besides a number of saloons (the Empire being the finest and most popular), by 1853 Nevada had added another newspaper, the *Nevada City Democrat*, the New York Hotel was accepting guests, and Dramatic Hall on Broad and Pine streets was hosting dramas performed by locals, as well as programs by celebrities making the gold camp circuits. The census taken that year paints a fairly clear picture of life in the settlement Plummer had chosen for his new home. The entire population of Nevada County consisted of 22,000 Indians, 21,000 whites (of which only 920 were female), and 4,000 Chinese. Other residents, listed in order of their prolificacy, were 4,200 hogs, 3,600 work oxen, 2,600 fowls, 2,200 beef cattle, 1,700 cows, 1,300 horses, and 800 mules. As for industry, thirty-three quartz mills were in operation, but many miners were already starting to become discouraged with the many dangers and difficulties involved in hardrock mining, such as cave-ins, floods, and other accidents, and were selling out to large companies who purchased individual 30- by 40-foot claims and consolidated them.[7]

Several astute miners, Plummer included, had also come to realize there was more money to be made on main street of Nevada than at the diggings anyhow. With his substantial profits, Plummer, now twenty-two years old, moved to town, purchased a house and lot on the south side of Spring Street, and invested in a business, whose advertisement from an April 1854 paper appears below:

UNITED STATES BAKERY

The proprietors of the United States Bakery, Pine Street, under the Dramatic Hall, return thanks to a generous public for the very, very liberal patronage heretofore bestowed upon them. They have recently fitted up . . . their building in a splendid order for the purpose of accommodating the public. Every article will be manufactured of the very best material with the utmost taste, care and cleanliness. The best assortment of bread, cake, and pastry to be found at all times on hand, together with a well selected stock of pie, fruits, etc., fresh peaches, apples, plums, figs, raisins, green peas, green corn, oysters, clams, sardines, tomatoes, and a good assortment of confectionaries, cigars, etc. Their aim is to make the best of everything and sell for a small profit. "Live and let live." PLUMER AND HEYER[8]

The ad definitely shows Plummer's touch: his taste for "the best," a near fastidiousness — the mention of "cleanliness" in food preparation — and the old Puritan idea he had brought with him from New England that it was not right for a businessman to make more than a "small profit." Of course the motto, "Live and let live," not so much described his way of doing business as his entire way of living, a tolerance for others combined with similar expectations from them. The business did well, only partly because of its location convenient to the "after-theater" crowd, and the next year the partners expanded, supplying "wedding parties, families, and restaurants" with "rich cake of every description, lemon, pound and sponge" and "every variety of bread and family pastry usually found in New York bakeries," the final words a tribute to the refinements that had been left behind in the East. The members of the *Journal* staff, who were provided a sample cake for their appraisal, reported it to be delicious.[9]

In February 1855, fire again struck Nevada City, this time destroying fifteen houses, a billiard saloon, the Hotel de Paris, and the competition's bakery. The United States Bakery was bypassed by the flames. The month following the fire Plummer bought out his partner and took over the business alone, only to receive such a good offer himself that he in turn sold out. Then he and Heyer repeated the exact process. They formed a new partnership, "fitted up in style the saloon known as the Polka," opened the City Bakery on Broad Street, and built it into a prosperous business, which Heyer sold to Plummer and which a short time later Plummer also sold. [10]

The year 1855 was not only a prosperous one for Plummer and Heyer, but also for the town as a whole, which had incorporated, elected a marshall, and built a two-cell jail out of sawed logs. Downtown boasted a total of twenty brick buildings now, all reputed to be fireproof, one of which was a towering three-story hotel, a "conspicuous ornament" that gave "an air of permanence to the place," the newspaper reported, "which no other mining town in the state" could equal. [11]

In November Plummer sold his house and lot to his former business partner, Henry Heyer, for the sum of $1,000, and the property deed provides conclusive proof of Plummer's legal name, despite the clerk's misspelling the surname by adding an extra "m." Though the document lists the seller as William H. Plummer, the notary public has written at the bottom, "Personally appeared Henry Plummer known to me to be the individual described in and who executed the foregoing instrument." [12]

The close of the year brought the town alive with advertisement of the approaching election of a new marshall, posters plastered about town in behalf of the several candidates, whom the *Journal* listed as Dave Johnson, U. S. Gregory, Sylvester McClintock, and Henry Plumer, "all gentlemen of nerve." Later the winner was announced as Dave Johnson, but in mentioning the fourth candidate, the reporter had made a prophetic error: the name should have been Asher, not Plumer. [13]

MARSHALL OF NEVADA CITY

Plummer had come West to put down roots, purchasing a home, setting up in business, and making friends it would be difficult to leave. But homesickness was said to be the most prevalent ailment on the frontier and he had a case. Selling everything he had acquired, he bid his friends farewell and traveled to San Francisco to book passage home on the next steamer. While he was waiting, though, he had second thoughts, not just about the many opportunities he was giving up or about leaving the California sunshine, but about a particular girl, and he changed his mind.[14] Returning to Nevada City, he again bought a home on Spring Street and formed a new partnership with Heyer.

Nevada City did not have all the advantages of the East; still it was flourishing and developing an "air of decided civilization," having cast the third largest vote in the state of California in the past election, plus it now offered the drinking crowd, who were in a decided majority, a choice of sixty-five different establishments when they had a yen to purchase "spirits."[15] Attempting to keep order in the county had proven to be an awesome, if not impossible, assignment, but Plummer had not followed the gold rush to become a businessman. Fitting out a frontier store that could serve the same fine pastries as a New York bakery had been an interesting challenge, but it did not suit Plummer's temperament all that well. In addition to his predilection for creating order out of chaos, he had a craving for action and excitement that was not being fulfilled. Early in the year he became active in the Democratic party, and when party officials offered him the position of city marshall on their spring ticket, he accepted. Party members realized the race would not be an easy one. The incumbent, David Johnson, had been energetic in going after the rowdy element and was himself respectable enough to earn the support of most of the townspeople.

Though the well-organized and ably led Democrats launched a vigorous campaign for the entire ticket, the outcome of the marshall race appeared too close to call. Johnson, bolstered by his good record and backed by influential friends as well as the *Journal*, was running on the American Party ticket, which was making every effort to hold on to its existing power. By morning of election day, 2 May 1856, the two candidates for marshall were running neck and neck and continued that way right down to poll closing that evening. When the final vote was tallied, it was discovered that Plummer had squeaked by Johnson with a majority of only seven votes — 424 to 417. The *Journal*, something of a sore loser, wrote that

> good citizens desirous of order, and not bigoted with so-called Democracy voted the American ticket. . . . Of all the men within the city proper, who pay to keep up a city organization, two-thirds voted for the American candidate for Marshal. But outsiders from Rough and Ready, Red Dog, Alpha, Rush Creek, and in short from almost

every mining camp in the county, would have beaten by hard swearing the "oldest man in the world." . . . The infallible symptoms of democracy — broken English, hiccuping, yelling — were too strong to put anyone at a loss to diagnose.[16]

Though, as the *Journal* was quick to point out, the election had not been the most orderly in the brief history of the town, Nevada residents could be thankful things were still not as out of hand as in other parts of the state. San Francisco, for example, had to request that the governor call out the state militia to suppress the vigilantes. Plummer had no reason to be ashamed of owing his victory to the miners; after all, mining was the industry that provided the wealth for the easily offended merchants. The girl responsible for Plummer's return to Nevada — as well as her merchant father — had to be impressed by the victory.

After the election, Plummer maintained the business partnership with Heyer and may have had mining partnerships as well. His salary as marshall was considerable, amounting to $1,200 a year plus 5 percent of taxes collected and fees levied in justice court. He was required to post a bond of $6,000 and was expected in his new role to fulfill four primary duties, not all of which were exciting. First, he was to keep an orderly town, that is, arrest persons breaching the peace, suppress riots, take into custody vagrants or "suspicious persons whose appearance and conduct may seem to justify their being called to account for their manner of living," and arrest any persons making threats of violence. For these purposes he was authorized to enter "any house in which may exist a riot or disturbance or other proceedings calculated to disturb the peace of the neighborhood."[17] A second duty was to prescribe rules for the protection of the town, especially from fire, and he was also responsible for collecting property taxes, issuing business and public performance licenses, and receiving payment of fines levied for violation of city ordinances. After recording accounts of monies collected in books that were at all times open to the inspection by the board of trustees and turning over all funds to the treasurer, he was to present to the board a monthly statement of the city's finances. His final duty was to enforce the following town ordinances:

1. Fast riding in town is not lawful: a horse, mule or any other animal must be held to a pace of a slow gallop or trot and to a walk over bridges. "Furious riding" will draw a fine of $50.

2. It shall not be lawful for any person to discharge in town any firearms or fireworks between the hours of 3 to 5 P.M.
3. It is unlawful to throw into streets any rubbish, such as "old boots, shoes, shavings, clothes, vegetables, meats, etc."
4. It is unlawful for hogs to run at large within the city limits.
5. "Any male or female who shall indecently expose himself or herself in the streets or in the doorways or windows of any house so as to be visible from the street or any female who shall dress and appear in the streets in men's clothing or any male who shall dress in female clothing and appear in the streets shall be fined."
6. Every store and house must have a stovepipe that extends at least twenty-four inches above the roof and must keep handy a ladder, barrel of water, and two buckets to extinguish sparks that might ignite the roof.

There were a few inherent difficulties in Plummer's carrying out the duties of his office, not the least of which was the fact that not only the rowdies, but the most respectable citizens as well, were often reluctant to relinquish the perfect freedom they had enjoyed earlier. There was often unwillingness if not open defiance to accepting the authority of a law officer, even if he had been elected by the people. Plummer was only twenty-four years old and though described as having "a prepossessing appearance,"[18] was of very slight build. In addition he was open to constant ridicule from true westerners for the eastern accent he apparently never lost. Shortly after taking office he was introduced to the type of problems generally involved in breaking up quarrels between armed men who had been drinking, and for his troubles he received the thanks of an article in the opposition newspaper criticizing his efforts.

Plummer and two friends had entered the billiard saloon one evening for a little recreation, but even before they could get a game going, a brawl broke out. When a Mr. Johnson pulled the nose of a Mr. Post and then pushed him against the bar, Plummer stepped in to restrain Johnson. But the owner of the saloon, Lewis, objected to the young marshall trying to keep order in his establishment, saying that "he would keep peace in his house, that he had always kept an orderly house, and would still do so, peaceably if he could, or by force." Though Plummer's companion, Jordan, who just that afternoon had been released on bail of $500 for breaking a teamster's jaw, suggested to Lewis that he allow Johnson and Post to fight it out, the owner did not want any more suggestions as to how he should run his saloon, and a new altercation broke out between him and Jordan. Bragging that he could whip Lewis anytime, Jordan followed after the owner as he attempted to retreat behind the bar, casually replying that it was not true that his customer could whip him. When Jordan insisted that he could whip him, Lewis responded that he was nothing but a liar, and Jordan, angered at the insult, called Lewis a "d----d son of a b---h," at the same time reaching across the counter to hit at him. Snatching up his gun, Lewis fired at Jordan, who had crouched down, peeking up over the bar with a glass tumbler in his hand as a weapon, and though Lewis missed Jordan, he did hit Johnson, the original troublemaker. Quickly firing again, Lewis this time struck Jordan in the chest, killing him immediately. Plummer now moved to arrest Lewis, but was prevented from doing so by the wounded Johnson, who was scrambling to obtain a pistol for himself. As Plummer was fending off Johnson with his police club, Lewis sent out for the county officers and surrendered himself to Sheriff Wright rather than give in to Marshall Plummer. During the moments the decision was being made as to who should arrest Lewis, Sheriff Wright or Plummer, Johnson took advantage of the opportunity to flee into the streets, complaining loudly of the bad treatment he had just received at Plummer's hands.[19] In reporting the incident, the *Journal* criticized the new marshall for not having arrested Johnson after he had hit him on the head with a club, but instead letting him wander the streets "raving and delirious from the effects of the blows" and thereby disturbing the "quiet of the town." Obviously, the quiet section of town referred to in the news item was nowhere in the close vicinity of the billiard saloon.

The following month saw the occurrence of a second sort of catastrophe Plummer was expected to prevent. The Great Fire of 1856 broke out late one afternoon in a blacksmith shop on Pine Street and within a half hour from the sounding of the alarm the entire town had been literally destroyed — four hundred wooden houses as well as the "believed fireproof" brick buildings. The new courthouse, recently completed at a cost of $50,000, was also gone and with it all county records, which must now be rerecorded. The loss of Plummer and Heyer's business was calculated at $1,600, and the total cost of the destruction to the town was estimated at 1.5 million dollars. Even worse, ten lives were lost, men who had trusted they would be safe inside the new brick structures after locking the iron window shutters.[20] It was clear the marshall would have to enforce the fire ordinance much more stringently.

Plummer's first two months in office, at least as reported by the *Journal*, were not a very auspicious beginning to a career as a peace officer, but evidently the Democratic party still held high hopes for him. In September they selected him as one of the twelve members of their executive committee, the ruling body of the party, and the same month nominated him as one of the delegates to the county convention, though he fell short of being one of the ten highest and therefore was not sent.[21] His big break came the next month.

For some time a young robber by the name of Jim Webster had been making Yuba County nearly unsafe to live in. Though Webster had at one time been a hard-working miner, when several men tried to jump his claim, he had shot them all and then fled rather than involve himself in the justice process. From that point, he followed a life of crime, robbing, chalking up several more murders, and in general inspiring fear in local residents. Plummer succeeded in bringing him in. Webster, reportedly a friend of the Tom Bell gang, was a desperate man and very prone to breaking jail, especially from a building of such low security as the one temporarily being used to replace the jail that had burned with the new courthouse. The present facility was secured only by a door fastened from the outside with a small padlock and guarded by a keeper who might be either absent or sleeping at any time during his watch. Webster was soon gone from the temporary jail, and Plummer was again sent after him. The *Democrat* reports the ensuing events:

> Jim Webster, who broke out of jail in this place, on Wednesday night last, was re-arrested by Mr. Plumer, our efficient city Marshal, on Saturday morning, and is again lodged in jail. Mr. Plumer had got intelligence that Lee Schell, the supposed accomplice of Webster, was at Empire Ranch, and on Friday evening, in company with Bruce Garvey started for that place, in the hope of finding Webster. On arriving at the ranch, they ascertained that two persons answering the description of Webster and Schell had left that place, and gone towards Marysville. They proceeded as far as Smartville, in Yuba county, where they overhauled them. When found, they were asleep in bed, with their pistols under their heads. The pistols were quietly removed, and the two worthies taken into custody, and brought back to this place the same day.[22]

Within two weeks, Webster had again broken jail, this time in the company of the two Farnsworth brothers, members of Tom Bell's gang who had been in jail awaiting trial. Though the padlock

Nevada City, California, Firehouse, built in 1861. Though a popular city marshall, after the Great Fire of 1856, Plummer alienated merchants by a stricter enforcement of fire ordinances, contributing to his upset in the race for state assemblyman. (Photo by Boswell, 1985)

had been picked sometime during the night, the jailer had not realized the men were missing until the next morning. On learning his prisoner had been lost a second time, Plummer informed the sheriff he would not go after Webster again without the county paying his expenses, complaining that on the previous occasion they had not so much as covered his horse hire. Offering to pay $300 for the return of all three of the escapees, Sheriff Wright insisted on going along on the hunt himself. Since Plummer had caught the public eye during the Webster escapades, Wright, as well as several other deputies and private citizens, wanted to be part of the next episode. Though a sort of friendly competition existed between the sheriff's department and that of the marshall, the former being in the habit of passing off petty complaints to the latter and keeping the more interesting assignments for itself, the recapture of Webster offered more of a challenge than Wright cared to take on alone. After reluctantly consenting that Wright come along with him and Garvey this time, Plummer suggested that having any more men along would not be wise, to which Wright agreed.

The last time Plummer and Garvey had brought in Webster, he had asked to stop off at the cabin of the friend who was to provide an alibi in his upcoming trial and Plummer had agreed. The marshall had now received a tip that Webster had gone to the same friend for help, and he and Wright were hoping to surprise him at the cabin. While Plummer, Garvey, and Sheriff Wright were making preparations to leave on the manhunt, the local Democrats were making preparations to hold a torchlight rally in connection with the upcoming national election in which their candidate, James Buchanan, was opposing the Republican, John Fremont. In the excitement preceding the gala event, few in town gave any thought to the danger that might lay ahead for the party on their way for a third try at bringing in Webster, but by nightfall, Sheriff Wright was to be dead, Deputy Dave Johnson wounded, and the torchlight parade and political speeches called off.

INQUEST INTO THE SHERIFF'S DEATH

Wright had been a family man and a popular sheriff, gruff but basically kindhearted, and all business houses closed for his funeral, the cortege of carriages and men on horseback being the longest ever seen in town. The inquest into the cause of his death conducted the same day as the funeral, though, brought out some surprises. For one thing, after agreeing with Plummer that the posse should be composed of no more than three men, the sheriff had secretly asked three others to come along, but trailing far enough behind so Plummer and Garvey would not notice. These three additional men were

Teal, Butterfield, and David Johnson, who since his defeat as marshall had been serving Wright as a deputy. But before the posse could get underway to the cabin where Webster was supposed to be hiding, a Mr. McCutchin brought news to Plummer of two horses, probably intended for the escape of the prisoners, being staked in a ravine on Gold Flat. Plummer and Wright decided to check the ravine before the cabin. [23]

McCutchin had been sent by Mr. Robinson, the first one to spot the horses, who said he would wait on a bank above the ravine until the sheriff arrived. McCutchin forgot to tell Plummer that Robinson was still guarding the horses, but it probably would not have helped anyhow since while Robinson was waiting on the bank above the ravine, a prominent citizen by the name of Wallace Williams had shown up, and jumping at the chance to play lawman had informed Robinson he would take over. Neglecting to tell Williams that the authorities had already been sent for, Robinson left, saying if he should return, he would whistle so he would not be mistaken for the prisoners and fired upon. After assuring the departing Robinson that he would be on the lookout for his possible return, Williams hastily recruited a party of volunteers — Baldwin, Armstrong, and Vanhook — armed them with revolvers and shotguns, concealed them behind trees and in a ditch so as to form a semicircle around the horses, and instructed them that when the wanted men came to mount the horses, he would give a command for those hidden to step out, order the prisoners to halt, and if they did not, all were to commence firing at them.

Wallace Williams was accustomed to giving orders. He was the only child and business partner of Squire Williams, one of the wealthiest men in town and owner of two ranches, a mine, the local waterworks, and several town properties that included Temperance Hall. The squire and his wife, both from aristocratic families, were busy laying plans to recapture the charm of the plantation life left behind by building a huge mansion for the family, a four-story brick castle to be set atop Prospect Hill. Wallace, who had been sent to law school by his parents and was just preparing to open an office, felt more than qualified to handle the recapture of Webster without involving the sheriff or marshall.

From the first, Plummer had told Wright he would prefer that the marshall's men handle the capture by themselves, but since

Wright insisted on coming, Plummer picked up the horses at the stable and then stopped by for the sheriff. Though the marshall was impatient to start, Wright dallied, Plummer growing more restless by the minute. Then the second messenger sent by Robinson before he had left appeared, this one named McCormick, who, seeing Plummer waiting in the street, told him to "go as quick as he could." Others in the street heard the message and expressed a desire to go with him, but Plummer turned them down, continuing his wait for the sheriff. When McCormick again urged "that he'd better be in a hurry," he reported that Plummer, who was already irate at the delay, had replied that he would have gone before this time, but it took the "God damned sheriffs about three hours to start, that he had waited about two hours already." Wright had still more things to tend to and, as Plummer later told the coroner's jury, "We went over the bridge and waited for Wright several minutes; he did not come and we went up on the hill and came back again to the bridge; whilst sitting there on horseback we saw Wright coming out of the stable with somebody else; I said that I supposed Boss was waiting for somebody when Garvey said, 'There is too many of us and don't let's us go.' "[24] The two of them headed back towards town, but Wright, riding alone, overtook them and asked them to turn back towards Gold Flat.

It was dark by the time they reached the spot where Wallace Williams and his men were concealed. As Wright, Plummer, and Garvey were dismounting and tying their horses, the three deputies caught up to them. "That was the first I knew of Johnson and the others coming at all," Plummer said. When Wright suggested that one person go first, the marshall started in alone and, on reaching the horses and seeing no sign of the prisoners, whistled for Wright and Garvey to follow. As the two men approached, they heard another whistle and a voice coming from the ditch below them. "Jim Webster's voice," Garvey said.

"I guess it is," Plummer answered. Garvey advanced in the direction of the voice, and Plummer raised his gun to cover him, calling to the man hidden in the ditch, who was not Webster as they believed but rather a member of Wallace Williams's volunteers named Baldwin, that if he moved, he would kill him. Sheriff Wright's three deputies were supposed to have spread out and worked their way down into the ravine so as to surround the horses, but they did not appear, and Plummer called out to them, "Dave, close down." As Dave Johnson approached the ravine, he stumbled onto another member of Williams's citizen party, Armstrong, and the two men fired at each other; at the same instant, Williams stepped out from behind a tree and commenced shooting at Wright and Plummer. "Wright and I turned about together," Plummer said, "I stepped back two or three feet towards the horses, Wright and I running side by side, the shots were coming fast and thick, I saw by the flash of a pistol a man jump behind a big stump near the middle of the ravine. Wright ran straight for him, this man put his pistol out in the direction of Wright and fired, Wright fell . . . I almost immediately recognized Wallace Williams by the flash of Garvey's pistol. I told him to stop, calling him by name."[25]

After Plummer called out, "Stop, for God's sake! You are shooting your friends," both sides ceased firing and, realizing their mistake, quickly began a search to determine who had been wounded. By the dim moonlight, they discovered Wright, fallen on his face across his own double-barreled shotgun and a pistol belonging to Dave Johnson. When they turned him over, he was still breathing and lay there working his mouth as someone was sent for help for him. The doctor who came washed the wounds by candlelight, but it was too late to save Wright, who had taken more than forty buckshot, which had perforated his neck, and a slug, which had broken his chin. Deputy Johnson was wounded in the chest but managed to make it to the nearest house, which turned out to be the home of Armstrong, the man who had shot him. Johnson asked Armstrong for some laudanum to relieve his pain, which was given to him, and then begged that the Masons be sent for. He survived only until the next afternoon.

Though Wallace Williams was a lawyer, his testimony at the inquest was filled with contradictions. He refused to admit that he had shot Wright, placing the blame on Baldwin and claiming he had only tried to strike the sheriff with the butt of his shotgun but missed. In addition, Williams took every opportunity to belittle the sheriff's posse for cowardice, accusing Teal of deserting the other deputies "quick after the firing" started, and adding, "I suppose Plumer took to his heels and ran after he fired." Though Baldwin had testified that Plummer came up right behind him when they first discovered Wright's body, Williams placed the marshall "in a north-east direction on the hill," only to reverse himself at another point by stating it was Plummer who had recognized him and put a stop to the shootout.

The grand jury reached the conclusion that Wright and Johnson's wounds "were given from guns or revolvers in the hands of Wallace Williams, T. L. Baldwin, and Geo. H. Armstrong, and were given accidentally and by mistake, in a collision that occurred, . . . both parties attempting to arrest prisoners escaped from the jail, and coming in contact in the night."[26] But the townspeople, shaken at the needless death of the sheriff and deputy, could not forgive Williams his lack of remorse. Whereas others in his party had admitted they had no authority to arrest the escaped prisoner, he had boldly closed his testimony with the contention that, "We had no legal writ to arrest the prisoners, but were acting as police to arrest them on our own hook, and as good citizens to sustain the law."[27] Williams never regained his stature in the community, and the Red Castle that the squire later constructed for his son on Prospect Hill was small comfort for the loss of a good reputation.

Plummer, feeling both the loss of Boss Wright, whom he genuinely admired, and a sense of guilt at being one of the survivors, wrote in a letter that he wished he could forget "all the events of the deplorable tragedy."[28] And in one special sense he was responsible for the entire disaster. Though he had tried to warn others of the danger that would come from involving several armed men in the search for Jim Webster, those who were so eager to participate were only hungry for a share of the glory he had received from his former exploits.

Before the incident, Plummer had been the hero of the county for bringing in Webster, but in the debacle of 3 November 1856, Jim Webster, who had come for the staked horses, stumbled onto the gunfight in progress and had escaped without leaving a trace. Even more humiliating, in the flurry of self-defense at the inquest, two derogatory remarks had been made about the marshall. McCormick, while being questioned as to why he had not informed the Williams party that he had contacted the officers, replied that he had not thought to go back to the ravine and tell the men waiting there, but he had told Plummer some men were guarding the horses. Plummer said he was certain that no one had told him. When McCormick was asked, however, if any of the men present in the street had heard him tell Plummer about the guards in the ravine, he admitted they had not. Still the damage had been done, leaving the impression that Plummer had been careless in leading the others into the ravine, though the results would have been the same since McCormick had no knowledge of the Williams party being concealed below the horses rather than on the bank above in plain view.

Adding insult to injury as far as the marshall's reputation was concerned, McCormick was also asked if he thought Plummer could have been drunk when he was given the message about men guarding the horses. McCormick responded "I cannot tell when Henry Plumer is drunk or not."[29] The answer could be construed as a backhanded compliment for being able to hold his liquor, but the fact that the question was asked at all created doubts about the new marshall's drinking habits.

Plummer apparently took no offense at the question of his drinking on duty, but he was angry at Williams for touching on the one spot where he was sensitive — the issue of his courage. The Democratic party was also concerned over the slipping popularity of their main drawing card. In way of remedy, the *Democrat* offered to publish a letter to the public from Plummer, hoping to rescue him from the same "notoriety" Williams was suffering.[30] Plummer's letter, written in the melodramatic style frequently employed in the paper rather than in the common speech of his inquest testimony, states, "I cannot permit the sneering insinuation of Williams to pass unnoticed. In his evidence he says he supposes I ran after firing my shots. As he gives no reason for this opinion, and his assertion varies materially from that of the other witnesses before the Coroner, I am compelled to regard this part of his evidence as a gratuitous insult to myself, in which he has falsified his testimony to inflict upon me an injury." The letter goes on to point out some of the discrepancies between Williams's testimony and that of others, closing with the rather poignant lines, "Unlike Mr. Williams my reputation for courage is dependent neither upon my own testimony, (although under oath) nor upon the trumpetings of the press. I shall leave this subject, hoping that Mr. Williams may enjoy that reputation for which he longs, and I, such as I may deserve. H. PLUMER, Marshal."[31] Plummer's career depended on his success in proving to the community once more the sort of reputation he did deserve.

REBUILDING

The *Journal* printed Wallace Williams's response to the letter. His antagonism toward Plummer, as reflected in his inquest testimony, had evidently come more from the fact they were complete opposites—Williams owing all he had to his father and Plummer being self-made—than from the happenings at Gold Ravine, and he regretted his slurs. Writing that he himself had not made the assertion about Plummer's cowardice, he explained he had only responded to a direct question and not intended any offense. To his way of thinking, he added, when a man was being fired upon from all sides, as Plummer was, running away would not have been cowardice anyhow, but wisdom.

After conducting the inquest into Wright's death, the coroner, John Grimes, believing he was next in line to fill the vacant position of sheriff, requested the marshall and three others to accompany him to the county offices, where he took possession of the property therein so as "to secure the interests of the county as well as litigants having monies in the hands of the Sheriff."[32] As it turned out, the board of supervisors selected not the coroner but Deputy Butterfield to succeed Wright, making it necessary for the coroner to surrender the appropriated property to the new appointee. Criticizing the coroner's premature action in assuming control of the office, the *Journal* characterized "the Coroner's posse," as they labeled it, as men who "doubtless consider themselves more honest and responsible . . . than other men" and therefore feel "self-responsible to guard the interests of individuals and the public. This is an assumption of superior virtue which, it is to be hoped, their future conduct will warrant."[33]

This criticism of Plummer, as one of the group, for assuming he was of "superior virtue" and therefore "self-responsible to guard the interests of individuals and the public" was most likely an accurate description of the marshall's character, and perhaps a prerequisite for any man who presumes to represent the law. But there was an ominous note of warning behind the newspaper's appraisal that Plummer would have done well to consider. Of course, being young, confident, and idealistic, he did not. Walking through the tight, winding little streets of Nevada City and feeling the pride of responsibility for their safety could produce a false sense of security, creating the illusion that the marshall and the law were synonymous.

A few months after the deaths of Wright and Johnson, the town narrowly averted yet another tragedy, this one brought on by a combination of the poorly laid plans of men and the assistance of nature. Heavy rains caused a wooden dam constructed on Deer Creek to burst, flooding the surrounding area to a depth of twenty feet and sweeping away bridges, sawmills, and any other buildings in its path. Stores located at the foot of Main and Broad streets had to be evacuated, occupants barely escaping with their lives. The usual rebuilding of the city commenced immediately after.

Plummer, who was also rebuilding his reputation, was constantly being written up in the local news items for his escapades in bringing in wanted men. In November of the prior year he had apprehended a robber named Sanford, and he started out the new year, in response to a description dispatched from Sacramento by telegraph, by arresting Fisher, wanted for larceny and garroting. In February he spent two fruitless days as part of a posse attempting to trace the robber Gehr, only to find on his return that Rattlesnake Dick, well-known leader of a robber gang, had escaped from the Nevada jail during his absence. He quickly rode in pursuit of Dick, gradually expanding the circle of his search until he received a cryptic suggestion from one of Dick's fellow escapees, whom he had already captured, that the further from Nevada he looked the less apt he would be to find Dick. Suspecting that he must still be hiding in Nevada, the marshall concentrated his search on the area surrounding the jail. Later, confederates revealed the miscreant had, shortly after his breakout, died from slipping into an abandoned mine shaft near the corner of Pine and Commercial streets. On the same day of learning Rattlesnake Dick's fate, Plummer interrupted a local theater performance to arrest Sullivan, sitting among the audience, on charges of having robbed some Chinese at Bear River of $500, and escorted him up the street to jail. In March he rode to Sacramento, successfully bringing back Nevils, suspected of having brutally attacked an old man in the mining camp of Alpha. April brought up the case of Myers, wanted for trying to burn down the entire town of Nevada in way of revenge for his acquired gambling losses as well as a strong grudge he held against his wife. As reported by the *Journal*, "Marshall Plummer and O'Brien arrived at Folsom . . . and arrested Myers in bed at the Mansion House," the opposition paper conceding "considerable ingenuity on the part of those who effected" the arrest.[34]

Plummer took the less exciting duties of his office, such as enforcing the fire ordinance, just as seriously as the manhunts, surprising merchants with an unannounced check for the required ladder, buckets, and barrel of water in their houses of business. Not expecting the marshall's men to cover the outskirts of town, the *Journal* editor was caught completely unprepared, but was fair enough about the matter to praise the marshall's efficiency in protecting the town from future fires. However, when informed of the fine levied for his violation, the editor printed a little piece grumbling about the difficulties of complying with the ordinance and the unfairness of the penalty for its violation. There was more grumbling to be heard in town when Plummer's men commenced the yearly tax collection, turning the amount of $4,936 into the city treasury in March with a balance of $3,000 to collect from the not so willing.[35]

Despite grudges built up against him and occasional protests from the opposition political party, Plummer was generally a popular marshall. Some of his acquaintances provided an anonymous journalist with the following assessment of his first year in office: "Business integrity had gained him many friends," and "it may be justly said of him, that as a public officer, he was not only prompt and energetic" but "when opposed in the performance of his official duties, he became as bold and determined as a lion." He was "also kind to such as the duties of office compelled him to oppress."[36] The image of the dashing young marshall built up by the press, a single issue sometimes carrying as many as three items on him, was not wasted on the girl he loved, who consented to marry him, or on the Democrats, who nominated him for a second term, even though, due to the number of enemies made during the discharge of duty, it was nearly impossible for a marshall to be reelected in Nevada. "Mr. Plummer has served one year as marshal," the *Democrat* wrote, "and has made an efficient and reliable officer. The immense majority which he received in the primary election for renomination is a flattering tribute of which he may well be proud, and shows plainly his great popularity with the masses of the Party."[37] The usual campaign posters went up and the hoopla was begun about Plummer and his opponent, S. Venard, whom he was expected to defeat handily. "The election on Monday passed off quietly," the press reported, "no rows nor evidences of ill feeling disgracing the day."

As predicted, Plummer defeated Venard, receiving 417 votes to the challenger's 305. On the evening of election day, as though it might be an omen of good times ahead for the city, a "beautiful phenomenon" occurred. A glowing meteor appeared in the night sky, circling the town in an arced path just above the level of the surrounding hills. [38]

The same month as the reelection, in nearby Washington Territory, Mount Saint Helens put on quite a flashy show by suddenly spewing out steam, molten lava, and hot cinder ash on the surrounding countryside, and Lola Montez created an almost equal stir among her disappointed audience by stomping off a theater stage and refusing to perform because she disliked the color of the stage carpet. Also, the usual spring cases of typhoid fever broke out in town, and Plummer made more news by travelling to outlying ranches to capture and bring in two cattle thieves, one of whom made a spirited attempt to resist arrest. [39] July was spent by all good Democrats in feverish preparation for the county convention, Plummer again being nominated as a delegate but again falling short of the required number of votes. Despite his defeat as a delegate, his political star had risen, and at the convention in August, he was overwhelmingly chosen as the candidate for the state legislature. The opposition news, though admitting that the nominees were "fair men," predicted trouble ahead for the party: "The Plumer wing of the party being vastly in the ascendancy had it all their own way. Outside of the delegates the soreheads were numerous and complaining. . . . This course is little calculated to produce harmony."[40] Refusing to acknowledge the warning about the split in the party, Democratic party regulars remained buoyed up with the enthusiasm for a coming victory generated at the convention. In their view, the temporarily disgruntled losers would soon relent, allowing the party to maintain their majority in the county, and in addition Plummer's opponent was considered a rather weak candidate. Jubilant over the prospects of sending one of the youngest men in history to a state assembly, the loyal workers eagerly commenced the campaign. Plummer, only twenty-five years old, seemed to be well on his way to a political career that might know no bounds.

During the hectic weeks of campaigning prior to election day, a race of another sort came off at Nevada City. Lucy, the local mule who had walked away with the purse at the Fourth of July celebration, had been challenged by a champion speedster from Gold Hill, who had no name, but because he belonged to a Mr. Job was simply called "Job's Mule." The outcome of the mule race was not just a matter of local pride. There were heavy bets riding on it, which continued to be placed almost up to the last moment. On a Sunday, the contest was held at a mile-long stretch just outside town, the purse being the substantial sum of $350. As predicted, Lucy took an early lead and held on to it to the three-quarter mark, but while three lengths ahead, she stubbed a hoof against a stone on the course and fell, Job's Mule streaking by her. Though Lucy gamely picked herself up and tried to catch her challenger, it was too late. She lost by over six feet. After their initial shock and disappointment over the upset had worn off, Lucy's supporters suggested doubling the bet in a rematch, but Mr. Job of Gold Hill would not even consider their offer.[41]

Since the Democrats were in a majority in the area, they had been expected to sweep the ticket in September, but their race was not going much better than Lucy's. Party officials had insisted at the start that "the most perfect harmony and good feeling prevailed and the friends of the defeated aspirants for the several offices submitted cheerfully to the will of the majority and pledged themselves to give the ticket a hearty support."[42] In reality, the party split that had developed at the convention, rather than healing, had broken wide open. Dissenting Democrats formed a coalition with the Know-Nothing Party, led by Squire Williams, and launched an extensive campaign against the candidates for the senate and assembly—Walsh and Plummer—the gist of it being that both men were part of a scheme to wrest the mines from local people and put them in the hands of foreign investors. Affidavits were printed in the newspapers and handbills passed out by the hundreds at mining camps swearing that Walsh was in favor of selling the mineral lands and reducing wages to $1.50 per day and quoting Plummer as saying he was "in favor of early spring rains," a weather condition unfavorable to river miners. The charges were believable because Judge Walsh had previously operated a mine for a British company and Plummer spoke with an accent frequently mistaken as British. Judge Walsh prepared a public letter, denying the charges against him and reminding the public he was a miner himself. The editor of the party-affiliated paper printed the following defense for Plummer:

> MR. PLUMER'S POSITION. — We understand that some inquisitive gentlemen of this place have ascertained that Mr. Plumer is in favor of early rains, and are using this fact with great effect against him with river miners. We are authorized to state, that Mr. Plumer has expressed no opinion about this question, and further, that he has not been in the last dog fight, and has had no hand in the next war; that he is in favor of good diggings, with the bed rock of a proper pitch, water the year round, an equitable temperature, an addition to our moonlight nights, and an immediate reform and general improvement in everything.[43]

The reference to "moonlight nights," included in the hopes that all the world loved a lover, was also a subtle reminder to the residents that even though Plummer talked like a foreigner, he was in love with a local girl.

In addition to the distrust being spread among the miners, the press reported that Plummer's reputation was also suffering badly at the hands of those who had built up a resentment against him during the past fifteen months in "the discharge of his duty. . . . Many persons who have been fined for violating city ordinances . . . have contracted a hatred against Mr. Plumer, and . . . they were using a great exertion to defeat him."[44] Plummer's combined enemies were doing a quite successful job of presenting him as a man of "bad character" through "constant abuse, fictitious affidavits, and lying handbills."[45]

For Plummer, who was by nature so sensitive to criticism that he felt uncomfortable with having a single enemy, the campaign weeks were particularly grueling. The result of the widespread propaganda was that both Plummer and Walsh went down to defeat, the *Journal* reporting that Plummer's name was "extensively erased" from the ballots, though there was "no open opposition to him like to Judge Walsh." Plummer received 1,888 votes to the winning candidate's 3,089.[46]

The election past, and with it Plummer's hopes for a career as a legislator as well as his good reputation, he resumed duties as usual. He had been taught a valuable lesson about being too enthusiastic in enforcing unpopular ordinances, but with his usual overoptimism he believed he could regain his lost popularity just as he had done before. However, small-town mentality does not lend itself to easily altering a once firmly entrenched opinion, as Wallace Williams had learned, and even before Plummer could get reestablished, he was drawn into the domestic tragedy of the Vedders, a young couple who rented his house near the foundry on Spring Street. Soon after moving in, the Vedders discovered they did not get along any better in Nevada City than they had out at Van Young's ranch, where their only child had been born, or than they had in Sacramento. For one thing, John Vedder seemed to attract bad luck. During his first five months in town, he had already been involved in a civil suit after nearly losing an eye from being struck in the forehead by a rocket set off at the Fourth of July celebration. In addition to having a bad temper and few friends, John was also losing money as a monte dealer in a gambling house.[47]

He and his wife, also named Lucy, may have hoped for a new start in Nevada City, but they quickly resumed the habit of carrying even the smallest quarrel past the point of reconciliation and then seeking outside help to remedy the situation. One day when John became more violent than usual, roughly setting Lucy down on her big trunk and telling her to use it, she walked up the hill to the courthouse and reported him to the county recorder, who, however, informed her that family problems were out of his line. In retaliation for the embarrassment she had caused him, John looked up an old acquaintance from Sacramento, a blacksmith named Rice, whose shop was located between the foundry and the Vedder residence, and asked him to go back to the house and send Lucy packing. John "had forgot to get some coal," as Rice reported the cause of the family discord, and "when he came back, she had a long face and looked black. He called her a God d----d son of a b---h, and she had called him a d----d whorehouse pimp." Rice, who had known Lucy for several years in Sacramento, went around to the house to talk to her, and she admitted to him that she liked John "better than any other man." By Rice's persuasion, the couple then "made up and kissed each other and said they loved each other."[48]

Lucy Vedder had first met Plummer when he removed his personal effects from the house, John introducing him as "the Marshall of Nevada City." The Vedders had rented the house furnished with the understanding that Plummer could also store inside it certain items he had no place for at his new quarters. Among them, John noticed a rifle, which he asked to borrow for some hunting, and Plummer agreed, stopping by with a friend a few days later to pick up the gun for his own use. On a second instance Plummer came to the door saying a friend wanted to borrow the fishing line and hooks he had left at the house. Though John worked nights and was still in bed, Lucy found the fishing equipment herself and handed it out the door to Plummer. The exchange took about three minutes. She did not see the marshall again until the next family crisis, which occurred just two weeks before John Vedder's death.

The Vedders had been married two years, and their little girl, who was of rather delicate health, was just learning to walk. Though Lucy cooked, sewed, and took the precaution of barring the back door of the kitchen with a low board so the baby would not fall down the steep back stairs, John did not consider her a good mother, suspecting that while he was working nights she left the baby alone and went out. When John hired a man to observe her, Lucy realized she was being followed and raised a row with John. During this encounter, he pulled a knife from his belt, held it to her throat, and told her if she did not go back to her parents in Sacramento, he would kill her. Not wanting to leave her husband for good, Lucy took the baby and found a room for the night and the next morning began asking around about the best way to obtain protection from her husband. She later reported that Mrs. Senner, whose husband owned a saloon the Vedders frequented, suggested she contact Plummer, explaining that "she always went to him for advice." Several other persons consulted agreed with Mrs. Senner that "if they wanted counsel they would speak to Mr. Plumer."[49] Lucy accordingly sent a note to the marshall, who, after dropping by to hear her trouble, went for his friend David Belden, a prominent attorney and fellow officer of the Democratic Club. Though Belden preferred that Lucy come to his office, when Plummer explained she was unable to leave her child, Belden agreed to visit her home, Plummer accompanying him for the purposes of introduction, then leaving.

"She told me her grievances," Belden said, "and why she wished to get a divorce. She said that John was very cruel and had

Hotel de Paris on Broad Street of Nevada City, California, where Henry Plummer and Pat Corbett took a room to protect Lucy Vedder against her husband. The bad reputation Plummer gained from his involvement with the Vedders followed him to Montana, causing leading citizens to doubt the Sheriff's integrity. (Courtesy of Searls Historical Library, Nevada City, California)

knocked her down and that he had been in the habit of abandoning and leaving her. She made a pitiful story and referred me to witnesses who had seen this treatment. When making the statement, she expressed herself as though John loved her and cried. I told her she did not want a divorce; the matter could be reconciled."[50]

After Belden left the house, Rice, who had observed what was taking place from his shop, went downtown to find John, informing him the marshall had brought a lawyer to their home. At first John refused to believe him, insisting Plummer had always been friendly to him. But since Belden had handled John's earlier civil suit and he was therefore acquainted with him, he paid a visit to his office to ask who the messenger was that had brought him to the house. Belden refused to say, but reported Vedder's inquiry to Plummer, who agreed to go and explain the situation to him. The outcome of the whole affair was a brief reconciliation, John notifying Belden to halt the divorce proceeding and commenting that she had "the G-d d----dest tongue, but that she was as good a wife as any."[51]

But just one week before he was killed, John again put Lucy out of the house, and an observant bystander ran for Pat Corbett, an ex-policeman, reporting to him that Mrs. Vedder was being beaten by a man. John had left by the time Corbett arrived, but he escorted Lucy and her child to the Hotel de Paris where she took a room. Despite the pretentious name, the hotel was a plain, one-story, wooden structure, appearing from the front to be about the size of a toolshed. It stretched out behind Broad Street a considerable distance, allowing enough space for several guest rooms, a dining area, and a saloon. It was particularly convenient for Lucy because she could go out the back door and through the alley to the house on Spring Street any time she wanted.

About an hour after his wife checked in at the hotel, Vedder showed up, angry and violent, and then rushed off to Belden's office, advising him to start the divorce again and adding, "She can go to hell her own way." In a short time, John returned to the hotel room, sat down on the bed, and began to play with the baby, but all the while threatening to take their small daughter to Mr. Ashmore's house of ill-fame to be raised. Apparently feeling no strong maternal instinct at the moment, Lucy replied she did not object to his taking the baby if he would put her in a respectable home.

During the week Lucy spent at the hotel, she continued to go to Spring Street to cook for John and make his bed, but the quarrel over the custody of the child continued. When on Wednesday John came to the hotel with a gun and forcibly took the baby, the hotel owner called for Plummer to settle the dispute. The marshall had a long talk with the Vedders, later explaining to one of their friends that "there was another party in the way and he was trying to fix it up between John and the woman." Though Plummer had warned of legal problems involved in taking the child away from the mother without first having her declared unfit, John paid no heed to the advice and took his daughter to the Van Young ranch, hiding her there and refusing to tell Lucy of her whereabouts. As tension between the couple continued to grow, Lucy went to Rice and confided she was "afraid for her life." That evening Rice went to Plummer, asking him if he would take care of Lucy, as marshall, but also warning that Vedder was angry over the child custody issue and had threatened to kill Plummer. The marshall answered that his men were already observing everything Vedder said or did and that he and Corbett had also taken a room across the hall from Lucy at the Hotel de Paris so as to keep an eye on her. As for Vedder harming him, Plummer thought John had always seemed friendly enough, and he doubted there would be any trouble. But after finishing his conversation with Plummer, Rice did a strange thing: he went to the gambling house where Vedder worked and informed him that each night when he went to work, Plummer came to his house. Flying into a rage, John borrowed Rice's gun and ran immediately to the house. Though Rice ran after him, overtaking him at the corner of Pine and Spring and attempting to stop him, Vedder, a large, strong man, pushed him away, shouting that he would make a "funeral pile" of the both of them. Finding only Lucy at the house, John grabbed her by the hair and held a knife to her throat until she begged for mercy and promised to leave town immediately after receiving the divorce bill.

On Friday morning, the last day of John's life, he came very early to Lucy's room to continue the quarrel, loudly threatening to hit her, and Plummer and Corbett heard the commotion from across the hall. Pushing the door open, Plummer asked John if he would not be ashamed to strike a woman, to which John answered he would strike his own mother if she used him as badly as his wife did. Continuing a conversation with Vedder until his temper had cooled, Plummer invited him to accompany him downtown, Lucy reporting after that the two men went out of the room together, "laughing, apparently good friends."[52]

Being completely broke, John next went to an old business partner, Mr. Draper, to borrow the money to pay lawyer Belden's fee. Draper said, "I hocked my watch on the day he was killed to raise money for his divorce suit." Insisting Belden complete the paperwork at once, Vedder walked to the courthouse with him, paid the fees, and received the summons, but when he tried to pay Belden, the lawyer refused, insisting the money must come from Lucy since she had started the suit and therefore they must go find her. As they walked down the hill from the courthouse, Vedder told Belden, "Now I'm a free man," going on about his plans to leave California and cross the plains, even inviting Belden to come along. On reaching the house, Vedder handed the money to his wife, who was in the processs of dismantling the house and preparing to vacate it. She in turn paid Belden the $20. At dusk, Belden again saw Vedder carting down Broad Street a large rocking chair that he tried to sell to him. Vedder took the lawyer's refusal good-naturedly enough,

saying "I've got my child and my dog, and that is all I care a damn about."

"That was the last I saw of him alive," Belden said.

Though Vedder actually intended on taking his daughter with him across the plains, he had nonetheless promised Lucy she could have custody, and she was expecting him to go to Van Young's ranch that evening so he could deliver the child to her before her departure to Sacramento. With his own plans in mind, however, Vedder entered a store and asked the owner to loan him a pistol, saying he "wanted to kill some son of a b---h in this town." The owner refused the loan of his gun and, after Vedder had left, called Plummer off the street to ask him if he knew why Vedder was so upset and who he was out to kill. "No one, I guess," Plummer responded.

But continuing his search, Vedder managed to find an acquaintance who was willing to confiscate the pistol of an absent owner, and pocketing it and gathering his possessions and dog from the house, he took them to Rice, disclosing that he was going to kill Plummer. When Rice tried to dissuade him, Vedder walked away from him, gun still in his coat pocket, and went to the restaurant at the Hotel de Paris for supper. Being too agitated to eat, he sat picking at his food until the owner noticed and asked if he were ill, but John replied nothing was the matter and left the dining room. He went to a stable to hire a horse and then rode to the ranch where he had left the child. Noticing Vedder's state, Van Young insisted he stay at the ranch that night, expressing concern that there would be serious trouble if he went back to town. Vedder responded he had no fear, however, warning Van Young as he left not to give up the child to Lucy or to Plummer if either should come for her. Vedder then rode to Nevada City, went straight to the station to check for Lucy's name on the stage list, and from there to the house. A little after midnight, residents of Spring Street were wakened by the screams of Lucy Vedder, who ran into the street crying that Marshall Plummer had shot her husband. Plummer's name would never again be clear.

THE PEOPLE VS. H. PLUMER

Plummer left the house on Spring Street just ahead of Lucy Vedder and on reaching the corner of Pine, blew his police whistle several times. Receiving no answer, he continued walking in the direction of

Broad Street until he found Garvey. Mrs. Vedder's words were being repeated in the streets almost immediately after she had made her accusation. People milling in the business section of town were already anxious over rumors that a crowd was on its way from Downieville to hang Butler, a prisoner recently convicted of murder and lodged in the Nevada City jail, and some began to say that Plummer should be hanged with Butler.[53]

Concluding that formation of a mob might be imminent, Garvey and Plummer walked to the jail and knocked. It was about fifteen minutes past midnight when they arrived, and Deputy Van Hagan informed them he had no empty beds but invited Plummer to sleep with him. Plummer refused, saying his place was inside the jail, and when Van Hagan asked why, told him he had just shot John Vedder though he did not know if he had killed him. As Van Hagan was opening the cell occupied by Butler so he could admit Plummer, the marshall asked him if there were sufficient arms to guard the jail; at that same moment someone outside stepped up to the window and reported that Vedder was dead. Butler turned to his new cellmate, "Afraid?" he asked.

"They can't scare me," Plummer answered, holding out his hand to Butler. "Not trembling, is it?"

The inquest into Vedder's death was conducted the next morning, and two weeks later Plummer was brought before a grand jury. Before the grand jury could reach a decision, the judge ordered them to take no further action since "many of them had formed opinion in the case."[54] However, the ruling was later reversed, and on 16 October 1857, the jury returned an indictment for murder, bail being set at $8,000. When Belden, representing Plummer, made application to have bail reduced, Judge Searls refused, and Plummer was left waiting in jail for the $8,000 bond to be raised. In the meantime, Belden entered a plea of not guilty on behalf of his client, and trial was scheduled for 21 December.

Local newspapers showed commendable restraint in the publicity they gave the shooting, stating they would withhold judgment until after the trial, but only one day after the inquest, the *Sacramento Union* carried an item claiming "an intimacy had existed between Plummer and Vedder's wife, which caused a separation between the married pair."[55] Belden, feeling it impossible for his client to receive an impartial trial in the area, especially after the prejudice aroused by the news article, moved for a change of venue, supporting his motion with several affidavits taken from residents concerning the kind of remarks being made at the mining claims. At Red Dog for instance, someone had said "that Henry Plummer ought to be hung, that he did not believe that a man ought to fool about another man's wife." Other affidavits swore to the "strong political and personal feeling" against Plummer that had come out of the recent political campaign.[56]

The court, ruling that before granting a change of venue an effort should be made to empanel a jury, summoned one hundred potential jurors, only seven of whom were found acceptable after examination. The court then offered Belden the opportunity to renew his motion to move the trial elsewhere, but he chose not to. One hundred more residents were summoned. Though it had taken two and one-half days to obtain a qualified jury, the testimony was completed in only one and one-half.

The most pertinent evidence came from the only witness to the shooting, Lucy Vedder, though others provided valuable background information, such as the scene of the crime. The shooting took place in the kitchen of the Spring Street house, a 12- by 12-foot room containing a table and lit candle, a stove with a chair on each side, a bedstead, and a straw mattress. Window curtains had been taken down, the front door stood open because the latch was broken, and the back door was closed.

Witness Barker explained the conflict had developed between Plummer and Vedder during the child custody dispute over Plummer's warning there would be legal problems if the child was taken away from its mother without first going to court. "If Johnny had waited a day or two longer," Plummer had told Barker, "I could have explained it to him satisfactorily."[57]

Witness Draper's testimony revealed the extent to which Vedder's hostility had built up. "Vedder said if he was to kill Plumer, he would have no show, as he had no friends here. He told me Mr. Wall said if he killed Plumer, he would go his security. But Plumer did not want to have any difficulty. He had abused Plumer, but did not think he would fight and thought he was a coward. Vedder had insulted him in every way in his power but he would not resent it; Plumer told him if he should spit in his face, he would not resent it."[58]

By the time Lucy Vedder took the stand, little had been left of her reputation. Tidbits dropped here and there throughout the testimony of others had informed the court that she "was in the habit of swearing," "was given to drink," and had "lived with" another man before John, who also had "known" her before marriage. Her husband was having her tailed because he had caught her talking with an unidentified man, and he had put the knife to her throat to force her to leave because he did not want to live in the same town with her. Though she had left for Auburn after the inquest, her problems had followed after her, a series of court battles with Vedder Senior over her daughter that had made the news. The *Sacramento Union* reported that

> Mrs. Vedder went to the house of her father-in-law on Sunday evening and under pretense of seeing her child got possession of it and took it to the residence of a friend. A crowd assembled and some one threatened to take the child by force and restore it to its grandfather. Both mother and child were taken to the station house where they remained over night. She consented in the morning to allow the child to remain in the possession of her father-in-law until a writ of habeas corpus which she had sued out for the custody of her child was heard and decided.[59]

Despite all the adverse publicity, Lucy's testimony at the trial showed a certain dignity and forthrightness, and nearly everything she said was verified by other witnesses. "I am very quick-tempered," she admitted, "I allow no one the wrong." Speaking of her relationship with John, she said, "I told Mr. Rice I lived happy. I also said Mr. Vedder provided for me. I never wanted anything from him but care. He used violence to me nearly every day. I called for help. A gentleman once offered to come in. Vedder said he would kill him."[60]

Vedder's violence to Lucy was corroborated by Rice, who spent considerable time in their home: "I have seen him knock her over and pinch her nose until she could scarcely get her breath."[61]

Lucy tells how the day before he was killed, John had offered to give up the house to her, saying "he would trouble her no more," and in turn she agreed to leave for Sacramento, on the understanding she could take their daughter and keep her as long as she "led a respectable life." After signing the list for the 2:00 A.M. stage, Lucy asked Plummer and Corbett if they would carry her trunk to the station when it was ready and they agreed. She ate supper at the hotel

and about 7:00 P.M. crossed the alley to pack the remaining possessions in the house, planning to return to the hotel afterwards to wait
for John to bring in their daughter from the Van Young ranch.

"At early candlelight," Rice stopped by the house to see her. On
the stand, Rice had already mentioned this visit, the prosecution
having asked him if he had worn a disguise at the time. Rice replied
that he had not. "I was always free with my jokes with her, but I
never was with her at Auburn. I have never been in a room with her
naked," Rice said. "I did not go to Plumer repeatedly to make him
believe Vedder was going to kill him, or to Vedder that Plumer
would kill him."[62] Rice had explained that he had only stopped by
that Friday evening to tell Lucy that John had gone to Van Young's
to see about the child, and the entire visit had lasted only about
twenty minutes.

Shortly after Rice left, Pat Corbett arrived. Lucy, who was taking down the drapes from the windows and packing them, thought
he had come by to keep her company because she was "lonely and in
trouble," but Corbett told the court otherwise. "I had orders from
Plumer, as Marshall, to watch her. He told me to go there to see that
no one harmed her." Corbett took a chair by the fire and waited for
Lucy to finish her packing. "She built a large fire and said it was
near time for her to go home," Corbett testified. "It was about 11 or
half past 11. He told me to watch her till I saw him." Plummer arrived at the house between 11:30 and midnight and asked Lucy if
she was ready to leave. When she replied that she was considering
staying at the house, Plummer asked her if she were not afraid Vedder might come back and "disturb" her. As Corbett stood up to go,
Plummer sat down in a chair by the fire, and Corbett went out the
kitchen door facing the street, leaving the door open behind him.[63]

Lucy continued the story from that point.

It was about 12 o'clock at night I think. I was sitting on one side of the
kitchen stove three or four feet from the back door; Mr. Plumer was
sitting on the other side about the same distance from the door. He
asked me whether I had made up my mind to leave the fire. I said I did
not like to leave a fire. He had been there but a few minutes when I
heard someone coming very quietly up the back stairs, very fast, did
not hesitate. I thought it was Mr. Vedder by his step. Mr. Plumer was
sitting with his hands over his eyes; he heard the step and started a
little. Mr. Vedder opened the door and stepped in, came over the
board. He got both feet over the door. I saw a pistol in his hand, saw a

flash from it. Saying to Mr. Plumer, "Your time is come," he fired a
pistol. Am positive as to the words he used, told him his time was
come. As he made the remark and fired the pistol, he stepped back.
Mr. Plumer raised out of his chair and fired at him as he was in the act
of stepping out the door. Mr. Plumer took aim and fired three or four
times. Vedder did not fire again. Plumer fired standing up; he did not
fire while retreating; he never spoke at all. He took one or two steps to
the door and fired all from one place, did not step over the board. Vedder may have been in the act of stepping down the first stair, can't say
how wide the platform is. Plumer then turned and left the house
through the front door without speaking a word to me. Neither of us
spoke. After Plumer left, I took a light and went to the back stairs. I
could not see Mr. Vedder very plain from the top of the stairs, could
not see him till I got most to him. He was lying on his back with his
head towards Deer Creek and his feet toward the stairs, his hands open
and within two or three feet of his head a pistol was lying. He was alive
when I got there and his eyes moved. He was breathing very hard. I
laid my hand on his hand and on his forehead. I thought he knew me
before he died. He lived but a short time. I went back upstairs and
went into the street and called for assistance; presently some gentlemen
came and carried Mr. Vedder upstairs. I then left the house.[64]

Plummer's first shots struck Vedder in the heart and arm; the
other two struck the back fence and privy. Vedder's shot passed
through the kitchen and out the front door, lodging in the gate.
Though Belden did not put Plummer on the stand, deputies
repeated the words he had spoken when he asked for admittance to
the jail. "He said he was in Vedder's house, talking, and Vedder
came up; there was a board there; he pushed it away, drew up his
arm with a pistol and told Plumer his time was come. Then Plumer
drew and fired; he said he shot at him and backed and shot twice as
he backed out, and said if he had not shot Vedder, Vedder would
have shot him. He did not know who shot first, but thinks he had the
first shot." When the deputies asked Plummer if he had killed Vedder, he had responded that he did not know.

The prosecution attempted to show a motive for Vedder's
murder by linking Lucy and Plummer, but were unable to provide
any witnesses who had seen them alone together other than on the
night of the shooting, 25 September. Neighbor women had not seen
Plummer come to the house when Lucy was there alone, and the
hotel keeper testified that Plummer had never been in Mrs. Vedder's
room other than when John was also present. The witness who had

unwittingly supplied Vedder with a gun swore John told him "he did not believe his wife had been unfaithful to him with Plumer."[65]

Failing to prove "intimacy," the prosecution called to the stand Vedder Senior, who claimed Rice had told him Plummer and Corbett wanted to kill his son so they could get his daughter-in-law to a "whore house."

Rice was brought back for further questioning. "I never told old Vedder that Plumer and Corbett murdered Vedder to get her to a whore house," he said. "I told him I thought they did *not* want to make a whore of her. I don't think they wanted her at all; I never saw Plumer put his hands on her."[66]

The courtroom was packed throughout the trial, and after the testimony had been completed on Christmas Eve, the session was adjourned until Saturday, allowing jury members to spend the holiday at home. The first day back was taken up entirely with lawyers' arguments, the court not charging the jury with its decision until 9:30 P.M. On Sunday at 1:30 P.M., the jury returned to announce their verdict to the overcrowded room. They found Plummer guilty of murder in the second degree.[67]

APPEAL TO THE SUPREME COURT

Immediately after the delivery of the verdict, Plummer was taken into custody. When he was brought to court for sentencing three days later, Belden produced evidence that two jurors, Denny and Getchell, the foreman, had the day after Vedder was shot publicly expressed the opinion that the defendant was guilty. Accordingly Belden made motion for a new trial, but Judge Searls refused, accepting the verdict as fair and sentencing Plummer to twelve years imprisonment.

On the hope he would be found innocent, Plummer had held on to his job as marshall to the last possible moment, but he now sent in a letter of resignation to the board, who appointed E. O. Tompkins to fill the remaining four months of his term.[68]

While attorneys prepared an appeal to a higher court, Plummer spent four months in the Nevada City jail. In May 1858, he was released on bond, and in June, his appeal was heard in Sacramento.[69] "Some three hundred jurors were summoned," his attorney told California Supreme Court justices, "to enable us to get twelve men, who pretended that they had not made up their minds defiinitely as to his guilt, and some of whom entertained the most bitter prejudices against him personally. A clearer case of an unjust verdict can scarcely be imagined. If this defendant is not entitled to come to this Court for redress against a great wrong, disguised by judicial forms, who can be?"[70]

After the deliberation, Chief Justice David Terry delivered the unanimous opinion of the court, which is quoted in detail not only because it is an eloquent defense of our legal heritage, but also because its content is so pertinent to the issues of justice involved in a consideration of the life of Henry Plummer.

One of the dearest rights guaranteed by our free Constitution is that of trial by jury. . . . A trial before a prejudiced jury, or one composed of men who had already prejudged the case, is a mere mockery of justice. . . . The very meaning of the word trial, which is an "examination by a test," shows that the triers are to act not upon previously formed opinions, but upon inquiry, first instituted and carried on before them. Moreover, if each juror forms his opinion before taking his seat, the case is, in reality, predetermined by persons who, at the time of making their decision, are not jurors. So that the wholesome restraint of the oath administered to the jurors—the solemn proceedings of the Court—the opportunity to observe the demeanor of the witnesses—the thorough public sifting and scrutiny of the evidence—the explanations of counsel—the instructions of the judge, and the deliberations of the jury, enlightened by private discussion after they have retired—are so many useless forms, and the parties have only the appearance of jury trial, without any of its benefits. . . . There are certain legal safeguards which must be preserved immaculate; the purity of the stream of justice is involved in it. One of these safeguards is that the jury shall be impartial and unbiased, their minds free from prejudgment. I must say that he who gives his consent to serve on a jury, when he must know that his mind is utterly disqualified from doing justice between the prisoner and the State, is guilty of gross misconduct. To convict one under such circumstances, is to perpetrate an offence little short of murder itself.

Can it be insisted that the juror was impartial; that he possessed that moral perception, that sense of justice, that integrity of character which would qualify him to pass upon the life of a fellow-citizen? The affidavit of Pulse stated that Getchell, soon after the killing with which defendant was charged, declared that "the people ought to take Plummer out of jail and hang him," and on other occasions expressed a belief that he was guilty of murder. In addition to the affidavits, witnesses were examined both by the accused and the prosecution, as to the facts alleged. The testimony of the witnesses corroborate the statement in the affidavits, and, we think, clearly establish that such a declaration was made by the juror.

The remark of Denny, as stated by Southwick, was that "Plummer ought to be hung, and if he was at the Bay he would be hung before night." Smith and Fraser both testify to hearing him say that Plummer ought to be hung. This conscientious juror does not seem to have troubled himself to inquire whether the defendant was guilty or not; with him, it appears that the accusation was sufficient; in the language of witness Smith, "He appeared to be down on all men situated as Plummer was."

It is clear that neither of these jurors was competent to sit upon the trial of defendant, if indeed they were competent to sit in any case involving the life or liberty of a citizen. A man who could so far forget his duty as a citizen, and his allegiance to the Constitution as to openly advocate taking the life of a citizen without the form of law, and deprive him of the chance of a jury trial, would not be likely to stop at any means to secure, under the forms of a legal trial, a result which he had publicly declared ought to be accomplished by an open violation of the law.

Judgment reversed, and a new trial ordered.[71]

After obtaining the opportunity for a new trial for Plummer, Belden, now a Nevada County judge-elect, moved for and received a change of venue. Judge W. T. Barbour of the district court in Marysville, Yuba County, scheduled the case to be heard on 6 September 1858, nearly one year after Vedder was shot. The second trial lasted four days, with little alteration of previously presented evidence except for a minor change by the prosecution to strengthen its contention that an intimate relationship had developed between Lucy and Plummer during the two-week period in which they were in frequent contact.

At the first trial, witness Holmes had reported seeing Plummer and Lucy walking down Broad Street about noon two days before the shooting. They approached a "daguerrean saloon," where they were met by John Vedder. Holmes approached Plummer, asking him "what woman that was." Plummer, after correcting him with, "what lady," answered that it was Mrs. Vedder. At the retrial, Holmes completely omitted the appearance of Mr. Vedder: "I saw Mrs. Vedder and Plummer pass through Broad Street a few days before the killing of Vedder, *together*. They went into a daguerrean saloon together. Plummer returned in a few minutes alone and told me that it was Mrs. Vedder."[72]

The prosecution had provided the romantic link that had been missing in their earlier case, and they followed it up by introducing a new witness. "I know Mrs. Vedder and have been in her company since the trial at Nevada," Mrs. St. John testified, "and I have seen in her possession a daguerrotype of a gentleman. She told me it was the picture of Henry Plummer. I only saw it once; it was about last Christmas."

Under cross-examination, Lucy denied Mrs. St. John's statement: "I have not at any time since the trial of this case at Nevada had a daguerrotype portrait of Henry Plummer. I never did have a portrait of him in my possession at any time."[73] Though Lucy insisted the picture did not exist, Vedder Senior, who was now supporting his daughter-in-law and sleeping, though not eating, at her house, claimed he had also seen the picture on one occasion. At the first trial, Vedder Senior had proven an unreliable witness, nearly all of his testimony being declared false by other witnesses, but in this instance his words were more believable since they agreed with those of Mrs. St. John.

Before the jury began deliberation on Thursday evening, Judge Barbour provided them with instructions. If the evidence showed the defendant killed the deceased in the necessary defense of his own life, they must acquit him; but if it showed the defendant's actions were unnecessary to defend his life but that he "followed up and designedly and premeditatedly killed John Vedder while Vedder was retreating and attempting to escape from a combat with Plummer," they must find the defendant guilty of murder in the second degree.

The decision facing the jury was whether the marshall, known as a peaceable man who brought in his prisoners alive, acted in self-defense when he shot a man who had threatened to kill him, borrowed a gun for that purpose, entered a house owned by the marshall, told him his time had come, and fired a shot at him. Doubts that Plummer's actions were strictly in self-defense were raised by the testimony of Lucy Vedder, the only eyewitness, that Vedder retreated immediately upon firing and that Plummer advanced two steps toward the door, which could be considered "following." Vedder, struck in the heart with the first shot, was obviously from that point on doing exactly what Judge Barbour had advised them about, "attempting to escape from a combat." Still, the case did not meet the judge's other stipulation that "premeditation" be present. The prosecution had made little attempt to show Plummer had planned beforehand to kill Vedder, other than the opinion Vedder Senior expressed that Corbett and Plummer had killed his son because they wanted to get Lucy to a house of ill-fame. However, even he had expressed bewilderment as to why they would want to kill his son on Friday night to be rid of him when he would be leaving town anyhow on Saturday morning.

But whether Plummer had made plans to murder Vedder was not necessarily the question debated by the jury during the hours they spent considering the case. They were more concerned with the issue of passion than that of violent death. Violence was a common means of settling disagreements, and one not necessarily frowned upon by much of the community, as proven by the instances of the two judges who heard Plummer's case.

Judge Barbour, while presiding over the Marysville trial, was himself under indictment for assaulting with a deadly weapon a man who had criticized his court decisions. Barbour had successfully postponed trial for four years with no apparent damage to his reputation as a judge, and even after eventually being found guilty of assault with intent to kill, he was the very next year nominated as a candidate for the assembly.[74] Likewise, Judge Terry of the supreme court, who had had a falling out with a legislator who had made insulting remarks about him, challenged his political foe to a duel. Terry won the duel, killing his opponent, and was indicted for murder. On the day of the trial, not a single witness appeared in court to testify for the prosecution, and the charge was dismissed for lack of evidence.[75]

Of course Plummer did not have the prestige or influence of either judge, but of more consequence to his case was the fact that the crime of which he was accused included a relationship with a married woman and was being decided by a jury composed mainly of miners, angry at him because during the last election it had been charged that he wished to join the state assembly for the purpose of destroying the opportunities of the small miner.

The jurors deliberating between a verdict of either self-defense or murder in the second degree were very much people of their own time, and it was a time when citizens of California believed that Holloway's Ointment was a cure-all for those at death's door, but did not necessarily subscribe to the belief that *all* men were created free and equal or that men had the right to deviate from accepted ways. The local prejudice can be detected in any issue of the newspapers, items slurring those who were different in any way — racial groups, new religions, or free thinkers. Name-calling was standard journalistic practice: "Greasers," "thieving celestials," and "niggers, the inferior race." Mormons were "ignorant and fanatical," Salt Lake City being "at best but a rendezvous of murderers, thieves, and fanatics." And Democrats could be easily recognized since they were the "party who swears in broken English." Plummer was not only a sort of foreigner accused of aiding and abetting foreign investors, but also the victim of another common prejudice of the day, especially in an area where such a shortage of women existed: hatred of a "seducer," a man who destroyed a home by tempting a wife to be unfaithful to her husband. The verdict reached by the Marysville jurors would hinge on whether they decided that Plummer fell into this category.[76]

Though the members of the jury understood that Plummer's involvement with Lucy Vedder had at first been only in the line of duty — protecting her against the violence of her husband and advising the couple about the custody of their child — Mrs. Vedder's reported possession of a daguerreotype of Plummer indicated that a personal relationship between the two had developed later. Prosecution lawyers were quite skillful at asking questions that created suspicions in the minds of the jurors, and even when a defense witness responded to such questions with denials, the impression made by each original question remained. A classic example is Rice's response to a question insinuating that he had once caught Plummer and Lucy together: "I did not tell Vedder that Plumer was setting on Mrs. Vedder's lap."[77]

Prosecuting lawyers also led Lucy into a series of denials that served to tell the story they were contending had taken place. "I had no quarrel about Plumer with Vedder," Lucy answered. "I did not see Plumer push Vedder out of my room. I knew Mrs. Phelan. I never told her that Plumer was to pay expenses for divorce and afterwards I would marry him. I never said that if Mr. Vedder caught me and Plumer in a bad house he would smother us both. I never said

Plumer advised me to get a little house a short way out of Nevada. There was no understanding I was to marry Plumer."[78] Keeping in separate compartments of the mind the insinuations offered by the prosecution and the denials made by the defense became a near impossible task for the jury. The lingering images left in their minds by the cross-examination confirmed suspicions that Lucy was a "loose" woman, one who looked on the Bible as a "novel," though she had denied that accusation. Plummer's enlightened handling of the problems of a battered wife had not only made it necessary for him to defend himself against the violence John Vedder had regularly been venting on Lucy, but also bewildered his other constituents. The only reasonable motive they could think of for Plumer defending a "bad" woman was that he was in love with her himself; either that or he wanted to "make a whore of her." It took them but a few hours to reach their decision. Plummer, who had been sick with consumption throughout the trial, was brought into court to hear the verdict: guilty of murder in the second degree.

During the time his attorneys were preparing a second appeal to the supreme court, Plummer was held in custody in Marysville, and while there received a letter from the girl he had planned to marry, saying she no longer loved him and was breaking off the engagement. The supreme court, after reviewing the second trial, agreed the questioning by the prosecution had not been "strictly proper," but concluded that a negative answer to an improper question prevents the prejudicing of a defendant's case. The supreme court therefore upheld the decision of the Marysville district court.[79]

The opinion of both the Nevada City and the Marysville juries in regards to the case of The People vs. Henry Plumer can be summed up by referring to a saloon conversation reported as part of the trial proceedings: "A man who could take another's wife away, and then shoot him down like a dog ought to be hung."[80]

Plummer had spent seventeen months in limbo, in and out of jail and in and out of court, while it was decided how he should be punished for firing back at Vedder and hitting him. Judge Barbour put a merciful end to the waiting by sentencing Plummer to ten years at state prison. On 22 February 1859, being celebrated as the birthday of the Nation's Father, Plummer was admitted to San Quentin.

SAN QUENTIN

The state prison stood on the slope of a misty, windswept hill on Point San Quentin, a peninsula jutting into San Francisco Bay about three miles from Marin Island. It was not the first time Plummer had seen San Quentin. He had been there before to deliver prisoners. The two-story structure with its single sentry box was intended to incarcerate about two hundred persons, the entire upper story being composed of two rows of cells separated by an aisle. The forty-eight cells, measuring 6 feet by 10 feet and designed to hold four persons each, were severely overcrowded, enrollment in 1859 being nearly three times the prison's normal capacity. To handle the overflow, one hundred of the less violent inmates were confined in one large room downstairs, the far end being used as a sick ward, though very few were allowed the luxury of its use. The lower story also held the guard's office, an armory, an apothecary shop, and a whipping room. A second building provided a tailor shop, kitchen, dining room, and quarters for female convicts. Inside of each heavy, plate-iron door, in both the cells and the downstairs room, was posted a copy of the state law that doubled the sentence of any convict caught attempting to escape. In spite of the warning, escapes were so common that residents of the area surrounding the prison were constantly writing letters expressing concern for their personal safety to members of the state legislature.[81]

The cosmopolitan population of San Quentin during the 1850s reflects the large number of states and foreign nations that had contributed to the California gold rush. Of the twenty-five countries represented there, the largest number of prisoners, excepting the United States, came from Mexico, Ireland, Chile, Germany, China, France, and England. More than forty of the inmates were mere boys under the age of seventeen.

Plummer entered this institution of correction as inmate number 1573, and on arrival was taken to a special room, where he and one Irish and one Australian prisoner admitted on the same day were stripped and then examined minutely for scars, birthmarks, or deformities that were recorded, along with other pertinent information, on the prison register. Plummer, listed as being twenty-seven years old and having worked as a clerk during the months he had been out on bail, was described as 5' 8½" tall, with light complexion, light brown hair, and gray eyes. He had two moles on the back of his neck and another under his left shoulder blade, as well as a scar on the right knee and another round one on the back of his right hand. The inside of his left forefinger was marked with a long scar, and the remaining three fingers of the left hand were permanently closed from a cut. Because of his lung disease, he was assigned a bed in the sick ward.[82]

The state prison had been leased to a private individual, who had the tendency to overwork chain gangs on the jobs contracted at the stone quarry and to scrimp on food and care for the prisoners. A year before Plummer entered, a concerned assemblyman had sent a committee to inspect the prison, and the findings of the group had shocked the entire state. The report told of "horrifying" overcrowding of prisoners, who had not been issued uniforms but were clad in the dirty, tattered remnants of the clothing they had worn on arrival. Over a hundred men went barefoot while others bound their feet in gunnysacks. Two light meals were served per day from cooking facilities so unsanitary as to cause frequent outbreaks of food poisoning. Sleeping quarters were "filthy," and little bed covering was available.[83]

On reading the report, Governor John Weller, the Democrat elected on the same ticket on which Plummer and Walsh were defeated, took possession of the prison and commenced reforms. Weller immediately ordered meals increased to three per day, sanitation in the cooking plant improved, uniforms issued to inmates, and hospital facilities upgraded. But before any further improvements could be made, the court ruled Governor Weller's takeover unconstitutional and reinstated the private lessee. Many problems still remained unresolved by February 1859: facilities were overcrowded; there were no bathing accommodations for prisoners; and cells were infested with bedbugs, fleas, and lice. Punishment was frequent and severe. Chinese prisoners had introduced the opium habit to other inmates; hard liquor was generally available to those having the price to pay; and gambling was carried on in the yard at every available opportunity. The diet was limited, frequently consisting of stale codfish and bread served in such small portions as to leave the prisoners nearly starving, and only one month before Plummer's admittance, three hundred had suffered poisoning from contaminated bread baked at the prison.

From his first day at San Quentin, Plummer's health deteriorated, and in July, prison doctors wrote Governor Weller concerning his condition:

> This is to certify that the person now confined in the penetentiary, by the name of Henry Plumer, is labouring under a disease which will in a short time prove fatal. On examination I find him to be affected with a disease of the lungs, commonly called consumption, and in all probability he will not be able to live, in his present situation, more than five or six months, at the furtherest, and I would recommend his speedy removal from confinement before it is too late. T. B. HEIRY, Physician in the State Prison, and ALFRED TALIAFERIO.[84]

When Plumer's friends in Nevada City learned of his condition, they prepared a petition requesting Governor Weller to issue a pardon, and on 14 August, Pat Corbett and Mr. Bullock traveled to Sacramento to personally present the request to the governor. It had been signed by one hundred ten officials of Nevada and Yuba counties, including officers of the court and members of the bar. With the petition Corbett carried a personal letter from Dr. Taliaferio that stated, "I write this on account of the solicitude of the friends of Henry Plummer who are constantly writing to me. . . . He has been declning ever since his imprisonment. I sympathize very deeply with him, and hope that you will pardon him out."

Though the doctor's letter presented grounds of poor health, the petitioners believed the pardon should be granted because Plummer was unjustly imprisoned:

> Henry Plumer is a young man having an excellent character, and was elected Marshall of the city of Nevada. The fatal occurrence took place without entraps other than the female, the cause of the tragedy. The deceased when discovered was found with a drawn pistol, one or two barrels of which had been discharged. The proof, as a portion of us knew, was entirely circumstantial as to who first drew a weapon. It is a case when the innocent may suffer the disgrace and mental and bodily suffering of a lengthy incarceration. We therefore urgently solicit your Excellency for this pardon.[85]

The list of petitioners was impressive, not necessarily because of its length, but because all those who had signed were leading citizens serving in positions that had given them the opportunity to deal with Plummer professionally and therefore became familiar with his character and his manner of carrying out his duties. And the one signature that is more significant than any of the rest, in an attempt to assess Plummer's character, is that of Phil Moore. In fact, it is surprising to find his name attached to a petition claiming Plummer's innocence, testifying to his "excellent character," and recommending his pardon, since Moore was the Democratic candidate for the state assembly Plummer had defeated in the 1857 primary. It was Moore's discontent that had provided much of the impetus for the party split and the resulting smear campaign that ruined the reputation of both Plummer and Judge Walsh. Moore's wounded pride extended beyond the realm of politics; Plummer had not only won from him the opportunity to compete for the state assembly seat but also the heart of the girl Moore had intended to marry. Thus Moore's signature on the request for a pardon for Plummer is undoubtedly a belated apology for the damage done to his reputation during the bitter campaign and its consequent influence on how the jury perceived Plummer's successful attempt to defend himself from John Vedder's attack. Though it is only speculation, Phil Moore's change of heart may have been due to more than pricks of conscience over the "lying handbills" spread through the camps; it is possible that when Plummer's fiancee broke off their engagement after his conviction at Marysville, she returned to her former love, thus eliminating his main source of hostility toward Plummer.

Shortly before the petition in Plummer's behalf was presented to the governor, Weller received a third letter of petition, a lonely effort by one of the prison guards, acting completely on his own, who had written a friend in Sacramento, asking him to deliver the plea to the governor:

> I have been acquainted with Mr. Plumer since my arrival here, and have through the medium of other gentlemen become familiar with the circumstances connected with his case, and it is impossible for me to witness his daily suffering without contributing my mile toward his speedy relief. Mine is an unsolicited impulse in his behalf, and I am sorry that *all* I can contribute is an assurance as to the good faith of Mr. Plumer's friends, and also to add my testimony to the correctness of the representation made by Mr. Plumer's physicians and friends in regard to his health condition. . . . Mr. Plumer is a gentleman worthy of sympathy and mercy . . . and it is for this reason I address you, and request you to hand to his Honor the Governor the inclosed letter, and if he does not remember me, I knew him in Ohio. . . . Bruce, I hope

you will attend to this for me. It will not do any harm, but on the other
hand may be additional testimony in Mr. Plumer's cause, and thereby
contribute to his good.

Truly your Friend,
THOMAS B. LEWIS

The day after receiving Pat Corbett and Mr. Bullock, who
delivered the petition signed by the officials of Nevada and Yuba
counties, Governor Weller signed a pardon, but not based on reason
of innocence as the petitioners had requested, but rather on the less
controversial reason of poor health. Plummer was released on 16
August 1859, having spent six months at San Quentin.

EXCONVICT

Both prison doctors had worried Plummer might die before the pardon was obtained, and he had also become concerned about the
disgrace to his family if he were to die in prison. Dr. Taliaferio wrote
Governor Weller, "I know that the idea of dying a convict presses
very heavily upon him." His condition was diagnosed as phthisis
pulmonary, a progressive wasting of the lungs resulting from the formation of scar tissue around invading bacteria. The effects were a
shortness of breath, sapping of strength, loss of weight, and general
deterioration of health; and prescribed treatment was a nutritious
diet and rest.[86]

After receiving the pardon, Plummer returned to the house at
94 Spring Street and was cared for by Mrs. Robinson, probably the
widow of his former partner at the Wilson Valley ranch. In way of
reminder to the community of his past services, his first act after a
month and half of recuperation was to make a citizen's arrest of "Ten
Year Smith," an escapee from San Quentin. Because of the many
letters inquiring about his health directed to prison doctors and the
petition presented to the governor by the officials of the county,
Plummer may have returned to Nevada City with hopes of regaining
the opportunities for a career that had formerly been open to him. If
so, he was soon disillusioned. The days when he had been a dashing
young marshall engaged to a respectable daughter of a merchant
were definitely over for good. Old prejudices were still alive and
were fueled by his exconvict status; many even held it against him
that he did not die after receiving a pardon on account of "precarious
health."[87]

Reconciling himself as best he could to his new status in the community, Plummer resumed the bakery partnership with Henry Heyer, optimistically refusing to believe he would not be allowed to make a new start. Nevada City had grown in his months of absence, new businesses downtown and new homes on the outskirts. Directly across from the National Hotel, on Broad Street, a bathing, haircutting, and shaving saloon had been opened, with both warm or cold baths available, and Squire Williams's Gothic Revival mansion on Prospect Hill was nearly completed. There was scarcely a house for rent to be found; even little cabins back in the hills were occupied, and rooms at the three-story U. S. Hotel could easily be filled at the price of 75 cents per night. [88]

Though all the wealth Plummer had accumulated during his four years in Nevada City enterprises had been used up by the expense of two trials and two appeals, there was still financial opportunity in the area, as Judge Walsh, Plummer's former running mate in the disastrous campaign of 1857, had just proven. As Walsh had attempted to convince the doubting Thomases during the campaign, he was himself a miner. In 1859, he had purchased several supposedly worthless claims in the Virginia Range of western Nevada from a Henry Comstock, claims that had proven impossible to work due to the presence of a pesky clay that stuck to pick and shovel and sucked at the digger's boots like quicksand. However, it was soon discovered that this gummy, bluish-gray clay that lay beneath the gold-bearing quartz, contained the richest silver deposits ever uncovered. As word of the silver's staggering worth spread, the town of Virginia City, Nevada, quickly sprang up near the lode. By early spring of 1860, the resulting silver stampede to the Comstock nearly drained Nevada City. In spite of an unusually heavy snowstorm as late as 6 April, Henness Pass was busy with the traffic of those who had caught silver fever — Plummer among them. Though most of the prospective silver miners drifted back dead broke in a matter of weeks and Nevada City again returned to overflowing, a few lucky investors stayed on in Virginia City to make their fortunes. One of these was William Stewart, the young lawyer who had served with Plummer and David Belden on the executive committee of the Democratic Club a few years earlier. After becoming a millionaire, Stewart got himself elected to the U.S. Senate and moved to Washington, where he constructed a three-story castle equipped with speaking tubes, a grand staircase, carved chandeliers, and a tapestried ballroom. The silver magnate's castle soon became a more popular tourist attraction than the White House itself.

Though Plummer maintained his residence in Nevada City, he kept claims in the Virginia City area for the next two years after discovery, making regular trips over the pass to visit his mines. Also, at Nevada City he became a partner in Cahalan & Company, a silver and gold mine located on Scott's Flat, and in the fall of 1860, he formed the Flora Temple Company, excavating gold in Kelsey Ravine, a lead of quartz nearly fifteen inches thick and only about ten feet down, so rich, according to the *Democrat* reporter who claimed to have seen quartz samples, that hardly a piece could be picked up that did not contain gold.[89]

In addition to his economic pursuits, Plummer once more involved himself in local political affairs, though his name never again came up as a nominee for office. In preparation for the coming national election, Nevada City Democrats met to form a Douglas and Johnson Club in support of the election of Stephen Douglas for president, and Plummer enrolled as a member. Their effort on Douglas's behalf was in vain; in November 1860, the Democratic candidate was defeated by Abraham Lincoln.[90]

As marshall, Plummer had been required to attend all the performances at the theater to keep order, but now he was free to go for the enjoyment, having a choice between serious drama, such as *Othello*, a "seriocomedy" of *Henry IV*, or vaudeville. The prime attractions at the Melodeon the fall of 1860 were Negro delineations, banjo solos, songs by Joe Taylor, mockingbird imitations, songs and dances of the Bingham girls, jigs, and bone solos. The *Democrat* recommended the program as well worth the half-dollar admission, the jig dancer and mockingbird imitator having "no superiors in their line."[91]

While leaving the Melodeon one evening in November, Plummer suffered a freak accident. During the final acts of the performance, he had been standing on a platform erected for the press, and when he jumped down at the close of the curtain, he hooked the little finger of his left hand, one permanently bent from a previous accident, over the back of a seat, breaking the bone and leaving the finger attached by nothing more than a strip of skin, a very painful ending to an evening's entertainment and the first in a series of accidents in store for him.[92]

Not all of the entertainment Plummer chose was as innocent as attending the theater. An editorial had recently appeared in the paper about the "increasing immorality of the people of our good city," with "business men, lawyers, judges, and the common bummer" gambling and drinking whiskey "from daylight till dark and even till the small hours of the morning."[93] No longer having the reputation of a law officer to uphold, Plummer was not long in joining the "immoral" crowd enjoying themselves until the early hours. Despite his bad reputation, there was a certain type of woman in town who still found Plummer attractive, and such women knew how to offer him consolation for what he had lost within the past year. But even this type of woman was in short supply with the city's ratio at eleven men to one woman, so there was always stiff competition and constant quarreling for their company. Plummer made a good target for hostile drunks because his imprisonment had earned him the contempt of half the town, he spoke with an eastern accent, and he was still frail from the bout of consumption. Due to his normally peaceful and quiet nature, he gave the appearance that he would not fight back, but he always did if pushed far enough.

In February 1861, he was involved in a fracas at the house of Irish Maggie on Pine Street. Because of conflicting rumors about what actually took place, some newspapers refrained from going into detail in printing the story, but the *Journal* had no compunction about writing up a detailed and damaging account, correct or not, of how Plummer had been "closeted" with a woman when W. J. Muldoon pounded on the door and demanded admittance. On being told that the woman was with another party and could not see him at the moment, he asked who she was with. When told it was Plummer, Muldoon referred to him by an epithet that so angered Plummer, he opened the closet door and attacked Muldoon. In the ensuing struggle, Plummer struck Muldoon on the head with a pistol, cutting a gash in his skull, but the police were not called in. Muldoon survived the blow, and Plummer, in his typical fashion, came around later to talk things over, and the two men made up their differences. His next skirmish at a house of entertainment would not end so favorably.[94]

The firing on Fort Sumter had taken place in April, and accordingly many of the disputes in the pleasure houses were brought on by the resulting tension between North and South. In May, Plummer was called as a trial witness to one such dispute in which one of the participants died from a knife wound. Speaking with his customary understatement, Plummer testified that the two men involved in the fatal controversy were "having some words."[95]

During this period of his nation's unrest and his own personal disgrace, Plummer formed a relationship with a woman, reportedly beautiful, who was employed by Mr. Ashmore, which would mean that she was probably either an actress or a prostitute. Though the woman assumed the name of Mrs. Plummer, no marriage ceremony ever took place. In October, while preparing to visit his lady friend at Ashmore's establishment, Plummer became involved in an argument with a Secessionist antagonist, and the resulting struggle delivered the coup de grace to his ill-fated attempt at a social and political comeback in Nevada City. "At about 2 o'clock last Sunday morning," the *Democrat* reported,

> a difficulty occurred at a house of ill-fame on Commercial Street between Henry Plumer and William Riley, resulting in the death of the latter. It appears that they had both been drinking pretty freely and got to quarreling in the entry when Riley struck Plumer on the head with a knife, cutting through his hat and inflicting a deep wound in his scalp. Plumer at the same time drew his revolver and fired at Riley. The ball took effect in his left side and must have killed him instantly. Plumer was taken into custody by officer Kennar and lodged in jail. Riley was a young man about 21 years of age and was formerly from Huntsville, Missouri. He had been living within the vicinity of Nevada for a year or two and we are informed was quarrelsome and dissipative.

Riley was the same man "who'd assailed a citizen of Blue Tent on the Fourth of July for firing a salute."[96]

A surgeon was called to the jail to tend Plummer's scalp wound, and the next afternoon "Mrs. Plummer" came to his cell to visit. While she was still there, a guard, on orders from a higher officer, opened both the cell and jail doors and turned away, allowing Plummer to walk out. Though officials claimed the incident had been an accident, Plummer, who had many friends among the law officers, was not apprehended as he walked away, and he did not leave town until evening. Officers told the reporter for the *Democrat*, "There is no prospect of his being caught. The circumstances connected to the killing of Riley as generally understood would hardly justify Plumer's conviction for murder. But this being the second man he has killed in Nevada and knowing there was a strong prejudice against him in the county, he doubtless thought it prudent not to risk a trial." The newspaper that had covered every one of Plummer's exploits as marshall, every capture of a wanted man or raid on a gambling den, now closed his career in Nevada City on a rather ungrateful note: "If Plumer shows as much tact in keeping away from the county as he did in leaving the jail, the community will have no particular occasion to deplore his departure, as the cost of an expensive trial would have probably resulted in still leaving him here, a most useless if not dangerous man."[97]

It is nearly impossible to overestimate the amount of hatred generated toward Plummer during the political campaign of 1857, but an idea of its magnitude came out during the two trials. Mr. Wall, a respectable merchant displeased over enforcement of city ordinances, informed John Vedder that if he wanted to shoot Plummer, he would "go his security," and Rice went to Wall saying he was a "friend of the prosecution," suggesting that someone get Lucy drunk to obtain more ammunition for the case against Plummer. Nevada City merchants had wanted law and order, but their idea of order was keeping the miners in line, not imposing fines against merchants who endangered the city by refusing to comply with fire ordinances. Even the editor of the *Journal*, who considered himself the public conscience, felt wronged at having to pay a fine for not owning the required fire prevention equipment. Out of such minor resentments came the campaign to sway the thinking of those who had elected Plummer in the two previous elections—the miners. Plummer's life story is a study in the complex relation between the law and the individual, and one of the issues it makes clear is how few good citizens expect the law should be applied to them personally. When two of the judges who presided over Plummer's case found themselves in a situation similar to his, they used their legal expertise to place themselves out of reach of the law. But Plummer, out of respect for the law, surrendered himself to the courts, believing he would receive justice; instead, he lost everything he had gained up to that point in his life. The verdict rendered by his jurors became his initiation into an understanding of the fallibility of individuals who carry out the processes of justice. As an initiate, he had no intention of again placing his fate in the hands of a local jury. As the news reporter commented, he would not risk a third trial in the area. By leaving before the inquest into Riley's death, Plummer became an outlaw; but the experiences of his last four years in Nevada City provided him with an insight into the justice system that few lawmen ever attain.

FROM CARSON CITY TO FLORENCE

When on the last day of October 1861 Plummer shook the dust of Nevada City from his feet, he made his way over the mountains to the newly organized territory of Nevada. The scalp wound he had received from Riley was severe, a three-inch gash that had required stitches, and on his arrival at Carson City he was in a weakened condition. According to Nevada historians, he first looked up Bill Mayfield, a professional gambler he had become acquainted with on visits to his mining claims in the area. Mayfield put Plummer up at his cabin, but word soon got out about his visitor. Since Plummer was too sick to travel further, Mayfield arranged to have him moved to the home of a friend, Jack Harris. By placing a bed across the rafters a hiding place was prepared in Harris's loft. After resting Plummer on the bed and placing provisions beside him, Mayfield and Harris sealed up the ceiling and left Plummer to recuperate as best he could on his own.

Though Nevada City officials did not have a murder case against Plummer and therefore did not want him back, Blackburn, the sheriff at Carson City, heard about the fugitive and went to search Mayfield's cabin, only to find Plummer already gone. Sheriff Blackburn, a staunch Unionist and reportedly a heavy drinker with a hot temper, was himself known as "the most reckless law-breaker" in the Territory of Nevada. Perturbed at being outwitted by Mayfield, whom he disliked for being a zealous Secessionist, Blackburn "proceeded to get drunk," his usual course of action, and then went to the St. Nicholas saloon to confront the gambler. When Mayfield informed the sheriff he could not arrest him without a warrant, Blackburn showed the temper he was famous for being unable to control. On a previous occasion when his authority had been challenged, Mayfield had shot a drunken man for failing to comply with his request to stop the boisterous singing. Saying he guessed the "son of a b----" would be quiet now, or so the story goes, Blackburn bought drinks for the cowed bystanders, clinking glasses with them "over the corpse of his victim" sprawled on the barroom floor.

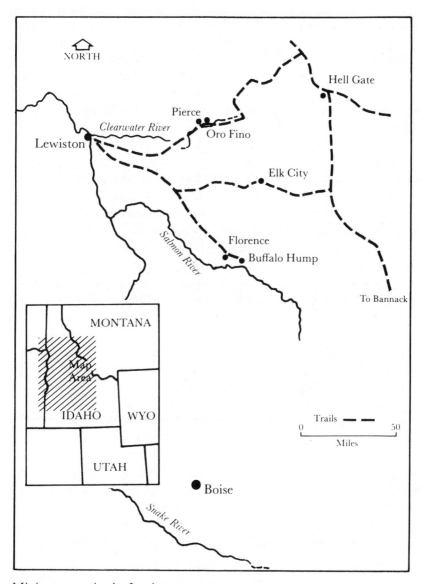

Mining camps in the Lewiston area.

In response to Mayfield's challenge of the authority to arrest him, Blackburn answered, "I tell you I can arrest you or anyone else, and d--- you, I'll arrest you anyhow." As the sheriff drew his pistol, Mayfield's friends caught Blackburn by the arms and dragged him toward the door, but he broke away and lunged for Mayfield, who drew his bowie knife and stabbed his assailant in the chest as he approached. Leaving the sheriff to die, Mayfield ran from the saloon and hid for the remainder of the night in a hogpen, not moving to a friend's cabin until daylight. An informant, tempted by the large reward offered, soon revealed Mayfield's whereabouts, and the sheriff-killer was arrested, tried for murder, and sentenced to hang. There being considerable public sympathy for the man who had rid the community of a sheriff as unpopular as Blackburn, several citizens arranged for Mayfield to escape from jail. Because of his love for a local woman, he tarried at Carson for several months, but was finally persuaded to relocate in Idaho Territory.[98]

As soon as he recovered his health, Plummer moved on to Walla Walla, according to rumor leading behind his horse a pack mule loaded down with the proceeds received from the sale of his mining claims. It is likely he left Nevada in the spring of 1862, travelling to San Francisco, where he purchased a double-barreled shotgun, booked passage on a steamer to Washington Territory, and reached the interior via the Columbia River.

The first actual record of Plummer being in what is now Idaho comes in July 1862, his signature on the register of the Luna House, the best hotel in Lewiston. Though later to become capital of the vast area to be organized as the Territory of Idaho, at the time, Lewiston was nothing more than a "rag town," whose buildings were constructed of wooden frames covered with white cotton blankets, but it was flourishing as a supply center for surrounding gold camps such as Florence, Oro Fino, Elk City, and Pierce. By night, candles and lanterns burning inside lit up the white cloth walls and ceilings of homes and businesses with a bright glow that illuminated the entire town.

The myth of Plummer's experiences as an outlaw chief in the Lewiston area goes like this:

> In the spring of 1861, among the daily arrivals at Lewiston, was a man of gentlemanly bearing and dignified deportment, accompanied by a lady, to all appearance his wife. He took quarters at the best hotel in town. Before the close of the second day after his arrival his character as a gambler was fully understood, and in less than a fortnight his abandonment of his female companion betrayed the illicit connection which had existed between them. . . . Soon, alas! she became one of the lowest inmates of a frontier brothel. . . . Every gambler or rough infesting the camp, either voluntarily or by threats was induced to unite in the enterprise; and thus originated the band of desperadoes

which, for the succeeding two years by their fearful atrocities, spread such terror through the northern mines. Plummer was their acknowledged leader. . . . He selected two points of rendezvous as bases for their operations. These were called "shebangs." They were enclosed by mountains, whose rugged fastnesses were available for refuge in case of an attack.

The account concludes with the death of one member of the notorious gang, Cherokee Bob, who was shot in Florence for his part in Plummer's seduction of red-haired Cynthia, the woman brought as his wife to the Luna House on his arrival in Lewiston.[99] So goes the myth that has been passed down as history.

In reality, Plummer spent not two years, but less than two months in what is now Idaho. Both his arrival and departure from the area are easily documented. If, as claimed by Langford, Dimsdale, and others, a gang with "designs of plunder and butchery" terrorized the Lewiston countryside for a period of two years beginning with the spring of 1861, Plummer, who spent 1861 at Nevada City, could not have had a part in the action. As noted earlier, his activities that year were closely followed by Nevada City newspapers.

Though the exact date of Plummer's recuperation and consequent departure from Carson City is not known, one thing that is certain is he did not spend the winter of 1861 and spring of 1862 operating as a road agent near Lewiston. In fact, there is good reason to believe no agents were working the roads leading from the northern Idaho mines during this period. The winter of 1861–62, one of the worst on record in the history of the Northwest, left most camps lying beneath as much as ten feet of snow from December 1861 through May 1862, nearly starving inhabitants unable to get out until late spring, and then usually on snowshoes. Under such severe weather conditions, little transport of gold and resulting road agent activity could have taken place.[100]

The limited records of Plummer's actual activities during the few weeks he spent in northern Idaho show that he arrived in Lewiston on 24 July 1862, signing the Luna House register as "Henry Plumer" and correctly listing his former residence as Nevada City, even though he had been invited to leave. He did not bring with him, as his wife, red-haired Cynthia. As the hotel register shows, the guest who signed on the lines directly above Plummer's name did have "a companion" with him, but Plummer did not.[101]

Hotel register, now housed in the Luna House Museum of Lewiston, Idaho. Plummer's only extant signature provides additional evidence in dispelling the myth that he headed a gang of road agents in Idaho. Plummer spent not two years, but less than two months in this area. Also, as shown above, he did not bring red-haired Cynthia to town with him, as charged, and register her at the Luna House as his wife. (Photo by Boswell, 1985)

The claim that Cynthia left behind in Walla Walla a "fond husband and three helpless children" to "mourn her loss" could not have been accurate anyhow since she already resided in Lewiston, being married to one of the more respectable citizens there. At some point, Cynthia, who had no connection to Plummer whatsoever, decided to leave her respectable husband and take up with Bill Mayfield and Cherokee Bob, but by the time she attended the famous ball in Florence that resulted in the shootout causing Bob's death, Plummer was gone. Early residents of Montana also disagree with the idea that Plummer followed the gambler's trade in Lewiston, arguing that he was so poor at the gaming tables he could not possibly have ever been a professional.

What Plummer actually did after his arrival, rather than gambling and organizing crime, was to join in the feverish rush to secure a claim at the fabulous diggings at Florence, situated on a mountaintop south of Lewiston. With the spring thaw that liberated the snowbound, Florence's five log houses, three stores, and two whiskey mills had blossomed into a bulging metropolis, boasting nine thousand citizens. In August, as evidenced from the same hotel register, Plummer again checked into the Luna House to spend a weekend in the city, this time in the company of five other miners from Florence: Charles Reeves, Jim Harris, L. A. Payne, James Wheeler, and Charles Ridgley. Shortly after their arrival, a guest destined soon to cross paths with Plummer, Reeves, and Ridgley, also signed in at the hotel, a Pat Ford, who had moved from Walla Walla to set up a string of saloons and dance halls in the camps.

During this weekend in Lewiston, Plummer is credited with preventing a lynching in the streets, standing up before an assembled mob to dissuade them from punishing suspected criminals without benefit of a trial. "My friends," Plummer said, "we must not in the beginning of this city do the very thing which we are gathered to prevent. These men may be guilty of the crime of murder, but we shall not be less guilty if we take the government in our own hands and put them to death other than by due process of law. Do not, I beseech you, take any steps that may bring disgrace and obloquy upon the name of our rising young commonwealth."[102] Though it is possible the speech is as fictional as much of the rest of the Idaho account, it is believable for the reasons that Plummer expressed similar ideas while at Bannack and that he had the habit of keeping the peace in the rowdy camps.

True or not that Plummer disbanded the vigilantes, Pat Ford, the new arrival from Walla Walla, held the former marshall responsible and retaliated a few days later by ordering Plummer, Reeves, and Ridgley out of his newly opened Spanish dance hall at Oro Fino, accusing them of making a "rough house," that is, breaking tumblers and upsetting tables. Though the three men promptly left the hall, Ford followed after them to the feeding lot where they had stabled their horses, and as they were mounting, fired eleven shots at them from the revolvers he held in both hands. Ridgley was shot twice through the leg, as was Plummer's horse, which later had to be destroyed. Ford was killed in the return fire of the three men, though Plummer, who was probably considered the best shot of the group, is usually blamed for Ford's death. [103]

An account of the Pat Ford incident, written up by a news correspondent and submitted to his paper, provides interesting information about Plummer's days in Idaho:

> I have been a resident of Washington Territory for over twelve months, and Henry Plumer or W. Mayfield were never arrested on any charge in Lewiston, Lillooet, or Florence. True, at Oro Fino, Plumer killed Ford, and had Plumer been caught at the time, the people might have executed him. Since that time, however, the true circumstances have been developed, and all unite in bearing testimony that Plumer acted on the defensive. . . . All reports that either Plumer or Mayfield are hung, or have ever been arrested for robbery are base lies, circulated for the purpose of injuring men who by the force of circumstances, have become fugitives from their country. I do not attempt to justify Plumer or Mayfield in any acts they may have done in California, for I am not acquainted with the circumstances. [104]

Though during the few weeks Plummer spent in northern Idaho there are no reports of gang activity, the month after he had left, a politically motivated incident did occur at Florence that was reported by the press as follows: "REBEL OR ROBBER RAID INTO FLORENCE CITY ON OCTOBER 6 — Raid into that city at 9 o'clock P.M. of that day being a gang of several hundred desperadoes headed by Bill Mayfield, the murderer of Blackburn of Nevada Territory, that made their entrance hurrahing for Jefferson Davis and the Southern Confederacy, and then proceeded to plunder the hotels, stores, saloons, and restaurants." [105]

Of course Plummer, who had left three weeks earlier and who was not a rebel anyhow, did not participate in the raid; by 6 October he had already reached Fort Benton, but this incident at Florence mentioned by the Sacramento reporter is undoubtedly the source of later rumors of the existence of a road agent gang near Lewiston. Though the news item specifically named Mayfield as the leader of the attack, with time Plummer's name evidently supplanted Mayfield's, not only because of their previous association in Carson City, but because after the Bannack hangings Plummer's name was better known than Mayfield's. Because of his known leadership ability, Plummer also seemed a more likely candidate as the rebel's projected Emperor of the West.

Plummer had left northern Idaho three weeks before the raid in the company of Charles Reeves, on 15 September to be exact, less than two months after his arrival at the Luna House on 24 July, and the Stuart brothers noted his appearance on the other side of the mountain in their diary, explaining how somewhere in the timbered mountain range between Elk City and Beaver Dam Hill, he had broken his shotgun and how they had mended it for him. After spending four days at Gold Creek with the Stuarts, Plummer decided against going on to the Grasshopper, and parting with Reeves, moved on towards the headwaters of the Missouri, planning to return East. At Fort Benton he met James Vail, who was searching for men to come back and help him protect his family against a feared attack by the Blackfeet. Following his natural bent as a law officer, Plummer agreed to return to the Sun River mission to help Vail defend the four women and children stranded there. But that story has already been told.

EPILOGUE

PLUMMER'S WIDOW, THE VAILS, AND THE EDGERTONS

After Plummer was hanged, Francis Thompson wrote a letter informing Electa of her husband's death but received no answer. Thompson had in his possession "quite a little sum of money" that Plummer had deposited with him, and not being sure what to do with it, he consulted Edgerton and Sanders. In accordance with vigilante bylaws, an executor was to be appointed for Plummer's estate, who was to pay the expenses incurred in carrying out the execution. Thompson, however, did not claim to be this executor. He explained only how he spent the sum left with him, a portion of it, $42.50, going for "a coffin and the expenses of a decent burial."[1] By a decent burial, he meant having the coffin placed in a gully above the gallows with rocks piled on top of it, thus leaving it vulnerable to vandalism. It is said the grave was broken into twice, first by Dr. Glick, who out of curiosity severed the right arm from the corpse to search for Crawford's bullet, reporting he found it "worn smooth and polished by the bones turning upon it." The second violation is attributed to strangers passing through town, who, after spending a few hours at a local bar, hit on the idea of digging up the grave. To prove their bravery, they detached the skull and carried it back to the Bank Exchange Saloon, where it was kept on display for several years, eventually being consumed in the fire that destroyed the building.[2]

After Thompson paid the carpenter for building a coffin and performing the burial, he sent the remainder of the money left with him to Electa, though if she ever received it, she refused to so acknowledge, giving some hint of her opinion of Thompson for the friendship he had developed with the vigilantes. Excepting the shotgun claimed by Goodrich, no record exists of the disposal of Plummer's property other than the funds left with Thompson, though the estate was undoubtedly considerable, one of his last requests having been time to settle his business affairs. The vigilantes made no accounting to the public as to how Plummer's mining claims were disposed of, but it is doubtful his widow received any of the proceeds.

On learning of her husband's death, Electa claimed he was innocent, that he had been the victim of a conspiracy, and the idea of his innocence was shared by others, though not freely expressed because of the watchful attitude of vigilantes. One news correspondent did send an item back to his paper, a month after the hanging, that Plummer's close associates "profess the greatest astonishment at the charge preferred against him — of being the chief of this organized band of fiends." However, there is no record of Electa ever having made any attempt to clear her husband's name.[3]

Plummer's ordeal with the vigilantes on 10 January 1864 was brief compared to the subsequent experiences of his widow, who survived to carry in her mind for nearly fifty years the moments of his death. The degree of tragedy is said to be measured by the sufferer's capacity to feel pain, and Electa mourned the loss of her husband through ten years of widowhood. When she had left Bannack a few months after their marriage, it was evidently not because she loved him too little to stay, as he had probably believed, but because she loved him too much to share with others. A romantic, Electa had been attracted at Sun River by Plummer's appearance, his confidence, and his mysterious past. But from the intense romantic love she felt for the man who had first appeared in her life as a protector against the Indians, she expected practical things, such as the security of home and family. She knew he had been through a period of disillusionment, but their love had restored his faith in the order of things, and she sensed in him a basic commitment to traditional values. After marriage, however, Plummer's dedication to his job and his sympathy for the needs of anyone who came to him for help left her alone and with the feeling she was not loved enough. For all her good traits, she was possessive of the man she had chosen, wanted him to herself, and left him, feeling confident that her loss would cause him to give up his position and, as she told Thompson, follow after her. Once she had made up her mind to go, she stubbornly refused to listen to reason. Going against Martha's advice, Electa persisted in her own course and then suffered the consequences. She had the rest of her days to regret not spending the last months of her husband's life with him.

Over the years, doubts may have eaten away at her once unshakable faith in her husband's good character, but if that is the case, she did not speak of it to anyone, never reaching the point where she could discuss her life in Montana, not even with family members.[4]

Martha and James Vail left Bannack and returned to Sun River farm, but were "turned out" by the Piegans the following winter, true to the prediction made in the newspapers at the commencement of the project.[5] The Vails then moved to South Dakota to take out homestead land, and Electa, making no particular show of her grief, left Iowa to join them, taking a teaching position at the town of Emory and spending vacations with the Vails on their farm located on the Missouri River near Vermillion.[6]

Life in Dakota Territory was not easy. To build homes on the vast, untimbered plains, farmers tilled up thick strips of sod, which they cut into blocks and mortared together with a mixture of mud and dry grass. The houses were snug enough except during rainy weather, when roofs tended to become soggy and leak muddy water. Winters were cold, as low as thirty-five degrees below in January and February, sometimes freezing the Missouri to a depth of three feet. It was not unusual for early settlers to go without sufficient clothing during the cold months or to run out of the two main staples they had raised and stored: wheat and corn. With spring thaws came flooding, followed by summer's hot winds that carried the constant threat of prairie fire. Crop failure was frequent. The scorching heat of summer sometimes arrived early, withering tender green corn shoots, or in those seasons when the wheat grew tall and its heads were plump with grain, a horde of grasshoppers might come to invade the lush fields, leaving nothing standing but a few broken stems. The farmers who had been forced to borrow against the expected crop to survive were often faced with foreclosure of their homesteaded land.[7]

But there were also good years when plentiful harvests were gratefully celebrated with corn huskings, quilting bees, and church socials. Churches had been established early in the area around Vermillion, and Electa and the Vails were regular attenders, James acting as superintendent of the Sunday school for several years.

Like the South Dakota homesteaders, Electa was a survivor, emotionally as well as physically. After ten years as a widow, she chose a second husband, again showing a flair for the exotic combined with an appreciation for financial security. James Maxwell was a foreigner and a prosperous farmer, but unlike Plummer, he offered the companionship and security of a large family. He and his wife, Christian, had migrated from Ireland, and at her death, Maxwell was left with six children, an older son and five young daughters. Electa's second marriage was a happy one that supposedly left her little time for recalling the past, though who can say that there were no lingering memories, bathed in the golden glow of the Indian summer spent at Sun River, of the man, destined to remain eternally young, whom she had loved and who had loved her.

As a mother of the Maxwell household, Electa found herself in a situation very similar to that of her own childhood—a large family of girls growing up on a farm. Having been a stepdaughter herself, she had an understanding of the children in her care, and as adults they wrote of her, "She was a fine, noble woman, and we children were indeed fortunate to have so kind and good a mother to take the place of our own mother, whom we lost when we were very young." In this same letter, her stepdaughters put an end to persistent rumors that Electa had a son by Plummer and that when the child was eight years old, she returned to Montana to search for treasure buried by Plummer on the Ford ranch just before he and Cleveland rode to Bannack. "She had no children by Henry Plummer," they wrote. "She never returned to Montana after leaving there, and there is no truth in the story that she did."[8]

Electa and James Maxwell had three sons of their own, the youngest dying in infancy and two living to adulthood, marrying and settling in Iowa. During the last years of her life, Electa suffered badly from rheumatism and died from the effects of a fall, resulting in a hip fracture that would not heal, only three days before her seventieth birthday. She was buried at Wakonda, South Dakota, being survived by her husband, two married sons, and five married stepdaughters, who described her as "an unusually devoted wife and mother," whose "home life was her delight and it was there that her tender womanliness and loving sympathy were best shown."[9]

Electa showed her mettle, rising above personal tragedy to dedicate the rest of her life to family, church, and school, but few remember her for these contributions. Her fascination lies in being the woman Henry Plummer loved, the woman who was not there when he most needed her.

Though Electa spent the remainder of her life in South Dakota, the Vails returned to their native Ohio, thus making the full circle back to Hancock County, their point of departure for Sun River in 1862. James also returned to schoolteaching, the occupation he had followed in Hancock County when he and Martha had first married. At the time of the Bannack hangings, Martha had been expecting their third child, Rena, a daughter who did not survive childhood. They also lost another child, an infant born while they were homesteading near Vermillion. After leaving Dakota, Martha had their fifth and last child, Suzie, who survived to womanhood. When James died in 1882, at the age of forty-four, Martha moved into nearby Findlay to accept a job as matron of a home for orphans, hiring Suzie, her youngest daughter, as the assistant matron. With the help of a nurse and a seamstress, who both resided at the orphanage also, Martha and Suzie shared the care of thirty-two children ranging in age from two to sixteen.[10]

Though at the government farm Martha had been outspoken in her criticism of Plummer and by at first rejecting him as a brother-in-law had not shown her usual optimism, at Bannack she had come to be numbered among his loyal supporters, spending twice as many months with him as Electa had, and it was she rather than Electa who domesticated Plummer and provided him with the months of family life he enjoyed before his death. When in town, he was regularly seen crossing the log bridge to her home several times daily, and during his sicknesses Martha cared for him. It is likely he was again suffering from consumption during the winter of 1863–64, and references to his "fleshless" cheeks, a "dead" look to the eyes, and a form that had become almost "effeminate" in its frailness suggest that his health had continued to deteriorate ever since he had left San Quentin.[11] With James absent from the home much of the time, Martha and Plummer seemed to live together compatibly, planning and hosting the most extravagant banquet ever held in Bannack. Plummer spent the last day of his life in Martha's home and was still there when they came for him at ten o'clock that night. The words he spoke to her as he left the cabin provide an answer to the mystery his accusers have never satisfactorily explained — why he did not leave the area, as Reeves and others did, when the vigilantes first began their vigorous roundup.

When the armed party appeared at the door of the Vail cabin that night, Plummer had no reason to suspect they had come for him. As he told them while they walked, he had done nothing to be hanged for. He told Martha, just as they had told him, that the party was searching for Dutch John, who had been hidden by Howie and Fetherstun in a cabin on Yankee Flat. He went along with them to see that the right thing was done, stopping off first at Sanders's cabin for additional support in preventing a lynching of John. Sanders put out the light and did not answer the knock, and at this point the determination behind the real intentions of the hastily assembled group was beginning to crumble. Sanders quickly appeared and gave the military order to proceed with the prescribed death sentence, bringing on Martha's alarm.

Martha's attempt to save Plummer and her fainting at the news he had been hanged have been used by some as argument that she was in love with her brother-in-law, perhaps as early as Sun River. This theory supposedly explains her motivation in opposing Electa's marriage to Plummer and her following the couple to Bannack and inviting them to take their meals at her home. The theory is unsupported by evidence and therefore hardly worth mentioning, except for its implications as far as Plummer's having left any descendants. There is some indication that Martha and James Vail were having their problems — a land deed on file in the county in which the couple homesteaded, whereby Martha sold James a piece of land on the Vermillion River. There is also a bit of mystery surrounding their third child, Rena, born several months after Plummer's death. Neighbors who homesteaded next to the Vails reported that James and Martha arrived from Sun River with only two children, Mary and Harvey, though Rena had been born by that time. Also, they report the death of the Vails' infant, but not the death of Rena, who lived beyond the age of six. Not only is Rena not mentioned by the Vails' neighbors in South Dakota, but at her death she disappears without leaving any trace in vital statistic records. Even more mysterious is her birthplace. Rena was born in Iowa, but it was not Martha who was in Iowa in 1864, but Electa, thus leading to speculation that the child was actually Electa's and only raised by the Vails, perhaps so the child would not have to bear the Plummer name after her father's being branded an outlaw. Regardless of who was the child's true mother, Martha or Electa, and who was her true father, Henry Plummer or James Vail, little Rena died without continuing family lines. As for Martha's feelings for Plummer, whether they were those of a family member or of a lover will probably never be known.

Of all the members of the two families involved in the tragedy, Plummer was the only one to remain permanently in the town of Bannack. Like the Vails, the Edgertons made the full circle back to their home in Ohio. Edgerton's career in Montana Territory had come to a standstill and his efforts to get Wilbur Sanders elected as Montana's first delegate to Congress had failed. Still he had enjoyed his days of glory, persuading Lincoln to sign the bill making the area east of the mountains the new Territory of Montana and to appoint him to reign over it as its first governor. The Edgerton cabin became a beehive of activity as the new legislature came into session, late night compromises over card games held in one curtained-off room and daily visits from lobbyists bearing gifts. The two Edgerton boys were selected to serve as pages to the two houses of the legislature and voted a wage of $5 per day, a sum nearly equal to that earned by the miners. The boys' visions of the peppermint sticks and candy beans they would buy with their new wealth did not materialize, however. Mary advised them that when and if funds finally arrived from Washington, she could "find ways enough to use the money when flour is twenty-eight dollars a sack and sugar is one dollar a pound." To meet the high living expenses, the legislature doubled the governor's salary, and in way of thanks he busied himself passing out political favors earned since his arrival in Bannack; Dimsdale was appointed as the first superintendent of public instruction and a petition was sent to Washington requesting Francis Thompson be made secretary of the territory.[12]

With Edgerton's backing, the government elected by the miners had been successfully overthrown—Sheriff Plummer backing up the miner's courts—and replaced by the vigilante justice system. But from the outset, the scales had been tilted in Edgerton's favor. Bringing with him a reputation for respectability that Plummer did not have, he had arrived in the territory as the first representative of the U.S. government. However, as territorial governor, he soon aroused antagonism by forcing the resignation of a respected member of the house, a Democrat, who had once served in the state militia of Missouri and was therefore unacceptable, thus upsetting the delicate balance that had existed before his interference: A Republican majority of one in the Council and a Democratic majority of one in the House of Representatives. Throughout his term of office he continued to offend the "Copperheads," as he called them. Also, his early affiliation with the vigilantes led to the charge that his administration was under their control, he being nothing more than a figurehead. But probably the greatest factor influencing his decision to resign as governor of the Territory of Montana was the complete lack of financing for the territorial government. President Andrew Johnson readily accepted Edgerton's resignation.

Back in Tallmadge, Ohio, the Edgertons bought a fine home and settled down, being welcomed back in town by an article in the local paper stating that though the Montana experience had been a "losing venture" for the governor politically, it had been quite a success financially despite his never having received a salary. "Mining interests" from seventy-five claims and other "investments" were reported to have been sufficient to "richly repay himself and family for the inconveniences and privations" suffered in the West.[13]

Sanders stayed on in Montana, eventually overcoming his earlier unpopularity, to become the state's first senator and also serving as head of the Montana Historical Society.

Though in 1863 Plummer had written letters to his sister and brother saying he, as a Unionist, was in constant danger from the Secessionist majority in the area, he did not seem to recognize the danger Edgerton and Sanders presented. Like both of them, he saw the opportunity for a career in the developing territory, but his unusual sensitivity to the needs of others made him more than just a politician. He shared many of the qualities of the family he married into, the Vails, who dedicated their entire lives to the service of others.

THE PLUMMER MYTH

Probably more myths have collected around Plummer than any other hero or villain of the West, stories still existing of his buried loot, totalling three or four million dollars. Whereas Dimsdale attributed every crime committed in the mining area east of the Rockies to Plummer, the author of the *Banditti* book included those on the west side also, embellishing them with details of mutilation of the victims. A robbery took on much more public interest if committed by a big-time operator like Plummer, who was laying plans to take over as Emperor of the West, rather than by some relatively unknown bummer temporarily down on his luck, such as Dutch John or Steve Marshland. Typical proof that Plummer was secretly pulling all the strings from behind the scene ranges from Dimsdale's simple "intuition" to the more firmly based "suspicions" mentioned by the following historian: "While Henry Plummer has never been directly connected with the Magruder murder, there has always been a well-founded suspicion that he was the instigator of this most dreadful crime."[14] "Never been directly connected" means that Billy Page, the territory's sole informant regarding the crime, made no mention of Plummer whatsoever in his testimony, but the meaning of "well-founded suspicion" remains vague since the writer provided no additional clarification. Not only is Plummer held responsible for every robbery and murder committed during his career, but also every other unrelated wrongdoing that occurred, whether it be a rumor that was spread or a wife who ran away with another man.

Because Plummer broke his rifle grip crossing the mountains to the Deer Lodge Valley, Dimsdale accused the Plummer gang of committing the attempted robbery of a Wells Fargo stage in Washoe County, Nevada, more than a year earlier — even placing the famous barrel that fell off the stock of the rifle in Plummer's hands. Items in local newspapers at the time of the robbery, however, gave the correct name of the gunman who was so unfortunate as to have his piece fall apart on him just at the critical moment — an exconvict who had served time in San Quentin for robbery and had been released by the governor after receiving an impassioned plea from the young man's parents in Ohio. Even Dimsdale should have recognized that such a botched job showed no similarity to the success with which Plummer brought in prisoners while he was serving as a law officer.

Myths of Plummer's outstanding abilities exist side by side with his supposed record of bungled robberies; he was "the best" at everything: dancing, selecting a wardrobe, seducing women, planning and organizing, leading men, riding a horse, and shooting, even though he had two crippled hands. Forgetting the myths and taking a more practical look at Plummer, we see a man who obtained his gold dust, not by waylaying passing travelers, but by excavating the earth. We have examined Plummer's alleged tendency to violence, and it is not appropriate to label a man violent for defending himself in two instances in which he would have been killed otherwise, first by John Vedder's borrowed revolver and second by William Riley's knife. Testimony at the Vedder trial revealed that Plummer's strong streak of pacifism had prevented previous trouble with John.

Looking at the two halves of Plummer's career — California and Montana — we note they fit into the same pattern. He came to both Nevada City and Bannack with intentions of settling down to family life: first buying a home and next making plans to marry. For financial security at both locations he relied on mining, but followed the profession of a law enforcement officer. In both instances, his downfall was brought on by his being too democratic to make a successful politician, becoming involved with helping social outcasts such as Lucy Vedder and George Hilderman and granting them the same respect as influential citizens. Skeptics might attribute his kindness to others as a method of getting votes, but a good indication of the sincerity of his sympathy for others comes during the last moments of his life, when he noticed the distress of Joseph Swift, who was crying because he could not save Plummer, and threw his scarf to his young friend.

A second way of making sense of the two separate parts of Plummer's career is to use details provided by Nevada City newspapers and trial records to give additional meaning to the abstract assessments of his character that have been left to us by

Dimsdale and Langford. There are few records of his actions as sheriff of Bannack, but we can assume they were similar to those reported in Nevada City, where he spent days on the road carrying out manhunts yet still earning a reputation for efficiency and business integrity by, at the age of twenty-four, being in charge of the finances of a city of several thousand. And we understand the leadership qualities Langford claimed in noting that Pat Corbett, even though no longer a policeman, obeyed Plummer's order to watch over Lucy Vedder to see no harm came to her on her final night in town. But probably nothing could better illustrate the courtesy and gentleness referred to by Montana writers than the words Plummer chose in urging Lucy Vedder to leave his house and return to her hotel room: "Have you made up your mind to leave the fire?"[15]

In contrast to those in both California and Montana who pre-judged Plummer, he stands out for his calm refusal to prejudge those he was called upon to arrest. Open minded and gentle mannered, yet flamboyantly courageous, Plummer assumed an important leadership role in civilizing the mining frontier, and his downfall is therefore a true tragedy, in the literary sense of the word, brought on mainly by his being too tolerant for his times, that is, showing a lack of discrimination in the regard he held for others. He was unusual not only for his leadership qualities and his seemingly opposite traits, such as aristocratic tastes and democratic ways, but for a distinctive manner of doing whatever he chose to do which sets him apart from others, as for instance, on the morning when he rode alongside Electa's stage wagon as she was leaving him.

Plummer's basic philosophy of life can be described as a subscription to fundamental Christian precepts adapted to fit the gold rush environment. Though he admitted to being a man who "wanted no trouble," the dominant way of life during his times involved both intemperance and violence. Turning the other cheek so John Vedder could spit on it or making peace between Cleveland and Perkins would not be particularly easy. Neither was it a simple matter to enforce law in a community whose members valued personal freedoms to the extent that they selected to obey those laws that proved convenient and then undercut elected authority by acting as law officers themselves whenever the notion took them. In way of examples, Wallace Williams laid plans to recapture Webster instead of notifying authorities; Neil Howie held Dutch John in his own custody instead of delivering him to the jail; Alex Toponce turned the deputies away instead of allowing Buck Stinson to serve a warrant on a member of his freighting party; and Sanders organized a vigilance movement instead of recognizing the authority of the miners' courts.

Though Sanders criticized the miners' courts for being slow, expensive, and imperfect in judgments reached, all of which was true, their replacement by the secret vigilante courts was of such little value as to provide posterity with nothing more than a negative example. Plummer's trials also point up the weaknesses of our justice system, the main one being the near impossibility of finding jurors who have moral perception and a sense of justice and who are free from prejudgments. Still, even the most cynical critics of our justice system would have to acknowledge the beauty of the concepts behind the system as presented by Judge Terry after reviewing the Nevada City trial. He said, in part, "One of the dearest rights guaranteed by our free Constitution is that of trial by jury—the right which every citizen has to demand that all offences charged against him shall be submitted to a tribunal composed of honest and unprejudiced men, who will do equal and exact justice between the government and the accused, and in order to do this, weigh impartially every fact disclosed by the evidence."[16]

In 1864, Plummer was deprived of this "dearest right," and he is again deprived of it by historians who accept the untried judgment passed down. Having read the standard histories, and therefore having formed prejudgments, disqualifies the present generation from being acceptable jurors for Plummer's case. There are at the present time no minds "as free as unsunned snow from any previous impressions" in regards to Plummer.[17] It may take a new generation with a new historical perspective to reach a fair verdict, to be able to see that Plummer was exactly what he seemed to be and nothing more. He admitted to killing men in self-defense and to forming bad associations, but laws were not intended to hinder a man from using past experiences to lead a more productive life. As Langford rightly claimed, Plummer possessed outstanding executive ability and a remarkable power over other men. He was a gifted leader whose peculiar background on both sides of the bar of justice left him in a position of making a special contribution to the growth and development of the West, if he had been allowed to live out his natural years rather than being killed in the thirty-second year of his life.

THE MYSTERY OF PLUMMER'S BIRTHPLACE

Drawing any conclusions about Henry Plummer's life inevitably leads back to the mystery surrounding his early days. Langford, who claimed Plummer was born in Connecticut in 1836, was the only writer to meet the Plummer family. He and Mr. Purple held an interview with Plummer's sister and brother in New York City in the summer of 1869 and learned that Plummer had maintained correspondence with his family up to the time of his death. According to Langford, the family "mourned his loss not only as a brother, but as a martyr in the cause of his country." Langford found the Plummers to be "well-educated, cultivated people," who "were eager in their desire to find and punish the murderers of their brother, and repeatedly avowed their intention to leave, almost immediately, in pursuit of them." To prevent their leaving for Montana, Langford gave them a copy of Dimsdale's book, which he happened to have with him, assuring them that "all it contained relative to their brother was true." He and Purple followed up their attempt to halt the Plummers' mission by calling on them again the next day, reporting the brother informed them, in a voice broken with emotion, that the sister was "prostrated with grief" and could not greet them. [18]

On reading Langford's account, Mattie Edgerton raised the question of how Langford and the Plummers happened to meet in the first place. The probable explanation is that Langford and Purple located the family, after several years of searching, for the express purpose of delivering the book to their hands. Dimsdale, who received as rewards for writing his book a political appointment from Edgerton and a gold-handled pistol from the vigilantes, never intended the book as a Bible for historians of the territories of Idaho and Montana. He wrote it to stem current criticism of the vigilantes' activities from both the West and East and to deter investigations into the events of 1864 that might prove embarrassing to participants. The visit to the Plummers, like the book, was part of a cover-up of the fact that men were hanged without sufficient evidence of their guilt. Langford hints that a similar visit was paid to

Electa to make certain she did not pursue the issue of her husband's innocence. In the effort to see that the story, as related by Dimsdale, was passed down to posterity intact, the control the Sanders family maintained over the Montana Historical Society for two generations was no handicap.

Dimsdale's brief biography of Plummer disagrees with Langford's suggestion that the place of birth was Connecticut. After sorting through "the most contradictory accounts," Dimsdale gave up on solving the riddle. "Many believe he was from Boston, originally; others declare that he was an Englishman by birth, and came to America quite young," he wrote, but "the most probable is that he came to the West from Wisconsin."[19] Dimsdale has in mind the theory put forth by Matilda Dalton Thibadeau and seconded by Mattie Edgerton. Mrs. Thibadeau claimed Henry Plummer was born in Maine and moved to Wisconsin with his family, the Rial Plummers, taking a farm next to the Daltons. In 1853 her father, Mr. Dalton, ran into Plummer in California and again met him in Bannack in 1863.[20] Mrs. Thibadeau's theory has been so widely accepted that Plummer is cataloged in such prestigious libraries as the Bancroft under the name she gave him: Henry Amos. But when Mr. Dalton spoke to Plummer regarding the old days in Wisconsin, Plummer responded he had never been there in his entire life. Though Dalton did not believe him, Plummer was telling the truth. Amos Plummer, son of Rial and neighbor to the Daltons, was never marshall of Nevada City or sheriff of Bannack, but a farmer in Wisconsin, as confirmed by his living descendants and other vital records. The 1880 census lists the Amos Plummer who was born in Maine in 1832 and subsequently moved to Wisconsin as being alive and well, supporting a wife and children on his farm, sixteen years after the hanging at Bannack.[21]

A second theory can be discarded for the same reason. *The Plumer Genealogy* compiled by Sidney Perley lists a Henry Plumer who married an Eliza Bryant. This William Henry, the son of Jones, was born in 1835 in Winchester, New Hampshire, but, like Amos, also lived long past the year 1864. Likewise, a third possibility, a William H. Plumer born in Maine in 1832, the correct year as based on both the San Quentin and the census records, is disqualified by a town record showing his selection to the office of hog reeve for Alna, Maine, in the year 1859, the period Henry Plummer spent in San Quentin. A final claim worth mentioning is that Plummer was the son of a baker who lived in East Boston, but Plummer families still residing in Boston deny this is true, and census records confirm their denial. [22]

Though for over one hundred twenty years the William Henry Plummer who was hanged at Bannack in 1864 has proven impossible to trace, we will at this point present the findings of our genealogical search. When he was admitted to San Quentin, Plummer gave his place of birth as Maine, and throughout our extensive research we have not found a single instance in which he told anything other than the truth. We therefore presumed that Maine was indeed his native state, a fact we have verified by an affidavit taken from the foreman of the jury at the Nevada City trial, George S. Getchell, who swore that Henry Plumer was "born and reared" in the state of Maine, and "in the immediate neighborhood" of Getchell's former residence. This statement was introduced as evidence to the California State Supreme Court in an attempt to prove that this juror, being from Plummer's home county, was not prejudiced against the defendant, and Plummer's attorney, when referring to the Getchell affidavit, did not refute its contents. [23] Being granted a new trial depended upon discrediting Getchell as a fair juror, and therefore beyond a doubt the attorney would have pointed out to the court any untruths in the affidavit as further support for his argument that Getchell was unfit. Since he did not, we conclude that the portion of the affidavit dealing with Plummer's place of birth and rearing is true and correct. This assumption also makes clear the defense attorneys' reasoning in their selection of Getchell in the first place from among the three hundred residents summoned for possible jury duty, a belief that Getchell's being from the same region as Plummer would free him of prejudice against the defendant's peculiarities as a native of the state of Maine. Even the theory Matilda Thibadeau Dalton proposed, if seen in the proper light, supports Getchell's claim of Plummer's birthplace. When Mr. Dalton met Henry Plummer at Nevada City, he assumed he had been his former neighbor in Wisconsin because Henry, like Amos Plummer, had been born in Maine. Though Matilda stated, in an effort at disparaging Plummer's veracity, that the sheriff, when he spoke to her father had forgotten all about his residence in Wisconsin, she did not state that he had forgotten anything about Maine, the place of his

birth. As explained earlier, Plummer could not recall the days back
in Wisconsin with Dalton because he had never been there; neither
could he forget Maine because it had been his home since the day he
was born until the day he sailed to Panama en route to the gold fields
of California.

Though he was attracted to this strange new world of the gold
frontier and was flexible enough to adopt many of its ways, Plummer neither gave up the pride in his original home nor forsook the
identity acquired during the days of a childhood and youth spent in
rural Maine. Having grown up in an area where the common speech
retained a strong flavor of the language as brought over from
England, Plummer's word patterns and manner of expressing
himself were quite noticeable to others. The typical Yankee tacitur-
nity, understatement, and ironic wit come through in nearly every
instance in which he speaks, as in his answer to Garvey's exclama-
tion that Jim Webster's voice was rising up out of the darkness of
Gold Ravine, "I guess it is"; or on being asked who Vedder was
going to kill, "No one, I guess"; and finally, in response to Cleveland's provocations, "I'm tired of this." Judge Rheem's belabored ex-
position of Plummer's unusual vocal qualities, the wary monotone
and lack of expressiveness, is nothing more than an attempt to
describe the rhythms and tone peculiar to a speaker from as far
"down East" as it is possible to be.

These regional traits provide the key to interpreting much of
Plummer's behavior; he was a man who relied not on discourse as
much as action as a means of communication. His tendency to be
sparing with words was no asset in resolving the problem of Electa's
loneliness after their marriage, and he evidently expressed his deep
sense of loss at her leaving only by riding day after day alongside the
cumbersome, slow-moving wagon. Even the prejudice he attracted
during the state assembly race in California and during the incep-
tion of the vigilance movement in Montana arose partially from
local suspicions that he had something to hide because of his hesi-
tancy in volunteering information and his refusal to waste words in
his own defense, trusting instead that he would be judged on the
efficiency and dedication with which he performed his duties. As
stated in the letter to the *Democrat*, he asked for nothing more than
the reputation he deserved based not on his own assertions or on the
accounts of the press, but on his past performance.

Recognized as a "polished gentleman" who "had a brain" and a keen "power of analysis," Plummer was undoubtedly intelligent and cultivated enough to be, when he deemed the occasion appropriate, both charming and persuasive. Despite a belief that words were not to be wasted on idle chatter and that familiarity with strangers was a breach of good manners, he realized that while entertaining Thanksgiving dinner guests, not laconic responses but cordial conversation was called for, and though it was not genteel to brag about one's own integrity or achievements, a moment of eloquence could be required to prevent an injustice from occurring in the streets of Lewiston.

Plummer was in no way provincial, as evidenced by his appreciation for the refinements of life, but he did display several traits in addition to those mentioned above that are also characteristic of the social mores of rural Maine: an independence and need for privacy that left him willing to "live and let live"; a self-assurance combined with humility that aroused the allegiance of other men; a dislike for pretension that attracted him to Electa Bryan; a genuine concern for others that caused him to go out of his way to help even those at the bottom of the social scale; a stubborn honesty and forthrightness that forced him to risk his freedom by listing Nevada City, California, as his former residence even though a fugitive from justice in that city; and lastly, a trust in the social and political institutions passed down by his ancestors.

The neighboring community in Maine in which Plummer was born and reared, as referred to by jury foreman George Getchell in his affidavit, was Addison, located between the Pleasant River and the Atlantic Coast and settled in 1764 while still part of the Massachusetts Bay Province. In 1770, the sixty families residing in the Pleasant River area delivered a petition to Governor Hutchinson, complaining of the disorderly condition reigning in their isolated region — cursing, fighting, and mobbing — that left decent citizens afraid to go to sleep at night and requesting that a justice of the peace be appointed. The first signature on the petition was that of Moses Plumer. Three generations of Plumers had inherited the hundreds of acres of both cultivated and timbered land as well as salt marshes reclaimed from the sea by the construction of dikes by the year of 1832, when the last child was born to the family of Jeremiah, the son of Moses III. The child's mother, Elizabeth Handy Plumer, following a custom very popular in her family, christened her youngest son as a namesake for a member of her own family, William Henry Handy, calling the boy Handy at home, but William Henry outside the home.[24]

William Henry Handy Plumer grew up in a new state much more liberal than its parent state of Massachusetts, but one in which a bitter boundary dispute with Acadian neighbors in Canada was raging. During the boy's tenth year, a compromise was reached, allowing tranquility to return to the troubled countryside. The Plumers' large family home was located but a few miles from the treacherous rocks, alternating with peaceful coves, lining the coast of the easternmost tip of the United States, almost to the Canadian border. Shipping lumber from the extensive surrounding forests and building the graceful schooners that transported it were the main industries of the area. Though they invested in nearby sawmills, the Plumers were in the main sea captains, men with a compulsion to explore and a resulting familiarity with the cosmopolitan ways of the two local ports of Boston and New York, as well as more exotic ones, such as the Madeira Islands, where Captain William Handy had contracted a tropical fever, causing his death aboard ship in Boston. Still the Plumer family found time for civic and social affairs in their hometown, serving as selectmen and school board trustees, joining the Masonic lodge, and attending the Methodist Episcopal church.

The household of Jeremiah was a prosperous one, having one member who belonged to a learned profession. His wife, Elizabeth, as well had come from a family of doctors and professional men. Though the couple had six children older than William Henry — three sons and three daughters — the youngest son of the aging parents, lavished with care and given special education, grew into a leader, a young man of unusual sympathy for others. Because of his rather delicate health, having contracted tuberculosis in childhood, the boy was not sent to sea, but allowed to pursue his studies and work the family farm. While he was still in his teens, his father, Jeremiah, died, and two of the older children returned to make their home with the widowed mother, a sea captain and a daughter married to a sea captain. After the death of Jeremiah, the family fortune gradually took a turn for the worse, and William Henry, hearing of a company of gold seekers who had left Maine for California, persuaded the family to allow him to join the rush also, promising to alleviate the financial problems at home. The hard winters of the area provided a strong incentive for a mother concerned over her son's consumption, and she gave her consent to his migrating to the more temperate climate. Being seafaring people, the family selected not the more popular overland route, but the mail steamer as being the better means of transportation. After the departure of his nineteen-year-old brother, the captain gave up the sea and worked the family farm for his mother.[25]

The Plumers of Addison, who originally came to Maine from Massachusetts, descend from a Francis Plumer, a linen weaver from England, who came to Massachusetts Bay in 1634 and joined others in creating a settlement in the fertile wilderness west of Plum Island. Francis Plumer was a bit of a rebel, distinguishing himself by signing a petition criticizing the local court for its religious intolerance and requesting the restoration of the due rights of a certain citizen who had been disfranchised. Of the fifty-five petitioners, Francis Plumer and his two sons were among those who refused to back down during the ensuing investigation, continuing instead to assert their right to petition. Francis's younger son was reported to the court and bound over for trial for his part in the matter, though no further action was ever taken against him. Other than this one showing as an early advocate of civil rights, Francis was a model puritan who remained a church member in good standing up to his death. His estate, valued at over four hundred pounds, and which included the following, provides an interesting picture of life during his times: thirty-five acres of land, an orchard, a barn, five horses, four oxen, eight cattle, twenty-five sheep, four swine, a shop containing a weaver's loom and twenty-five pounds of wool, and a dairy house filled with butter, bacon and pork, and twenty-eight pounds of cheese. In the parlor of the dwelling house was a feather bed with bolster, pillows, blanket and coverlet; in the hall, a table, cupboard, and chest; and in another room a bed with coverings. Kitchen furnishings included chairs and table, iron kettles, pewter dishes, wooden platters, brass candlesticks, and a smoothing iron. In a hall chamber were bushels of barley, rye, wheat, oats, peas, beans, and malt for beer.[26] From this typical puritan household descended William Henry Handy Plumer, and his values and ways of thinking did not stray as far from these roots as we have formerly been led to believe.

NOTES

MONTANA

1. *Wakonda Monitor* (Wakonda, South Dakota), 9 May 1912, p. 1.
2. Francis Thompson, "Reminiscences of Four Score Years," *Massachusetts Magazine*, 5 Supplement (January 1912)1: 141–67.
3. Ibid., 6 (October 1913) 4: 161–67.
4. Ibid., 6 (July 1913) 3: 158.
5. Ibid., 6 (October 1913) 4: 165.
6. Ibid., 6 (July 1913) 3: 115–16.
7. Henry Howe, "Hancock County," *Historical Collections of Ohio* (Cincinnati: C. J. Krehbiel, 1900), 867–74.
8. Court Records, Hancock County, Ohio.
9. Marriage Records, Hancock County, Ohio.
10. U.S. Bureau of the Census, *Eighth Census of U.S.: 1860 Population Schedule of Hancock County, Ohio.*
11. Granville Stuart, *Forty Years on the Frontier*, ed. Paul C. Phillips (Cleveland: Arthur H. Clark, 1925), 223n.
12. Thompson, 6 (July 1913) 3: 124.
13. Ibid., 118, 124.
14. Thomas J. Dimsdale, *The Vigilantes of Montana* (Norman: University of Oklahoma Press, 1953), 11.

15. Thompson, 6 (July 1913) 3: 124.

16. Ibid., 6 (October 1913) 4: 159.

17. Stuart, 231.

18. Barzilla W. Clark, *Bonneville County in the Making* (Idaho Falls: Author, 1941), 6–7.

19. Wilbur F. Sanders, "Early History of Montana," MS., Montana Historical Society Archives, 217.

20. *Register and Descriptive List of Convicts Under Sentence of Imprisonment in the State Prison*, California State Archives, Sacramento.

21. Dimsdale, 151.

22. Ibid., 31–32.

23. Ibid., 27–30; Nathaniel Pitt Langford, *Vigilante Days and Ways* (Boston: J. G. Cupples, 1890), 1: 242–46.

24. Dimsdale, 25.

25. Langford, 1: 246.

26. Dimsdale, 28.

27. Stuart, 235n.

28. Ibid., 237.

29. Langford, 1: 247.

30. Dimsdale, 12–14.

31. Sarah Wadams Howard, "Reminiscences of a Pioneer," *Souvenir Booklet Commemorating Bannack, First Territorial Capital of Montana*, Dedication and Pageant, 15 August 1954, Montana Historical Society Archives, n. p.

32. Clyde McLemore, ed., "Bannack and Gallatin City in 1862–1863: A Letter by Mrs. Emily R. Meredith," in *Historical Reprints* (Missoula: Montana State University, n. d.) 2, 9.

33. Helen F. Sanders, ed., *X. Beidler: Vigilante* (Norman: University of Oklahoma Press, 1957), 10.

34. Dimsdale, 36; Langford, 1: 254.

35. Harry S. Drago, *Road Agents and Train Robbers* (New York: Dodd Mead, 1973), 97, 224.

36. Langford, 1: 242.

37. Dimsdale, 41.

38. Dan Cushman, *Montana: The Gold Frontier* (Great Falls: Stay Away, Joe, Publishers, 1973), 70. Cushman is one of the authors who points out the general acclaim of Colonel Connor's attack on the Shoshoni at the Bear River.

39. Cushman, 219. Cushman describes the stamp mill, and the Sacramento correspondent identifies it as Plummer's. (See note 47.)

40. Dimsdale, 39–46; Langford, 1: 269–85.

41. Howard, n. p.

42. Hoffman Birney, *Vigilantes* (Philadelphia: Penn Publishing, 1929), 93.

43. Langford, 1: 289.

44. Ibid., 1: 242.

45. Ibid.

46. Birney, 91–101.

47. *Sacramento Daily Union*, 17 June 1863.

48. Langford, 1: 288.

49. Ibid., 1: 275–76.

50. Thompson, 6 (July 1913) 3: 116–19; 6 (October 1913) 4: 160–61.

51. Ibid., 6 (July 1913) 3: 160.

52. Ibid.

53. Langford, 1: 290.

54. Thompson, 6 (July 1913) 3: 118–19.

55. *Wakonda Monitor*, 9 May 1912, p. 1.

56. Dimsdale, 18.

57. Stuart, 233.

58. Michael McLatchy, "From Wisconsin to Montana and Life in the West, 1863–1889: The Reminiscences of Robert Kirkpatrick" (Dissertation, Montana State University, 1961), 159.

59. Howard, n. p.

60. Howe, 867–74.

61. Langford, 1:242.

62. Dimsdale, 78.

63. William Y. Pemberton, "A Short Reminiscence," William Y. Pemberton Papers, SC. 629, Montana Historical Society Archives, n. p.

64. Margaret Ronan, *Frontier Woman: The Story of Mary Ronan*, ed. H. G. Merriam (Missoula: University of Montana, 1973), 20.

65. N. H. Webster, "Journal of N. H. Webster," *Contributions to the Historical Society of Montana* (Helena: State Publishing, 1900), 3: 329.

66. Webster, 327–29.

67. *Beidler*, Sanders, 23.

68. A. C. McClure, "Wilbur Fisk Sanders," *Contributions to the Historical Society of Montana* (Helena: State Publishing, 1917), 8: 30.

69. Birney, 97.

70. Langford, 1: 382–84.

71. Wilbur F. Sanders, "The Story of George Ives," in Sanders, *Beidler*, 47.

72. Sanders, *Beidler*, 22.

73. Langford, 1: 147.

74. Ibid., 1: 326.

75. Thompson, 6 (July 1913) 3: 119–23.

76. Ibid., 120.

77. Ibid., 123.

78. Ibid., 6 (October 1913) 4: 162.

79. Ibid., 7 (January 1914) 1: 21.

80. Martha Edgerton Plassmann, "Judge Edgerton's Daughter," MS. 78, Montana Historical Society Archives, 118.

81. Martha Edgerton Plassmann, "Unidentified Article," quoted in Birney, 102.

82. James L. Thane Jr., *A Governor's Wife on the Mining Frontier: The Letters of Mary Edgerton from Montana, 1863–1865* (Salt Lake City: University of Utah Library, 1976), 14, 17, 79; Plassman, 113; Harriet Sanders, "Reminiscences of My Trip Across the Plains and of My Early Life in Montana," SC. 1254, Montana Historical Society Archives, 84.

83. Thane, 65.

84. Plassmann, 113–14.

85. Ibid., 115–16.

86. Thane, 80, 91, 102–6.

87. Ibid., 106.

88. Plassmann, 134.

89. Thane, 72, 76, 100.

90. Plassmann, 131; Thane, 115.

91. Thane, 125.

92. Sanders, "George Ives, " 62.

93. Thompson, 6 (October 1913) 4: 184.

94. Ibid., 167; Plassmann, 127.

95. Plassmann, 123.

96. Thompson, 6 (October 1913) 4: 169.

97. Plassmann, 122.

98. Langford, 2: 9–11.

99. Plassmann, 122–23.

100. Ibid., 118.

101. Thane, 67, 74.

102. Sanders, "Early Life in Montana," 86–88.

103. Langford, 1: 326.

104. Helen F. Sanders, *A History of Montana* (Chicago: Lewis Publishing, 1913), 1: 219.

105. Plassmann, 145.

106. Sanders, *History of Montana*, 188.

107. Plassmann, 145.

108. Sanders, *History of Montana*, 188–92.

109. Sanders, "George Ives," 40–79.

110. Ibid., 59.

111. John W. Grannis, "Diary—1863–1864," TS., Montana Historical Society Archives, Book I, p. 23.

112. Langford, 2: 81–82.

113. Dimsdale, 121; Langford, 2: 84.

114. Dimsdale, 125–35; Langford, 2: 84–96.

115. Dimsdale, 131.

116. Langford, 2: 158–59.

117. Plassmann, 124–25.

118. Thompson, 6 (October 1913) 4: 180.

119. Ibid., 180–83.

120. Dimsdale, 145–50.

121. Thompson, 6 (October 1913) 4: 183; Plassmann, "Unidentified Article."

122. Thompson, 6 (October 1913) 4: 183.

123. Plassmann, 127; Thompson, 6 (October 1913) 4: 183.

124. Plassmann, 127.

125. Howard, n. p.

126. Dorothy M. Johnson, *The Bloody Bozeman: The Perilous Trail to Montana's Gold* (New York: McGraw-Hill, 1971), 98–99.

127. "Unidentified Pencil Sketch," Henry Plummer Collection, SC. 651, Montana Historical Society Archives.

128. Sanders, *Beidler*, 22.

129. Langford, 2: 175–77.

130. Thompson, 6 (October 1913) 4: 185.

131. Plassmann, 126.

132. Ibid.

133. Dimsdale, 154.

134. "Unidentified Newspaper Item," Henry Plummer File, Montana Historical Society Archives, n. p.

135. "Unidentified Account," Henry Plummer Collection, SC. 651, Montana Historical Society Archives, n. p.

136. Dimsdale, 155–56; Langford, 1: 179–83.

137. Grannis, 2: 2.

138. George A. Bruffey, *Eighty-One Years in the West* (Butte: Butte Miner Printers, 1925), 38.

139. Dimsdale, 180.

140. K. Ross Toole, *Montana: An Uncommon Land* (Norman: University of Oklahoma Press, 1959), 78.

141. Dimsdale, 224–27.

142. Amede Bessette, "The Last Bandit Hanged in Bannack by the Vigilantes," TS., Montana Historical Society Archives, 1–3.

143. "Notes of W. Y. Pemberton's Lecture before Unity Club, May 12, 1908," William Y. Pemberton Papers, Handwritten MS., SC. 629, Montana Historical Society Archives, 13.

144. Alexander Toponce, *Reminiscences of Alexander Toponce* (Salt Lake City: Katie Toponce, Century Printing, 1923), 78.

145. James Miller, *The Road to Virginia City: The Diary of James Knox Polk Miller* (Norman: University of Oklahoma Press, 1960), 78.

146. Walter N. Davis, "Hung for Contempt of Court," Handwritten MS., SC. 1826, Montana Historical Society Archives, 12.

147. Wilbur F. Sanders, "Notes to H. H. Bancroft," Handwritten MS., H. H. Bancroft Collection, Bancroft Library, University of California, Berkeley, 7.

148. Lew L. Callaway, *Montana's Righteous Hangmen* (Norman: University of Oklahoma Press, 1982), 46–49.

149. Thane, 61.

150. Maurice Kildare, "Henry Plummer's Golden Loot," *Frontier Times*, April–May 1965, p. 8.

151. J. W. Smurr, "Afterthoughts on the Vigilantes," *Montana: Magazine of Western History* 8 (1958) 2: 17.

152. Sanders, *Beidler*, 32; Dimsdale, 168.

153. Sanders, *Beidler*, 32.

154. Smurr, 17.

155. Dimsdale, 25.

156. Toponce, 73–74.

157. Dimsdale, 257.

158. Ibid., 148.

159. "E. J. Porter Article," *Helena Independent*, 24 March 1886, in Sanders, *Beidler*, 93.

160. J. Holleman, Statement to H. H. Bancroft, September 1, 1887, Handwritten MS., H. H. Bancroft Collection, Bancroft Library, University of California, Berkeley, n. p.

161. Sanders, *History of Montana*, 219.

162. Dimsdale, 58–56.

163. Plassmann, 121–22.

164. "Unidentified News Article, August 13, 1925," Henry Plummer File, Montana Historical Society Archives.

165. Sanders, *History of Montana*, 192–93.

166. Thompson, 6 (October 1913) 4: 169.

167. Langford, 2: 35.

168. Ibid., 2: 10–11.

169. Plassmann, 118–19.

170. Dimsdale, 125–35; Sanders, *Beidler*, 84–85.

171. Ronan, 19–20.

172. McClure, 31.

173. Callaway, 52.

174. *Sacramento Daily Union*, 24 February 1864, p. 4. Reprinted from *Golden Age* (Lewiston, Idaho); 23 and 27 January 1864.

175. Cushman, 105, 119.

176. Bruffey, 39.

177. Thane, 74.

178. Bruffey, 36.

179. Dimsdale, 144–45.

180. Plassmann, 126.

181. Cushman, 119.

182. Langford, 1: 242, 289–90.

183. Thompson, 6 (October 1913) 4: 184.

CALIFORNIA, NEVADA, AND IDAHO

1. John Codman, *The Round Trip by Way of Panama* (New York: Putnam's Sons, 1879), 1–33.

2. Louis J. Rasmussen, *San Francisco Ship Passenger Lists* (Baltimore: Dedford, 1965), 73–80.

3. *Directory of San Francisco for 1853*, Sutro Library, San Francisco.

4. *Nevada Journal* (Nevada City, California), 3 July 1853.

5. Ibid., 14 October 1853.

6. *History of Nevada County, California* (Berkeley: Howell-North, 1970), 8.

7. State of California. Census of 1853.

8. *Nevada Journal*, 18 April 1855.

9. Ibid., 13 April 1855.

10. Ibid., 17 August 1855.

11. Ibid., 26 October 1855.

12. Nevada County Deed Records.

13. *Nevada Journal*, 30 November 1855.

14. The name of this girl is unknown. In other works about Plummer's life, she is referred to as "Miss B." The initial "B" is false as well, offering no clue.

15. Ibid., 26 October and 2 November 1855.

16. Ibid., 9 May 1856.

17. Ibid., 10 March 1854.

18. *Boise News*, 26 March 1864.

19. *Nevada Journal*, 13 June 1856.

20. *Nevada Democrat* (Nevada City, California), 19 July 1856.

21. Ibid., 3 September 1856.

22. Ibid., 15 October and 4 November 1856.

23. "Evidence Taken Before the Coroner," *Nevada Journal*, 7 November 1856.

24. Ibid.

25. Ibid.

26. Ibid.

27. Ibid.

28. *Nevada Democrat*, 19 November 1856.

29. "Evidence Taken Before the Coroner," *Nevada Journal*, 7 November 1856.

30. *Nevada Democrat*, 19 November 1856.

31. Ibid.

32. *Nevada Journal*, 14 November 1856.

33. Ibid.

34. Ibid., 28 November 1856; *Nevada Democrat*, 8 January; 4 and 18 February; 11 March; and *Nevada Journal*, 15 April 1857.

35. *Nevada Democrat*, 25 March 1857.

36. This information was supplied by residents of Nevada City to the anonymous author of Jerome Peltier, ed., *The Banditti of the Rocky Mountains and Vigilance Committee in Idaho* (Minneapolis: Ross and Haines, 1964), 43. Though he turned his work into a piece of sensational fiction, the author had some reliable informants in California.

37. *Nevada Democrat*, 22 April 1857.

38. *Nevada Journal*, 8 May 1857.

39. Ibid., 13 and 20 May and 3 June 1857.

40. Ibid., 21 August 1857.

41. *Nevada Democrat*, 19 August 1857.

42. Ibid.

43. Ibid., 26 August 1857.

44. Ibid., 9 September 1857.

45. Ibid.

46. *Nevada Journal*, 4 and 11 September 1857.

47. *Nevada Democrat*, 8 July 1857.

48. Trial Records of The People of the State of California vs. Henry Plumer in Nevada County in 1857, California State Archives, Sacramento.

49. Nevada County Trial Records.

50. Ibid.

51. Ibid.

52. Ibid.

53. "Examination of Plumer Before Justice Clark at Nevada City, September 26, 27, 1857," *Nevada Democrat*, 29 September 1857; Plummer Trial Records of Nevada County, and Trial Records of The People vs. Henry Plummer in Yuba County in 1858, California State Archives, Sacramento.

54. *Nevada Journal*, 9 October 1857.

55. *Sacramento Daily Union*, 28 September 1857, p. 2.

56. Affidavits with Plumer Trial Records of Nevada County.

57. Plumer Trial Records of Nevada County.

58. Ibid.

59. *Nevada Journal*, 16 October 1857, Information rewritten from *Sacramento Bee*.

60. Plumer Trial Records of Nevada County.

61. "Examination of Plumer Before Justice Clark at Nevada City," *Nevada Democrat*, 29 September 1857.

62. Plumer Trial Records of Nevada County.

63. Ibid.

64. Lucy Vedder's testimony is a compilation from the preliminary examination, the Nevada County trial, and the Yuba County trial, without the use of ellipsis marking. In some instances where the court recorder has obviously omitted the word "I," it is inserted without notation.

65. Plumer Trial Records of Yuba County.

66. Plumer Trial Records of Nevada County.

67. *Nevada Journal*, 30 December 1857.

68. *Nevada Democrat*, 13 January 1858.

69. Ibid., 12 May; 30 June; and 11 August 1858; "Supreme Court–April Term 1858," *California Reports*, IX, 298–313, State Law Library, Sacramento.

70. "Supreme Court–April Term 1858," *California Reports*, IX, 298–313.

71. Ibid.

72. Plumer Trial Records of Yuba County.

73. Ibid.

74. *Nevada Journal*, 15 May 1854 and 7 September 1860.

75. *Nevada Democrat*, 30 September 1859; *Nevada Journal*, 9, 16, and 23 September 1859 and 13 July 1860.

76. *Nevada Democrat*, 8 July and 20 November 1857; *Nevada Journal*, 24 February 1854; 1 May 1857; and 13 and 25 January and 3 February 1860.

77. Plumer Trial Records of Nevada County.

78. Ibid.

79. "Supreme Court–January Term 1859," *California Reports*, XII, 256, State Law Library, Sacramento.

80. "Supreme Court–April Term 1858," *California Reports*, IX, 309.

81. James H. Wilkins, "The Evolution of a State Prison," *San Francisco Bulletin*, 1 and 6 July 1918.

82. *Register and Descriptive List of Convicts*.

83. Wilkins, 6 July 1918.

84. Governor's File on Henry Plummer, California State Archives, Sacramento.

85. Ibid.

86. Ibid.

87. *Nevada Democrat*, 23 September 1859; *Eighth Census of U.S.: 1860 Population Schedule for Nevada County, California*.

88. *Nevada Journal*, 23 September and 21 October 1859.

89. *Nevada Democrat*, 9 October 1860.

90. Ibid., 5 September 1860.

91. *Nevada Journal*, 27 January 1860; *Nevada Democrat*, 24 October and 1 November 1860.

92. *Nevada Democrat*, 29 November 1860.

93. *Nevada Journal*, 2 December 1859.

94. *Morning Transcript* (Nevada City, California), 15 February 1861; *Nevada Democrat*, 14 February 1861.

95. *Morning Transcript*, 6 May 1861.

96. Ibid., 29 October 1861; *Nevada Democrat*, 29 October 1861.

97. *Nevada Democrat*, 31 October 1861.

98. Sam P. Davis, ed., *The History of Nevada* (Reno: Elms Publishing, 1913), 1: 252–54.

99. Langford, 1: 78–83; Dimsdale, 259.

100. "Fabulous Florence," *Idaho Yesterdays*, 6 (1962) 2: 23–31; Byron Defenbach, *Idaho: The Place and Its People* (Chicago: American Historical Society, 1933), 1: 274.

101. *Luna House Register*, Luna House Museum, Nez Perce County Historical Society, Lewiston, Idaho.

102. Defenbach, 1: 324.

103. Ibid., 1: 318–40.

104. *Sacramento Daily Union*, 17 June 1863.

105. Ibid., 1 November 1862, p. 2.

EPILOGUE

1. Thompson, 6 (October 1913) 4: 186.

2. Ibid.; George D. French, "Carpentry Receipt," SC. 297, Montana Historical Society Archives; Fielding H. Graves, "The Gallows and Grave of Henry Plummer," TS., Montana Historical Society Archives.

3. Langford, 2: 170; *Sacramento Daily Union*, 15 February 1864, p. 3.

4. Russell Maxwell, Letter to Harold W. Plummer, quoted by Harold W. Plummer in Letter to Arthur Pauley, 19 August 1980; Harold W. Plummer, Letter to Ruth Morgan, 9 January 1985.

5. "Bradley Manuscript," *Contributions to the Historical Society of Montana* (Helena: State Publishing, 1917), 8: 155; Thompson, 7 (January 1914) 1: 28.

6. Arthur Harris, Letter to Hoffman Birney, n. d., Montana Historical Society Archives; *Ninth Census of U.S.: 1870 Population Schedule of Clay County, South Dakota*.

7. Royal G. Sweely, *Wakonda Community History*, Church of Jesus Christ of Latter-day Saints Genealogical Library, Salt Lake City, n. d., 4–16; South Dakota, Clay County Deed Records.

8. Mrs. Stafford and Mrs. Slattery, Letter to David Hilger, n. d., Montana Historical Society Archives; *Wakonda Community History*, 61.

9. *Wakonda Monitor*, 9 May 1912, p. 1.

10. Arthur Harris Letter; *Tenth* and *Twelfth Census of U.S.: 1880* and *1900 Population Schedule of Hancock County, Ohio*.

11. Langford, 1: 290; Dimsdale, 117.

12. Thane, 108, 120.

13. Ibid., 60–61.

14. Defenbach, 1: 332.

15. Plumer Trial Records of Nevada County.

16. "Supreme Court–April Term 1858," 309–10.

17. Ibid., 305.

18. Langford, 2: 170–72.

19. Dimsdale, 256.

20. Matilda Dalton Thibadeau Papers, SC. 835, Montana Historical Society Archives.

21. *Tenth Census of U.S.: 1880 Population Schedule of Monroe County, Wisconsin*.

22. Sidney Perley, *The Plumer Genealogy* (Salem: Essex Institute, 1917), 192; New Hampshire, Belknap County Marriage Records; Maine, Alna Town Records; *Seventh Census of U.S.: 1850 Population Schedule of Boston*.

23. Plumer Trial Records of Nevada County and Appeal to Supreme Court.

24. Maine, Machias Vital Records, Hannah Weston Chapter of DAR; *Getchell Family Records*, DAR, Machias, Maine.

25. *Sixth, Seventh, Eight,* and *Ninth Census of U.S.: 1840, 1850, 1860,*

and *1870 Population Schedule of Washington County, Maine*; Maine, Washington County Court and Marriage Records; Maine, Addison Town Records.

26. Perley, 1–19; Plummer Family Records, Film at Church of Jesus Christ of Latter-day Saints Genealogical Library, Salt Lake City.

BIBLIOGRAPHY

BOOKS

Birney, Hoffman. *Vigilantes*. Philadelphia: Penn Publishing, 1929.
"Bradley Manuscript." *Contributions to the Historical Society of Montana* 8. Helena: State Publishing, 1917.
Bruffey, George A. *Eighty-One Years in the West*. Butte: Butte Miner Printers, 1925.
Callaway, Lew L. *Montana's Righteous Hangmen*. Norman: University of Oklahoma Press, 1982.
Clark, Barzilla W. *Bonneville County in the Making*. Idaho Falls: Author, 1941.
Codman, John. *The Round Trip by Way of Panama*. New York: Putnam's Sons, 1879.
Cushman, Dan. *Montana: The Gold Frontier*. Great Falls: Stay Away, Joe, Publishers, 1973.
Davis, Sam P., ed. *The History of Nevada*. Reno: Elms Publishing, 1913.
Defenbach, Byron. *Idaho: The Place and Its People*. 2 vols. Chicago: American Historical Society, 1933.
Dimsdale, Thomas J. *The Vigilantes of Montana*. Norman: University of Oklahoma Press, 1953.

Directory of San Francisco for 1853. Sutro Library, San Francisco.

Drago, Harry S. *Road Agents and Train Robbers*. New York: Dodd Mead, 1973.

French, Hiram T. *History of Idaho*. Chicago: Lewis Publishing, 1914.

History of Nevada County, California. Berkeley: Howell–North, 1970.

Howard, Sarah Wadams. "Reminiscences of a Pioneer." *Souvenir Booklet Commemorating Bannack, First Territorial Capital of Montana*, Dedication and Pageant, 15 August 1954, Montana Historical Society Archives.

Howe, Henry. "Hancock County." *Historical Collections of Ohio*. Cincinnati: C. J. Krehbiel, 1900.

Johnson, Dorothy M. *The Bloody Bozeman: The Perilous Trail to Montana's Gold*. New York: McGraw-Hill, 1971.

Langford, Nathaniel Pitt. *Vigilante Days and Ways*. 2 vols. Boston: J. G. Cupples, 1890.

McClure, A. C. "Wilbur Fisk Sanders." *Contributions to the Historical Society of Montana* 8. Helena: State Publishing, 1917.

McLemore, Clyde, ed. "Bannack and Gallatin City in 1862–1863: A Letter by Mrs. Emily R. Meredith." In *Historical Reprints*. Missoula: Montana State University, n. d.

Miller, James. *The Road to Virginia City: The Diary of James Knox Polk Miller*. Norman: University of Oklahoma Press, 1960.

Pauley, Arthur. *Henry Plummer: Lawman and Outlaw*. White Sulphur Springs, Montana: The Meagher County News, 1980.

Peltier, Jerome, ed. *The Banditti of the Rocky Mountains and Vigilance Committee in Idaho*. Minneapolis: Ross and Haines, 1964.

Perley, Sidney. *The Plumer Genealogy*. Salem: Essex Institute, 1917.

Porter, E. J. "Article." *Helena Independent*. 24 March 1886. In Helen Sanders, ed. *X. Beidler: Vigilante*. Norman: University of Oklahoma Press, 1957.

Rasmussen, Louis J. *San Francisco Ship Passenger Lists*. Baltimore: Dedford, 1965.

Ronan, Margaret. *Frontier Woman: The Story of Mary Ronan*. Edited by H. G. Merriam. Missoula: University of Montana, 1973.

Sanders, Helen F. *A History of Montana*. Chicago: Lewis Publishing, 1913.

Sanders, Helen F., ed. *X. Beidler: Vigilante*. Norman: University of Oklahoma Press, 1957.

Sanders, Wilbur F. "The Story of George Ives." In Helen Sanders, ed. *X. Beidler: Vigilante*. Norman: University of Oklahoma Press, 1957.

Stuart, Granville. *Forty Years on the Frontier*. Edited by Paul C. Phillips. Cleveland: Arthur H. Clark, 1925.

Sweely, Royal G. *Wakonda Community History*. Salt Lake City: Church of Jesus Christ of Latter-day Saints Genealogical Library, n. d.

Thane, James L., Jr. *A Governor's Wife on the Mining Frontier: The Letters of Mary Edgerton from Montana, 1863–1865*. Salt Lake City: University of Utah Library, 1976.

Toole, K. Ross. *Montana: An Uncommon Land*. Norman: University of Oklahoma Press, 1959.

Toponce, Alexander. *Reminiscences of Alexander Toponce.* Salt Lake City: Katie Toponce, Century Printing, 1923.

Webster, N. H. "Journal of N. H. Webster." *Contributions to the Historical Society of Montana* 3. Helena: State Publishing, 1900.

ARTICLES AND NEWSPAPERS

Boise News. 1864.

"Fabulous Florence." *Idaho Yesterdays* 6 (1962) 2: 23–31.

Kildare, Maurice. "Henry Plummer's Golden Loot." *Frontier Times*, April–May 1965, 6–58.

Montana Post. 1865.

Morning Transcript (Nevada City, California). 1861.

Nevada Democrat (Nevada City, California). 1853–1862.

Nevada Journal (Nevada City, California). 1853–1862.

Sacramento Daily Union. 1857–1864.

Smurr, J. W. "Afterthoughts on the Vigilantes." *Montana: Magazine of Western History* 8 (1958) 2: 8–20.

Thompson, Francis. "Reminiscences of Four Score Years." *Massachusetts Magazine* 5 Supplement (January 1912) 1: 141–67; 6 (July 1913) 3, (October 1913) 4: 114–90; 7 (January 1914) 1: 11–29.

Wakonda Monitor (Wakonda, South Dakota). 1912.

Wilkins, James H. "The Evolution of a State Prison." *San Francisco Bulletin*, 1 and 6 July 1918.

UNPUBLISHED MATERIAL

Bessette, Amede. "The Last Bandit Hanged in Bannack by the Vigilantes." TS., Montana Historical Society Archives.

Davis, Walter N. "Hung for Contempt of Court." Handwritten MS., SC. 1826, Montana Historical Society Archives.

French, George D. "Carpentry Receipt." SC. 297, Montana Historical Society Archives.

Getchell Family Records, Hannah Weston Chapter of DAR, Machias, Maine.

Grannis, John W. "Diary–1863–1864." 2 books. TS., Montana Historical Society Archives.

Graves, Fielding H. "The Gallows and Grave of Henry Plummer." TS., Montana Historical Society Archives.

Harris, Arthur. Letter to Hoffman Birney, n. d. Montana Historical Society Archives.

Holleman, J. Statement to H. H. Bancroft, 1 September 1887. Handwritten MS., H. H. Bancroft Collection, Bancroft Library, University of California, Berkeley.

Luna House Register. Luna House Museum, Nez Perce County Historical Society, Lewiston, Idaho.

Maxwell, Russell. Letter to Harold W. Plummer, n. d. Quoted by Harold W. Plummer in Letter to Arthur Pauley, 19 August 1980.

McLatchy, Michael. "From Wisconsin to Montana and Life in the West, 1863–1889: The Reminiscences of Robert Kirkpatrick." Dissertation, Montana State University, 1961.

Pemberton, William Y. "A Short Reminiscence" and "Notes of W. Y. Pemberton's Lecture before Unity Club, May 12, 1908." William Y. Pemberton Papers. SC. 629, Montana Historical Society Archives.

Plassmann, Martha Edgerton. "Judge Edgerton's Daughter." MS. 78, Montana Historical Society Archives.

————. "Unidentified Article." Quoted in Hoffman Birney. *Vigilantes*. Philadelphia: Penn Publishing, 1929.

Plummer, Harold W. Letter to Ruth Morgan. 9 January 1985.

Plummer, Henry. Henry Plummer Collection Unidentified Account and Pencil Sketch. SC. 651, Montana Historical Society Archives.

————. Henry Plummer File Unidentified News Articles. Montana Historical Society Archives.

Plummer Family Records. Film at Church of Jesus Christ of Latter-day Saints Genealogical Library, Salt Lake City.

Sanders, Harriet. "Reminiscences of My Trip Across the Plains and of My Early Life in Montana." SC. 1254, Montana Historical Society Archives.

Sanders, Wilbur F. "Early History of Montana." MS., Montana Historical Society Archives.

————. "Notes to H. H. Bancroft." Handwritten MS., H. H. Bancroft Collection, Bancroft Library, University of California, Berkeley.

Stafford, Mrs., and Mrs. Slattery. Letter to David Hilger, n. d. Montana Historical Society Archives.

Thibadeau, Matilda Dalton. Matilda Dalton Thibadeau Papers. SC. 835, Montana Historical Society Archives.

PUBLIC DOCUMENTS

California. *Census of 1853*.

California. Governor's File on Henry Plummer. California State Archives, Sacramento.

California. *Register and Descriptive List of Convicts Under Sentence of Imprisonment in the State Prison*. California State Archives, Sacramento.

California. *Reports*. Supreme Court Term 1858 and 1859. Vols. IX and XII. State Law Library, Sacramento.

California. Trial Records of The People of the State of California vs. Henry Plumer in Nevada County in 1857 and The People vs. Henry Plummer in Yuba County in 1858. California State Archives, Sacramento.

California. Nevada County Deed Records.

Maine. Addison Town Records.

Maine. Alna Town Records.

Maine. Machias Vital Records. Hannah Weston Chapter of DAR.

Maine. Washington County Court and Marriage Records.

New Hampshire. Belknap County Marriage Records.

Ohio. Hancock County Court and Marriage Records.

South Dakota. Clay County Deed Records.

U. S. Bureau of the Census. *Sixth Census of U.S.: 1840 Population Schedule.*

_____. *Seventh Census of U.S.: 1850 Population Schedule.*

_____. *Eighth Census of U.S.: 1860 Population Schedule.*

_____. *Ninth Census of U.S.: 1870 Population Schedule.*

_____. *Tenth Census of U.S.: 1880 Population Schedule.*

_____. *Twelfth Census of U.S.: 1900 Population Schedule.*

INDEX

A

Acapulco, Mexico, 121
Alder Gulch, gold strikes in, 51–52
American Party ticket, Plummer and, 126
Armstrong, George H., 133, 135–36
Ashmore, Mr., 170
Aspinwall, Panama, description of, 120

B

Bagg, Charles: description of, 78; recollections of, 112
Baldwin, T. L., 133–34, 136
Ball, Smith, 36; wounding of, 90
Bancroft, H. H., 96, 102
Banfield (card player), 32, 100
Bank Exchange Saloon (Bannack), 182
Bannack: dances at, 49–51; description of, 36, 47, 64; disease at, 32–33; first winter at, 22–23, 32–33, 50; hanging in, 4; houses in 47–49; miners and merchants of, 115–16; robberies in, 5, 67, 76
Barbour, Judge W. T., 157–59, 161; indictment of, 159
Barker (witness), testimony of, 151
Baume, Tom, 97
Bear River, massacre at, 27–28

Beidler, X., 79, 82, 83, 85, 89, 97, 98, 101, 110, 114; as hangman, 91; memoirs of, 28, 56, 108, 109
Belden, David, 145, 148–51, 157, 167; legal defense by, 154
Bell, Tom, 130
Bessette, Amede, memoirs of, 93
Biddle, Dr., 24
Biddle, Mrs., story about, 24
Birney, Hoffman: writings of, 35, 54
Bissell, Dr., 32
Blackburn, Sheriff: death of, 174; encounter with Mayfield, 173–74; reputation of, 172
Blackfeet Indian agency, 13
Blackfeet Indians, 9, 14, 43; religious ceremonies of, 14
Brocky Pete, story of, 53
Brown, George, 98; accusation of, 81, 82; hanging of, 82, 109; legends about, 112
Bruffey, George, 92, 112; recollections of, 113
Bryan, Electa, 4, 33, 36, 38, 40–42, 44, 57, 59, 181, 187, 191, 194, 196, 197; character of, 7; courtship of, 19, 20; departure of, 60–62, 64; description of, 20, 21, 56, 62;